Private Funds, Public Purpose

Philanthropic Foundations in International Perspective

NONPROFIT AND CIVIL SOCIETY STUDIES
An International Multidisciplinary Series

Series Editor: Helmut K. Anheier
London School of Economics and Political Science
London, United Kingdom

PRIVATE FUNDS, PUBLIC PURPOSE
Philanthropic Foundations in International Perspective
Edited by Helmut K. Anheier and Stefan Toepler

A Continuation Order Plan is available for this series. A continuation order will bring delivery of each new volume immediately upon publication. Volumes are billed only upon actual shipment. For further information please contact the publisher.

Private Funds, Public Purpose

Philanthropic Foundations in International Perspective

Edited by

HELMUT K. ANHEIER

London School of Economics and Political Science
London, United Kingdom

and

STEFAN TOEPLER

Johns Hopkins University
Baltimore, Maryland

KLUWER ACADEMIC / PLENUM PUBLISHERS
NEW YORK, BOSTON, DORDRECHT, LONDON, MOSCOW

Library of Congress Cataloging-in-Publication Data

Private funds, public purpose : philanthropic foundations in
   international perspective / edited by Helmut K. Anheier and Stefan
   Toepler.
        p.   cm. -- (Nonprofit and civil society studies)
   Includes bibliographical references and index.
   ISBN 0-306-45946-9. -- ISBN 0-306-45947-7 (pbk.)
   1. Charities--Cross-cultural studies.   I. Anheier, Helmut K.,
   1954-   . II. Toepler, Stefan. III. Series.
   HV40.P69 1998
   361.7--dc21   98-45464
                                                                   CIP

ISBN 0-306-45946-9 (Hardbound)
ISBN 0-306-45947-7 (Paperback)

© 1999 Kluwer Academic / Plenum Publishers, New York
233 Spring Street, New York, N.Y. 10013

10 9 8 7 6 5 4 3 2 1

A C.I.P. record for this book is available from the Library of Congress.

Printed in the United States of America

Contributors

Helmut K. Anheier • Director, Centre for Voluntary Organisation, London School of Economics and Political Science, London, WC2A 2AE, United Kingdom

Edith Archambault • Professor of Economics and Director of the Laboratoire d'Economie sociale, University of Paris 1 Sorbonne, 75013, Paris, France

Gian Paolo Barbetta • Research Scientist, Department of Economics and Finance, Università Cattolica del Sacro Cuore and Istituto per la Ricerca Sociale 20135, Milan, Italy

Heinrich Beyer • Economics Program, Bertelsmann Foundation, 33311, Gütersloh, Germany

Judith Boumendil • Research Assistant, Laboratoire d'Economie sociale, University of Paris 1 Sorbonne, 75013, Paris, France

Martin Bulmer • Professor of Sociology, University of Surrey, Guildford, Surrey GU2 5XH United Kingdom

William A. Diaz • Senior Fellow, Hubert H. Humphrey Institute of Public Affairs, University of Minnesota, Minneapolis, Minnesota 55455

Diana Leat • Visiting Senior Fellow, VOLPROF, City University Business School, London, EC2Y 8HB, United Kingdom

Tymen J. van der Ploeg • Faculty of Law, Vrije Universiteit, De Boelelaan, 1105, 1081HV, Amsterdam, The Netherlands

Nancy E. Popson • Senior Program Associate, Kennan Institute, Woodrow Wilson International Center for Scholars, Washington, D.C. 20523

Kevin F. F. Quigley • Vice President, Policy and Business Programs, Asia Society, New York, New York 10021

Frank P. Romo • Associate Professor, Department of Sociology, State University of New York at Stony Brook, Stony Brook, New York 11794-4356

Rupert Graf Strachwitz • Director, Maecenata Institute for Third Sector Studies, Berlin, Germany

Stefan Toepler • Research Associate and Lecturer, Institute for Policy Studies, Johns Hopkins University, Baltimore, Maryland 21218-2688

Sylvie Tsyboula • President of Fondation de Jouques, and Former Deputy Director, Fondation de France, c/o LES–University of Paris I Sorbonne, 75013, Paris, France

Preface

Private Funds, Public Purpose finds its initial motivation in what has emerged as a curious imbalance of current scholarship on nonprofit organizations at the international level (that is, the set of institutions located between the market firm and the state agency). While research on nonprofit organizations, voluntary associations, and civil society have gained much momentum in recent years, little attention has been paid to private philanthropic foundations. Similarly, whereas systematic information on the nonprofit sector in countries as different as the United States, Germany, France, or Italy is becoming increasingly available, we know much less about foundations. This neglect is the more surprising when we consider that foundations themselves are frequently seen as major "financiers" of nonprofit activity, both domestically and abroad. What is more, the lack of knowledge about foundations stands in marked contrast to the increasingly international character of the philanthropic communities in the United States, Japan, and Europe, and the contributions they are making to the social and economic transformation in regions as different as the European Union, Central and Eastern Europe, and the developing world.

Indeed, as the evidence presented in this volume makes clear, foundations have been increasing in numbers in many countries since the 1970s and they have expanded the scope of their activities and introduced new forms of support. Research activities, however, have not kept pace with these developments. The little research that has taken place in the past usually looked at foundations in the context of a particular country, typically the United States, the United Kingdom, or Germany. Yet comparative international issues remained unexplored. We have little systematic understanding of the different types of foundations that exist cross-nationally, the activities they engage in, the legal backgrounds in which they operate, and the historical events and processes that encourage or retard their growth and development. As a result,

vii

few comparative statistics exist, and our knowledge of foundations remains sparse and narrowly based on the experience of just a few countries.

Thus, the purpose of this volume is to begin to fill the gap in our understanding of foundations and to stimulate research and policy analysis of their current and future role in society. The effort began with "Foundations: An International Research Symposium," organized by the journal *Voluntas* and the Laboratoire d'Économic Sociale at the University of Paris 1–Sorbonne, which took place in Paris in October 1993. For the first time ever, the symposium brought together researchers for the explicit purpose of studying foundations cross-nationally. Over forty researchers and foundation representatives from ten countries attended the meeting. Some of the papers presented at the Sorbonne became part of a special *Voluntas* issue called "Foundations: International Perspectives," published in 1995. Three of the contributions included in that issue are also part of this volume, although the papers have been significantly revised and expanded from their original versions. The chapters are Martin Bulmer's comparative–historical analysis of foundations in the United States and Great Britain, Tymen van der Ploeg's comparative analysis of foundation law, and Diana Leat's discussion of grant management. The chapters by Helmut K. Anheier and Frank Romo comparing U.S. and German foundations, and by Heinrich Beyer on foundation management, were also presented at the Sorbonne meeting but were not included in the *Voluntas* issue. All other chapters were especially commissioned for this volume: William Diaz's analysis of models of organizational behavior among grantmaking foundations; Stefan Toepler's analysis of operating foundations; and the chapters on France by Edith Archambault, Judith Boumendil, and Sylvie Tsyboula, on Italy by Paolo Barbetta, on Eastern Germany by Rupert Graf Strachwitz, and on the role of foundations in Eastern and Central Europe by Kevin Quigley and Nancy Popson.

In working on this project, we were fortunate to benefit from the advice and support of many people. Edith Archambault (Sorbonne) and Stanley Katz (Princeton University) provided early encouragement, and Lester M. Salamon (Johns Hopkins University), Estelle James (the World Bank), Martin Knapp (London School of Economics), and Woody Powell (University of Arizona) offered useful advice on earlier versions of some of the chapters included here. We also gratefully acknowledge the support of the Ford Foundation (USA), the Foundation Library Center of Japan, the Fondation de France, the Thyssen Foundation (Germany), the Fondazione Sanpaolo di Torino (Italy), and the Charities Aid Foundation (United Kingdom) for the initial *Voluntas* conference.

Of course, the responsibility for the current volume rests with us alone. Finally, in working on this book and with its various authors, we have become aware of how important comparative research on foundations has become in recent years, and how much remains to be done if we want to gain a fuller understanding of what the potential contributions of future philanthropy can be to an increasingly international and interconnected world. In this sense, the present volume will meet its purpose to the extent to which it stimulates future scholarship on philanthropic foundations cross-nationally.

Contents

PART IV. COUNTRY STUDIES

PART V. CONCLUSION

Part I

Introduction

Chapter 1

Philanthropic Foundations

An International Perspective

HELMUT K. ANHEIER AND STEFAN TOEPLER

INTRODUCTION

In recent years, we have experienced a renewed interest in philanthropic foundations in countries as different as the United States, Japan, Italy, Germany, Sweden, and Turkey or Brazil. In the early 1980s, observers began to note a reversal in a trend of relative decline in the overall size and importance of the foundation sector that characterized the previous two decades (see Odendahl, 1987; Boris, 1987; Rudney, 1987; Neuhoff, 1978; Biermann, Cannon, & Klainberg, 1992; Arias Foundation, 1992). As part of a general reappraisal of the role of the state in modern society (Salamon & Anheier, 1996), foundations were discovered and rediscovered by donors and policymakers alike, and it now seems as if foundations are experiencing a kind of renaissance (Renz, Mandler, & Tran, 1997; Neuhoff, 1992; Strachwitz & Toepler, 1996). In some European countries, observers such as Berkel, Neuhoff, Schindler, and Steinsdörfer (1989) foresaw a new, third "foundation wave," after a first growth period in the late Middle Ages, along with the rise of commerce and finance, and a second one in the late nineteenth century, following the Industrial Revolution.

HELMUT K. ANHEIER • Director, Centre for Voluntary Organisation, London School of Economics and Political Science, London WC2A 2AE, United Kingdom. STEFAN TOEPLER • Research Associate and Lecturer, Institute for Policy Studies, Johns Hopkins University, Baltimore Maryland 21218-2688.

Private Funds, Public Purpose: Philanthropic Foundations in an International Perspective, edited by Helmut K. Anheier and Stefan Toepler. New York, Plenum Press, 1999.

This interest is held by governments, corporations, and private citizens alike. For the state, foundations tend to be vehicles either for semiprivatizing certain tasks that are not as easily or as efficiently accomplished within the bounds of the regular state administration (Strachwitz, Chapter 11), or for leveraging private money for public purposes, as was the case of the *Foundation de France,* or, in part, the Arts Foundation of the German States. Accordingly, some countries have begun to enact legislation aimed at encouraging the establishment of foundations, including the French Law on the Promotion of Maecenatism of 1987, the German Law on the Promotion of Culture and Foundations of 1990, the Austrian Law on Private Law Foundations of 1993, and the recent Swedish Act on Foundations of 1996. At the European level, the Commission of the European Union has called on member states to support the establishment and operations of foundations in fostering a "New Europe" (European Commission, 1997).

What is more, local communities and municipalities around the world are increasingly turning to the idea of community foundations to deliver services. What began as a local experiment in Cleveland, Ohio, in 1914, to combine small trusts with irrelevant or outdated purposes in order to streamline the funding and provision of services to urban neighborhoods under the guidance of a board of community leaders (Hall, 1989), has since been adapted by many other cities and metropolitan areas. Indeed, community foundations have been among the fastest growing segments of American philanthropy over the past two decades (Renz et al., 1997). Today, there are community foundations not only in the United States, but also in Canada and the United Kingdom, Japan and Australia, and first forays in countries such as Germany, Slovakia, Bulgaria, and Russia (Workshop, 1997), with more being established every year. Indeed, after a somewhat bumpy start in the 1980s, the British community trusts and foundations, of which there are close to forty now, are beginning to show consistent growth and a promise similar to the U.S. situation (Pharoah, 1996).

Corporations, too, are making more frequent use of foundations. For one, they established foundations as part of their corporate giving and outreach strategy, as is the case for the AT&T or IBM Foundations in the United States, and the Hitachi and Santory Foundations in Japan. Less frequently, we find that foundations assume legal ownership of significant parts of corporate assets; in some cases, they even become owner of the for-profit enterprise as such. Examples include the Wallenberg Foundation, which owns large holdings of private firms in Sweden, or the Bertelsmann Foundation in Germany, which holds larger portions of the Bertelsmann Media Corporation.

Of course, the most frequent founders of foundations are private citizens. In the United States, they created 89 percent of all foundations (Renz et al., 1997), and 78 percent in Germany (Brummer, 1996, p. 22). Moreover, the number of newly created foundations has increased significantly in recent years, particularly since 1980, suggesting that interest in philanthropic foundations among private citizens has also heightened. The apparent greater willingness among citizens to invest parts of their private fortunes in foundations might be related to attempts to reclaim societal space for a functioning civil society from what conservative observers such as Olasky (1992) regard as an overextended welfare state.

What is more, these political and ideological currents are amplified by the volume of private wealth that has accumulated in developed market economies to levels unprecedented in recent history. In most of these economies, the number of private fortunes is at an all-time high. For example, in the United States, personal savings increased from $162 billion in 1980 to $241 billion in 1995 (U.S. Bureau of the Census, 1996). The comparative figures for Germany, Europe's largest and richest economy, are DM 85 billion in 1980, DM 169 billion in 1989, the year prior to reunification, and DM 267 billion in 1996 (Statistisches Bundesamt, 1992, 1997); and, for the United Kingdom, £21 billion in 1980 and £55 billion in 1995 (Central Statistical Office, 1992; Office for National Statistics, 1997). Given these figures, it appears likely that the foundation sectors across many countries will benefit from these fortunes, as the establishment of foundations is one way to manage the imminent intergenerational transfer of wealth accumulated in the postwar period.

The apparent relationship between increases in private wealth and the number of newly established foundations, however, has also given rise to criticism in the past. Especially in the United States, the controversial public discussion in the 1950s and 1960s focused on the suspicion that foundations were mere tax shelters for the very rich. Tax policies benefiting private foundations were thus seen as favoring the rich rather than society at large (cf. Commission on Foundations and Private Philanthropy, 1970). One way to look at this proposition is to contrast the growth of private wealth and the number of foundations with income inequality. In fact, the Gini coefficient for U.S. income inequality jumped by about 10 percent, from .39 to .43 between 1969 and 1991, and the share of national income earned by the top 10 percent increased by 18 percent in the 1980s alone (see OECD, 1995). While this indicates that the growth in foundations seems to happen at a time of growing income inequality in the United States, can we extend this argument to other countries as well and propose that the rise in the number of philanthropic foundations is a function of economic and tax policies favoring the rich? Even a cursory survey does not lend much support to this proposition. Indeed, increases in the number of foundations are observable across a broad cross-section of countries where income inequalities have not risen as sharply as they have in the United States, or have remained relatively constant. In Germany, income inequality remained stable throughout the 1980s, even declined somewhat between 1980 and 1985, whereas the number of foundations created annually increased consistently by approximately 200 foundations (Strachwitz, 1994).[1] By comparison, income inequality in France developed similarly to that in Germany, while the number of foundations hardly grew at all (Archambault, Boumendil, & Tsyboula, Chapter 9). Apparently, when put in a comparative perspective, the recent rise in philanthropic foundations represents a far more complex picture than the U.S. case alone would suggest.

This indicates that significant growth and stronger interest in foundations have yet to translate into a better understanding of foundations as a social, political, and economic phenomenon. With the exception of the United States, where the foundation sector from its inception roughly a hundred years ago has been subject to intense, and oftentimes critical, public discourse, little is known about foundations in most parts of the world. Part of the problem has undoubtedly to do with the different actors (private citizens, corporations, government) that might be involved, and the great diversity of motives they represent. Moreover, foundations are relatively rare institutions compared to other forms of social or economic organization. Nonetheless, it is still somewhat surprising given the special and important roles foundations are often said to perform in modern societies (see below).

In addition, the lack of a significant body of knowledge about foundations outside the United States has also led to a lopsided view of foundations internationally for a different reason, as the American foundation sector often serves as point of reference for the few attempts to analyze foundations in other Western countries. As a result, American concepts and interpretations have become the yardstick to measure and evaluate foundations elsewhere. However, the historical and legal development of the U.S. foundation sector has been very different from the experiences in other parts of the world, which, in turn, raises a number of questions concerning the applicability of a particular paradigm based on the American experience when coming to terms with the foundation phenomenon in an international context. The purpose of this chapter is to raise some of the issues in an effort to develop a better comparative understanding of foundations.

AN AMERICAN PHENOMENON?

Historically, foundations are among the oldest existing social institutions, showing great longevity. It is, however, difficult to point to the precise moment when the first foundation was established, or which of the existing foundations today can look back farthest in time. Scholars, however, do not see the origin of foundations in early medieval times, but trace the "genealogy" of foundations back to antiquity (Coing, 1981). These roots include Plato's

Academy in Greece (Whitaker, 1974, p. 31) and the library of Alexandria in Egypt (Coon, 1938, p. 20).

Throughout the Middle Ages, foundations were largely synonymous with religious institutions operating in the fields of health and education, and operating orphanages, hospitals, schools, colleges, and the like. Integral part of the feudeal social structures, the governance and operations of foundation boards frequently combined both aristocracy and clergy. Indeed, foundations were the prototypical institutional mechanism for the delivery of educational, health, and social services under the feudal order. Beginning with the High Middle Ages, however, we find a stronger presence of the emerging urban middle class among founders of foundations, which were often linked, and dedicated, to particular trades or crafts guilds (Schiller, 1969). Gradually, the bourgeoisie began to replace the gentry and clergy as the dominant donor group—a trend that amplified with the process of industrialization in the nineteenth century.

However, as we will see in Chapter 9, not all countries saw growth in the number and influence of foundations during the early industrialization phase. Being identified with the *ancien regime,* foundations and associations remained banned in France after the Revolution of 1789, and faced a highly restrictive legal environment until the twentieth century. Indeed, the state kept a watchful, frequently distrustful eye on foundations in many countries. For example, in Austria, the state attempted to appropriate foundation assets to fill budget gaps at various times from the seventeenth to the nineteenth century, and transformed university foundations into governmental institutions during the eighteenth and nineteenth centuries (Euglia, 1895). In addition, for the first four decades of this century, the European foundation world suffered greatly from the political and economic upheavals, in particular from the impact of inflation, wars, and totalitarian regimes, which recently led the German President, Roman Herzog (1997, pp. 37–38), to speak of a still persisting "cultural loss" that France, Germany, and other European countries experienced at that time.[2]

By contrast, the American experience has been very different. Significantly, while Europe's foundations faced great uncertainty and frequent decline, the American foundation moved to the forefront of organized philanthropy. While foundations in various forms have existed throughout American history, perhaps the most important development occurred in the United States at the beginning of the twentieth century, with the emergence of large-scale philanthropic foundations. Historians such as Karl and Katz (1981, 1987) have shown that the first of these new foundations did not adopt the more traditional charitable approach of directly addressing social and other public problems, but aimed at exploring the causes of such problems systematically in view of generating long-term solutions rather than just alleviating them (see also Bulmer, Chapter 2; McCarthy, 1989). Given the significance of this new orientation of foundation work and the large amount of resources that went into it, the first of these foundations came to symbolize a new era of institutional philanthropy, pushing the more traditional aspects of foundation work to the background.

Accordingly, the modern foundation is often perceived as a genuinely American invention. As one American scholar noted as early as the 1930s, foundations are a "unique American answer" to the problem of excess wealth in a society with limited income redistribution. Although foundations existed before, it was suggested that "in no other civilization have such instruments been utilized so widely as in the United States. It may even be said that the foundation had become the ascendant American device for disposing of large accumulations of surplus wealth" (Lindeman, 1988, p. 8).

It becomes clear that the rise of American foundations in the early part of this century highlights their financial, redistributive function and neglects, if not outright discards, the service delivery function that was one of the major raisons d'être of the European foundations. It would indeed appear that Americans in the past have shown a high propensity to transfer excess wealth to private foundations serving public purposes; moreover, against the backdrop of low government social spending and a rudimentary social welfare system, foundations in the United States occupy a more prominent role in public life than in other countries. In addition, the international presence of such philanthropic giants as the Ford and Rockefeller Foundations has further emphasized this particular variant of "American Exceptionalism" not only in the United States, but also all over the globe.

However, public and scholarly concentration on a limited number of large grantmakers as the "prototypical" American foundations has led to a monolithic view of the U.S. foundation community and may have contributed to a certain mystification of the American foundation phenomenon. In this still widespread view, there are numerous large-scale foundations in the United States that are professionally organized and thrive in the absence of competition from an activist state. Compared to the perceived lack of proper incentives and the administrative barriers that foundations face in other parts of the world (van der Ploeg, Chapter 3), the United States appear to be the *El Dorado* of foundational activity.

The tendency to glorify the American foundation experience holds two potential dangers. First, we may overestimate the actual economic importance of foundations relative to government spending. Although U.S. foundations held nearly $227 billion in assets in 1995 (Renz et al., 1997), total foundation assets represent only a very small fraction of the national wealth (Margo, 1992). Against this background, Salamon (1992a, p. 17) observed that "although the overall scale of foundation assets seems quite large, it pales in comparison to the assets of other institutions in American society."

The second potential danger lies in downplaying other philanthropic traditions and styles. As the chapters in this volume show, other countries have developed a rich tapestry of foundation types, and can look back to a long history of philanthropic traditions. How, then, does the American experience compare internationally? In the following sections, we attempt to summarize what we know about foundations internationally in terms of size, prevailing types, and relationship with the state.

SIZE

At the most fundamental level, an accurate assessment of the size of the foundation sectors around the world is hampered by a lack of basic statistics. With the exception of the United States and its more than 40,000 foundations as of 1995, most countries can at best offer rough estimates of the number of foundations. This is true even for highly developed regions of Europe. According to the European Foundation Centre estimates, as many as 80,000 to 100,000 foundations might exist in all European countries together (Garonzik, 1997).

What this aggregate figure hides are the significant variations across countries (Strachwitz & Toepler, 1996). The British Directory of Grant-Making Trusts lists about 2,500 foundations (Leat, 1992; Kendall & Knapp, 1996); in Canada, we find about 850 (Canadian Center for Philanthropy, 1991); the Portuguese foundation directory lists about 250 (Fundacao Oriente, 1992), and the Australian Directory of Philanthropy includes about 400 trusts and foundations (Australian Association of Philanthropy, 1993). Moreover, there are about 7,000 foundations in Spain, yet less than 500 autonomous foundations in France (see Archambault et al., Chapter 9), and around 600 foundations in Austria (Badelt, 1997, p. 61).

At least three countries show a relatively high number of foundations. In Sweden, estimates reach as high as 50,000 (Lundström & Wijkström, 1997), although probably only around 8,000 are of any significant size; in the Netherlands, some 100,000 entities are registered as foundations (Burger, Dekker, van der Ploeg, & van Veen, 1997), and for Switzerland, Wagner (1997, p. 43) reports 21,500 foundations as of 1996. In each of these cases, foundations are typically not grantmaking institutions. In Sweden, foundations, particularly in the past, were a means of preserving family wealth (i.e., served a dynastic as well as a familial welfare function); in the Netherlands, foundations serve as the legal form for many social service providers and educational institutions, as well as church-related trusts. In Switzerland, nearly two-thirds of its foundations are social insurance and pension funds set up for employees (Wagner, 1997).

Our knowledge of the extent of foundation or foundation-like activities in other parts of the world is quite limited. However, such organizations appear to exist almost anywhere either as genuine institutional forms such as the *wakf* system in the Islamic world or as a result of the implementation of the civil or common law systems by the colonial powers in much of the developing world. If the estimates of about 1,700 foundations in Argentina (Goncebate, 1995) and 4,000 foundations in Korea (Park, 1994), or the fact that about 3,600 new foundations were established in Turkey over the last 30 years (Baloğlu, 1996), is any indication, however, it becomes clear that foundations are not a Western phenomenon.

Still, even in Western countries, little is known about foundations in solid empirical terms. We suggest that this lack of basic information has greatly contributed to a number of misconceptions about what foundations do and what their relative significance is in society. The German case constitutes one example for such misconceptions. Prior to the first full-scale survey of this foundation community in 1989–1990, it was widely assumed that the predominant majority of German foundations, or about 80 percent, were active in the area of social and human services, with another 10 percent each engaged in research, and arts and culture (Möller, 1989, p. 27). The survey, however, revealed quite a different and much more diversified picture. Indeed, less than one-third of all foundations pursued social purposes, but about one in five is active in education and training, another 13 percent in research, and approximately 10 percent in arts and culture, with the remainder involved in fields ranging from health to religion and the environment (Chapter 4 by Anheier & Romo; Strachwitz, 1994). What is more, the survey data also show that social services are not only the dominant field of foundation activity in Germany, but have also been steadily declining in importance over the past four decades, while arts and culture, and a host of other fields, including the environment, consistently gained ground (Toepler, 1996, 1998).

The development of better data, however, not only contributes to a more accurate understanding of foundations nationally but also allows us to put into context some of the myths that prevail at the international level. Using the German data to develop a comparison with the U.S. sector, Anheier and Romo (Chapter 4) are able to demonstrate that the structural differences between the German and U.S. foundation communities are in fact not as significant as commonly believed. Their results show that, as of 1991, in absolute terms, the U.S. sector is about five times larger in terms of number of entities (35,000 vs. 6,500 foundations), approximately eight times larger in terms of assets ($163 billion vs. $14–29 billion), and five times larger in terms of grants disbursed

($9 billion vs. $2–5 billion). The differences in size, however, diminish somewhat in relative terms. Relative to economic and demographic indicators such as Gross Domestic Product (GDP) and population size, the U.S. foundation sector appears to be less than twice the size of the foundation field in the Germany.

Furthermore, taking into account that substantial parts of the German foundation sector had likely been wiped out by hyperinflations after the world wars and the communist takeover of East Germany, it could be hypothesized that size differences between these two countries would further be reduced if corrected for differences in the recent economic–historical context. However, while this example indicates that in some countries, including most likely the Netherlands, Switzerland, or Sweden, we might find strong foundation communities that indeed compare in their relative size to the United States, it is also clear that in a number of other countries such traditions have not persisted as strongly, if at all. As Archambault et al. (Chapter 9) and Barbetta (Chapter 10) describe in more detail in their chapters, countries such as France and Italy are far from having a strong foundation presence.

DEFINITIONS AND PREVAILING TYPES

Besides issues of relative size and economic presence of foundations in various countries, we also find differences with respect to the definition of foundations and prevailing types. In its most basic form, the foundation idea is based on the transfer of property from a donor to an independent institution whose obligation it is to use such property, and any proceeds derived from it, for a specified purpose or purposes over an often undetermined period of time. Since this process involves the transfer of property rights, most countries provide a regulatory framework, which usually also holds some measure of definition.

However, the different legal definitions have limited applicability cross-nationally and are reflections of specific legal and national traditions. Under common law, foundations typically take the form of a *trust,* which is, legally speaking, not an organization but a relationship between property and trustees. Most common law countries use this rudimentary legal definition and leave the actual development of foundation law to case law. One exception is the United States, which, in 1969, established a precise, though negative, definition: Foundations are tax-exempt organizations under section 501(c)(3) of the Internal Revenue Code that are neither public charities nor otherwise exempted organizations. *In nuce,* this means that under American tax law, foundations are those charitable organizations that receive most of their resources from one source and are as such considered to be donor-controlled.

By contrast, in civil law countries, the essence of a foundation, as a legal personality, is its endowment, which is the fundamental difference to the other major type of nonprofit organization, the member-based voluntary association (see also the chapters by Archambault et al. and Barbetta). In most civil law countries, however, legal definitions of foundations are usually very broad. In the German and Austrian case, for instance, the Civil Code falls short of an explicit definition, but mentions three necessary characteristics: Foundations need to have (1) one or more specific purposes; (2) certain assets to be used to pursue the purpose(s); and (3) some kind of organizational arrangements to carry out the intended purpose(s). Similarly broad is the Dutch legal definition, according to which foundations are organizations without members, with the purpose to realize objectives specified in their charters by using property allocated to such objectives (Chapter 3, by van der Ploeg).

Yet in both the common and the civil law cases, the vagueness of the legal definition (or nondefinition) allows in principle a variety of different organizations to be considered foundations. There is thus a need to go beyond legal definitions of what constitutes a foundation. Already, during the 1950s, Andrews (1956, p. 11) proposed a definition that was later adopted by the New York–based Foundation Center, a clearing house for information on U.S. foundations. According to this definition, a foundation is

> a nongovernmental, nonprofit organization with its own funds (usually from a single source, either an individual, a family, or a corporation) and program managed by its own trustees and directors, established to maintain or aid educational, social, charitable, religious, or other activities serving the common welfare, primarily by making grants to other nonprofit organizations. (Renz et al., 1997, p. 111)

Within this framework, the Foundation Center distinguishes four categories of foundations:

1. Independent foundations, that is, organizations generally endowed by private individuals or families that primarily engage in grantmaking.
2. Company-sponsored foundations, which are similar to independent foundations but established by proprietary businesses.
3. Operating foundations, that is, foundations that primarily operate their own programs or projects but may also provide funds to other organizations.
4. Community foundations, which are grantmaking entities that receive their funds and endowments from a variety of sources.

Within these four types, private independent foundations account for the by far largest number of foundations. They range from multibillion-dollar endowments such as Ford, Rockefeller, Carnegie or Kellogg, to very small family foundations. Of the more than 40,000 U.S. foundations existing 1995, 89 percent were independent foundations. Corporate and operating foundations with approximately 5 percent each, and community foundations, with 1 percent, are of comparatively less importance (Renz et al., 1997).[3] Roughly the same proportions hold true with regard to assets and grants, although to a lesser degree.

This definition refers to the two basic types of foundations—grantmaking and operating—but puts considerably more attention to the grantmaking part of the sector by further dividing the grantmaking category by donor type (individual, corporate, and multiple sources). Given the Americentric paradigm, this definition and classification have been the benchmark for the development of typologies in other regions of the world. For instance, the European Foundation Centre has basically adopted the grantmaking focus and the orientation toward the origin of financial sources inherent in the U.S. definition, only adding the fund-raising and government-sponsored foundation types that are prevalent in many Western and Eastern European countries but do not exist in the United States.

However useful the U.S. approach to defining foundations has proven, a number of problems nevertheless remain. Importantly, this definition classifies foundations by their source of capital, which says little about how they achieve their goals (i.e., by making grants to third parties, organizing award competitions, or operating their own programs or institutions). Although such differences in foundation activities can have significant impacts on organization, management, and public relations, they are not reflected in the prevailing U.S. definition of foundations (Strachwitz, 1998). In dealing with the U.S. definition, it should therefore be kept in mind that it originated in an environment that put more emphasis on issues concerning the control of (grantmaking) foundations rather than the organization of foundation work.

The dominant focus on grantmaking has also led to an underappreciation of operating foundations in the international foundation debate (Toepler, Chapter 8; Strachwitz, 1998). However, in many countries, we find a quite strong presence of such organizations. This is the case not only in France and Italy, where operating foundations by far outnumber grantmaking ones, but also in Turkey, where many *wakfs* are dedicated to maintain mosques and historic sites. In Germany, about one-third of all foundations are operating. Here, we find not only a large share of foundations operating various types of institutions, but also a number of foundations dedicated to run their own programs and projects. Among the latter are some of the largest foundations.

A closer look at operating foundations, however, raises a host of new definitional problems, specifically in view of international comparisons (Chapter 8). As noted earlier, many civil law countries do not legally distinguish between grantmaking and operating foundations. From the point of view of the law, foundations are endowed organizations usually founded by single individuals or entities. Whether the endowment is in form of financial capital or in form of an institution, such as a museum or a hospital, is not of concern. In the United States, on the other hand, operating foundations are subject to very specific definitions of the tax law. While U.S. operating foundations are generally privately endowed organizations, not all endowed organizations are classified as such. For example, major universities, such as Harvard or Johns Hopkins Universities, may have substantial endowments but are classified as public charities. Although many endowed, U.S. nonprofit organizations would indeed not necessarily be taken for operating foundations in the civil law, Western European understanding of the term—due to the fact that they had not been founded by a single donor—many others nevertheless would. Given the current data situation, however, it is not possible actually to determine how substantial the "operating foundation sector" in the United States would be if a definition of operating foundation were to be applied that is more international in scope and less based on the vagaries of the U.S. tax code. Still, as Toepler indicates in this volume, the true size of the operating part of the U.S. foundation community could be much more significant than it appears today.

To summarize, as the discussion shows, significant work remains to be done in terms of developing a definition of foundations that goes beyond the few, and sometimes misleading, clues the law has to provide, and that takes better into account variations in the prevalence of different foundation types internationally.

THE FUNCTION AND OPERATION OF FOUNDATIONS

While we still know little about foundations at the macrolevel in most parts of the world and also lack a comprehensive, internationally valid definition, we know even less about the microlevel, that is, how foundations operate, how they are managed, and perhaps most significantly, how they behave as organizations and what impact they have. In the British case, Leat (Chapter 5) notes accordingly that the "[l]ack of clarity in financial data is more than matched by the lack of knowledge of how foundations operate," a statement that is equally true for a number of other countries. Even in the United States, as Diaz (Chapter 6) puts it, "foundations remain 'black boxes,' little known and even less understood."

Against this backdrop, what can we then suggest about the role and functions of foundations in modern society? To be sure, common assumptions have long ascribed to foundations a number of special roles that transcend their limited function as financial intermediaries of the nonprofit sector. Accordingly, the literature often suggests that foundations are uniquely qualified to enable innovation, take social risks, serve as philanthropic venture capital, and generally "have a special mandate to enter fields of controversy, where the explosive nature of the issues would make suspect the findings of less independent organizations and where needed financing from other sources might prove difficult (Andrews, 1956, p. 19).[4]

The argument that foundations have these special competencies rests on the assumption, unlike almost all other institutions, that foundations are largely free from direct external control, as they are not accountable to voters, members, consumers, shareholders, or other stakeholders. Typically self-supported by endowment income, foundations and their trustees are usually bound only by the donor's will, as laid down in the charter, of course, within the constraints of the overall legal and regulatory framework. This potential of endowed grantmaking foundations has long been recognized and also somewhat glorified. The 1949 report of a program and policy study committee of the Ford Foundation, for instance, noted that the "freedom from entanglements, pressures, restrictive legislation, and private interest endows a foundation with an inherent freedom of action possessed by few other organizations" (quoted in Andrews, 1956, p. 21).

However, the potential of foundations to exercise their functions does not necessarily mean that foundations do so to the fullest. Unfortunately, however, systematic research into the actual extent of the innovativeness of foundations has not been attempted yet.[5] Indeed, without a better and more differentiated understanding of how foundations operate and behave as organizations, a realistic assessment of the actual fulfillment of these unique functions might not be possible.

Nonetheless, we can suggest a few answers on the extent to which foundations perform their role or functions. In Chapter 5, Leat describes an exploratory study of British grantmaking trusts, which yielded three more or less distinct types of "grantmaking cultures." According to this study, foundations may act as "gift-givers," "investors," or "collaborative entrepreneurs," progressing from passive uninvolved funders to proactive social entrepreneurs that set their own tasks and work quite closely with their grantees to accomplish them. A similar distinction is made by Beyer (Chapter 7, this volume), who differentiates between an "administrative" and an "entrepreneurial" way of foundation management.

Arguably, the adoption of any of these distinct styles or cultures will influence foundation performance with regard to the functions commonly ascribed to these organizations. More specifically, the entrepreneurial style, that is, foundations that use "creative powers to discover social needs" (Beyer,

Chapter 7) or identify "a voluntary organization to work with to create what it wants" (Leat, Chapter 5), appear to be closely related to the innovation or venture or risk-capital function.

By contrast, the pursuit of innovative new concepts and ventures, and the taking of risks in doing so, may hardly be expected from passive "gift-givers" whose "gifts are gifts and success and failure are not really coming into it" (Chapter 5) or administrators, "where the management function is reduced to the bureaucratic execution and control of projects" (Chapter 7).

These findings seem to imply that the special functions of foundations are most pronounced when they adopt an entrepreneurial approach, and that their contributions are limited the more passively foundations approach their goal achievement. This further suggests that normative prescriptions are geared toward a more active approach to foundation management, involving longer-term relations with grantee organizations rather than short-term project support (Letts, Ryan, & Grossman, 1997) and stronger emphasis on evaluation (Council on Foundations, 1993).

However, such prescriptions are not without problems, as proactive, entrepreneurial foundation management requires a high degree of expertise, which many foundations tend to lack (see Leat, Chapter 5). Expertise, as well as close working relationships with grantees or the development of self-designed and executed programs and projects, also require a higher level of human resources and concomitant administrative expenses. This, in turn, poses a public accountability problem, making foundations vulnerable to criticisms concerning "self-absorption" (i.e., diverting too much of their resources to administration rather than maximizing their payouts) and inflexibility due to bureaucratization (Frumkin, 1997).

Perhaps more significantly, the majority of foundations in any given country might simply not control sufficient resources to pursue a strategy of philanthropic entrepreneurialism. In 1996, only 12.2 percent of U.S. foundations surveyed with less than $5 million in assets reported having paid staff (Renz et al., 1997, p. 19). Moreover, small foundations with assets up to $10 million controlled only 15.5 percent of total foundation assets, while accounting for 94 percent of all foundations (p. 14). Similar financial concentrations of the foundation sector are evident elsewhere (Anheier & Romo, Chapter 4; Leat, Chapter 5; Strachwitz & Toepler, 1996), indicating that the majority of foundations are limited in their ability to adopt proactive strategies seeking out innovative, high-impact funding ventures. Indeed, with regard to the British study, Leat (Chapter 5) concludes: "By far, the most common culture of grantmaking among the foundations studied was that of the gift-giver. Less systematic data on a wider range of foundations in Britain suggests that gift-giving is the generally dominant style of grantmaking." This suggests the need to adopt a more differentiated and less monolithic view of foundations. Different cultures may prevail in grantmaking as opposed to operating foundations, and in large as opposed to small foundations.

This implies foremost that the "venture capital paradigm" might apply to only a small number of well-endowed, professional foundations and cannot fairly be generalized across the whole foundation field. Yet what then would be the potential role of small foundations? To a large extent, their role would be to serve special constituencies and interests that would be underserved by tax-based public sector funds, or outside the scope of for-profit operations. Taken together, the sheer number of smaller foundations would contribute to pluralism in funding and provision, and expand the institutional choice available in a given society.

In summary, the study of foundation behavior as well as the relationships between societal functions and organizational characteristics leave fertile, but so far largely unexplored grounds for future study. This includes further analysis of the internal processes at work in foundations (Diaz, Chapter 6) and other determinants of specific organizational cultures in addition to size.[6]

FOUNDATIONS AND THE STATE

At various points in history, the relationships between the state and foundations were marked by conflict and occasionally led to state interventions that subsequently altered the development of foundations in different countries. Perhaps the most dramatic example is the French Revolution, which led to the dissolution of foundation property throughout France or the secularization of church property in the Napolenoic years throughout much of Europe. On a less dramatic scale, the relationship between the state and the foundation world, while sometimes strained, is regulated in most countries by law that spells out the extent of state supervision and discretionary power.

In Chapter 3, van der Ploeg shows the great variation that exists in the supervision of foundations across countries. France, having a small foundation sector, is a country with little explicit legislation on foundations, where the state has significant discretionary powers in the establishment and operation of foundations. By contrast, most other countries (United States, Germany) have extensive legal regulations in place that are largely concerned with the tax treatment of foundation assets and revenue. The state restricts itself to questions of overall formal legitimacy of purpose in granting the establishment of foundations, but otherwise has little or no discretionary power over foundation affairs. Other countries, such as the United Kingdom, the Netherlands, or Austria, have moved the supervision of foundations to the judiciary or independent agencies.

Next to governmental supervision, *direct government involvement* (i.e., state authorities as founder or operator of foundations) has shaped the foundation sectors in most parts of the world. While such foundations are generally recognized as legitimate parts of local foundation communities, they are set apart in the United States. Nevertheless, they exist in the United States, too, and include the Smithsonian Institution in Washington, DC—which is in many ways similar to the Prussian Cultural Heritage Foundation (*Stiftung Preußischer Kulturbesitz*) in Germany (see Strachwitz, Chapter 11), foundations controlled by state universities, and the National Science Foundation. While Andrews (1956, p. 34–37) still included governmental foundations in his typology in the 1950s, the recent emphasis on private foundations has pushed this aspect of the American landscape to the side.

In general, we find that governments in Europe show a greater tendency to establish and sponsor institutions, including different types of foundations, outside the direct state administration. In some cases, separate foundations are established to deal with public issues that are either highly politicized or controversial if kept within the realm of the public sector more narrowly defined.[7] Examples include the German AIDS Foundation, established by an act of parliament in the late 1980s, or the Swiss foundations set up to handle financial transactions associated with funds held in accounts owned by Holocaust victims and their families.

Civil law countries principally allow the incorporation of foundations under private as well as public law. In theory, public law foundations serve as vehicles to facilitate the provision of public services and are closely connected to the state administration. The state, however, is not bound to incorporate foundations under public law. To the contrary, government-sponsored foundations are increasingly constituted under private law to allow maximum flexibility in the pursuit of philanthropic or public benefit purposes. In fact, two of the largest German foundations, for instance, the Volkswagen Foundation and the Federal Foundation for the Protection of the Environment, are independent, private law foundations established by the state and endowed with proceeds resulting from the privatization of formerly state-owned enterprises (cf. Strachwitz, Chapter 11). Other state-sponsored foundations in Germany have only minimal endowments and are funded by government appropriations, allowances from state lotteries, and the like. Although government representatives are commonly represented on the governing boards and thus are able to exercise a high degree of influence on grantmaking policies and programs, government-sponsored private law foundations are constituted independently and legally separate from the state. As a matter of fact, the relationship between a state-sponsored private law foundation and the state is in many ways similar to the relationship between company-sponsored foundations and the sponsoring companies.

Governmental foundations are not only frequent, but they are also contro-versial. The main problem surrounding governmental foundations established under the private law concerns the issue of accountability, as these organiza-tions lie outside the direct parliamentary budgetary oversight to which other state agencies are subject. This lack of accountability in the government's use of foundations has been criticized in countries as diverse as the United Kingdom (Chapter 5), Germany (Strachwitz, 1998), Poland (Kurczewski, 1997, p. 254), and Brazil (Landim, 1997, p. 341).

Another issue relates to the control of foundations, which arises from the privatization of quasipublic enterprises. In the case of the Italian banking foundations, the argument has been that only truly private ownership arrange-ment will protect these foundations from expropriation of assets or stringent control by the government (Chapter 10, Barbetta). In the Hungarian case, at last, the reintroduction of public law associations and foundations in the Civil Code, in 1993, has led to fears that such organizations break the homogenous private character of the nonprofit sector, divert public resources and privileges away from truly private organizations, and might represent a renationalization of the sector (Kuti, 1996, pp. 67–68). Although a number of problems will continue to be associated with governmental foundations, they do constitute a significant aspect of the international foundation landscape that needs to be taken into account.

OVERVIEW OF THE BOOK

As has become apparent in the preceding sections, the issues that we have discussed are not unique to certain national contexts but are central to the foundation debate across different countries. In this respect, the themes laid out in this introduction resonate to varying degrees throughout the book. The presentations in this volume move from comparative studies to management and organizational issues, to an examination of foundations in specific nation-al and regional contexts. The first three chapters are explicitly comparative in focus and examine the historical development of foundations (Bulmer, Chap-ter 2, on the United States and Britain), their legal background in terms of governance and accountability (van der Ploeg, Chapter 3) in the United States, England, Germany, Austria, France, and the Netherlands, and their scope, activities, and growth patterns in two countries, and United States and Ger-many (Anheier & Romo, Chapter 4).

The following four chapters explore specific aspects of foundation man-agement and organizational behavior. In Chapter 5, Leat examines how British foundations manage grantmaking; Diaz, in Chapter 6, looks at different organzational models for philanthropic foundations; Beyer, in Chapter 7, analyzes the role of entrepreneurship in the foundation world; and in Chapter 8, Toepler explores an important variant of modern philanthropy, the operating foundation (i.e., foundations that fund and operate their own activities directly rather than indirectly through grantmaking).

The third section of the book includes several country studies: Archambault et al. (Chapter 9) report on France, a country where the role of foundations has historically been somewhat limited; Barbetta (Chapter 10) looks at Italy and, specifically the current changes in the legal treatment of foundations; Strachwitz (Chapter 11) explores the reemergence of foundations in East Germany in the aftermath of the fall of the Berlin Wall in 1989; and, similarly, Quigley and Popson (Chapter 12) describe the development of foundations and the role of philanthropy in the social and economic transition of Eastern and Central European countries. The book closes with a concluding chapter that summarizes some of the key insights that follow from the various chapters and outlines key facets of a continued research agenda on the role and impact of philanthropic foundations cross-nationally.

NOTES

1. While there are considerably fewer foundations created in Germany each year than in the United States, the actual growth rates of the German foundation sector have exceeded those of the United States since the 1970s (Toepler, 1996).
2. The real extent of this loss is hard to gauge but likely to be substantial. Although there might be problems of comparability, an 1895 directory counted in excess of 2,000 foundations and funds in the city of Vienna alone (Euglia, 1895), whereas the total number in the whole of Austria is currently estimated at 600 foundations (Badelt, 1997).
3. It should be noted that the data reported in *Foundation Giving* only refer to operating foundations that also make grants. Including those operating foundations in the United States that do not make grants to other organizations would increase their share to approximately 10 percent of all foundations (Toepler, Chapter 8).
4. In the American foundation community, the "venture" or "risk" capital concept may date back to the 1920s (see Kiger, 1954). While this understanding of the potential of foundations has long formed the foundation philosophy in the United States, it is also common elsewhere. Similar formulations can be found in the German literature (Flitner, 1972; Strachwitz, 1994; Toepler, 1996), and, as Leat in this volume shows, these ideas are also prevalent in the United Kingdom.
5. For one limited attempt to test the assumption, see Mahoney and Estes, 1987.
6. Odendahl, Boris, and Daniels (1985) point to the lifecycle of foundations. Other factors should include donor characteristics or the composition of foundation boards.
7. It is important to note that this is not a European phenomenon but also prevails in countries around the world with civil law legal systems.

REFERENCES

Andrews, F. E. (1956). *Philanthropic Foundations.* New York: Russell Sage Foundation.

Arias Foundation for Peace and Human Progress. (1992). *The State of Philanthropy in Central America.* San Jose, Costa Rica: Author.

Australian Association of Philanthropy. (1993). *The Australian Directory of Philanthropy.* Port Melbourne, Australia: Author.

Badelt, C. (1997). Der Nonprofit Sektor in Österreich. In C. Badelt (Ed.), *Handbuch der Nonprofit Organisationen* (pp. 51–70). Stuttgart: Poeschl.

Baloğlu, Z. (Ed.). (1996). *The Foundations of Turkey.* Istanbul, Turkey: TÜSEV.

Berkel, U., Neuhoff, K., Schindler, A., & Steinsdörfer, E. (1989). *Stiftungshandbuch.* Baden-Baden, Germany: Nomos.

Bierman, B., Cannon, L., & Klainberg, D. (1992). *A Survey of Endowed Grantmaking Development Foundations in Africa, Asia, Eastern Europe, Latin America, and the Caribbean.* New York: Synergos Institute (mimeo).

Boris, E. (1987). Creation and growth: A survey of private foundations. In T. Odendahl (Ed.), *America's Wealthy and the Future of Foundations* (pp. 65–126). New York: Foundation Center.

Brummer, E. (Ed.). (1996). *Statistiken zum Deutschen Stiftungswesen.* Munich: Maecenata.

Burger, A., Dekker, P., van der Ploeg, T., & van Veen, W. (1997). *Defining the Nonprofit Sector: The Netherlands.* Working Papers of the Johns Hopkins Comparative Nonprofit Sector Project, No. 23. Baltimore: Johns Hopkins Institute for Policy Studies.

Canadian Center for Philanthropy. (1991). *Canadian Directory to Foundations.* Toronto: Author.

Central Statistical Office. (1992). *Annual Abstract of Statistics.* London: Her Majesty's Stationer's Office.

Coing, H. (1981). Remarks on the history of foundations and their role in the promotion of learning. *Minerva,* 19(2), 271–281.

Commission on Foundations and Private Philanthropy. (1970). *Foundations, Private Giving, and Public Policy.* Chicago: University of Chicago Press.

Coon, H. (1938). *Money to Burn.* London–New York–Toronto: Longmans, Green.

Council on Foundations. (Ed.). (1993). *Evaluation for Foundations.* San Francisco: Jossey-Bass.

Euglia, E. (1895). Einleitung. In C. F. Mautner Ritter von Markhof (Ed.), *Die Wiener Stiftungen* (pp. 11–43). Vienna: Carl Gerold's Sohn.

European Commission. (1997). *Communication from the Commission on Promoting the Role of Voluntary Organisations and Foundations in Europe.* COM 97/241. Luxembourg: Office for Official Publications of the European Communities.

Flitner, H. (1972). *Stiftungsprofile.* Baden-Baden, Germany: Nomos.

Frumkin, P. (1997). Three obstacles to effective foundation philanthropy. In J. Barry, & B. Manno (Eds.), *Giving Better, Giving Smarter: Working Papers of the National Commission on Philanthropy and Civic Renewal.* Washington, DC: National Commission on Philanthropy and Civic Renewal.

Fundacao Oriente. (1992). *Guia das Fundacoes Portuguesas:* Lisbon: Romos Afonso & Moita.

Garonzik, E. (1997). Foundation funding: Venture capital for civil society. In Civicus (Ed.), *Sustaining Civil Society: Strategies for Resource Mobilization* (pp. 45–78). Washington, DC: Civicus.

Goncebate, R. (1995). Foundations in periods of political and economic uncertainty: The Latin American link and the Argentine case. *Voluntas,* 6(3), 330–344.

Hall, P. D. (1989). The Community foundation in America, 1914–1987. In R. Magat (Ed.), *Philanthropic Giving: Studies in Varieties and Goals* (pp. 180–199). New York and Oxford, UK: Oxford University Press.

Herzog, R. (1997). Zur Bedeutung von Stiftungen in unserer Zeit. In Bertelsmann Stiftung (Ed.), *Operative Stiftungsarbeit*. Gütersloh, Germany: Verlag Bertelsmann Stiftung.

Karl, B. D., & Katz, S. N. (1981). The American private foundation and the public sphere, 1890–1930. *Minerva, 19*(2), 236–269.

Karl, B. D., & Katz, S. N. (1987). Foundations and ruling class elites. *Daedalus, 116*(1), 1–40.

Kendall, J., & Knapp, M. (1996). *The Nonprofit in the United Kingdom*. Manchester, UK: Manchester University Press.

Kiger, J. (1954). *Operating Principles of the Larger Foundations*. New York: Russell Sage Foundation.

Kurczewski, J. (1997). Poland. In L. M. Salamon (Ed.), *International Guide to Nonprofit Law* (pp. 246–254). New York: Wiley.

Kuti, E. (1996). *The nonprofit sector in Hungary*. Manchester, UK: Manchester University Press.

Landim, L. (1997). Brazil. In L. M. Salamon & H. K. Anheier (Eds.), *Defining the Nonprofit Sector* (pp. 323–349). Manchester, UK: Manchester University Press.

Leat, D. (1992). *Trusts in Transition: The Policy and Practice of Grant-Making Trusts*. York, UK: Joseph Rowntree Foundation.

Letts, C., Ryan, W., & Grossman, A. (1997). Virtous capital: What foundations can learn from venture capitalists. *Harvard Business Review, 2*, 36–44.

Lindeman, E. C. (1988) [1936]. *Wealth and Culture*. Reprint, Society ad Philanthropy Series. New Brunswick, NJ & Oxford, UK: Transaction Books.

Lundström, T., & Wijkström, F. (1997). *The Nonprofit in Sweden*. Manchester, UK: Manchester University Press.

Mahoney, C., & Estes, C. (1987). The changing role of private foundations: Business as usual or creative innovation? *Journal of Voluntary Action Research, 16*(4), 22–31.

Margo, R. (1992). Foundations. In C. T. Clotfelter (Ed.), *Who Benefits from the Nonprofit Sector?* (pp. 207–234). Chicago: University of Chicago Press.

McCarthy, K. D. (1989). The gospel of wealth: American giving in theory and practice. In R. Magat (Ed.), *Philanthropic Giving: Studies in Varieties and Goals* (pp. 46–62). New York & Oxford, UK: Oxford University Press.

Möller, R. (1989). Aktuelle Probleme des deutschen Stiftungswesens. In Ludwig-Erhard-Stiftung (Eds.), *Markt, Staat und Stiftungen* (pp. 25–36). Stuttgart, New York: Gustav Fischer.

Neuhoff, K. (1978). Sonderdruck aus SOERGEL—*Kommentar zum Bürgerlichen Gesetzbuch* (11. Auflage), Band 1: Allgemeiner Teil. Essen, Germany: Stifterverband.

Neuhoff, K. (1992). Stiftung and Stiftungsrecht. In R. Bauer (Ed.), *Lexikon des Sozial und Gesundheitswesens* (pp. 1967–1974). Munich and Vienna: Oldenbourg.

Nielsen, W. A. (1972). *The Big Foundations*. New York: Columbia University Press.

Odendahl, T. (1987). Independent foundations and the wealthy donors: An overview. In T. Odendahl (Ed.), *America's Wealthy and the Future of Foundations* (pp. 1–26). New York: Foundation Center.

Odendahl, T., Boris, E., & Daniels, A. (1987). *Working in Foundations: Career Patterns of Women and Men*. New York: Foundation Center.

Organization for Economic Cooperation and Development (OECD). (1995). *Income Distribution in OECD Countries*. Social Policy Studies No 18. Paris: Author.

Office for National Statistics. (1997). *Annual Abstract of Statistics*. London: Stationery Office.

Olasky, M. (1992). *The Tragedy of American Compassion*. Washington, DC: Regnery Gateway.

Park, T. (1994). Non-profit foundations in Korea. In K. Jung (Ed.), *Evolving Patterns of Asia-Pacific Philanthropy* (pp. 59–78). Seoul, Korea: Yonsei University Institute of East and West Studies.

Pharaoh, C. (1996). The growth of community trusts and foundations. In Charities Aid Foundation (Ed.), *Dimensions of the Voluntary Sector* (pp. 70–73). West Malling, UK: CAF.

Renz, L., Mandler, C., & Tran, T. (1997). *Foundation Giving. Yearbook of Facts and Figures on Private, Corporate and Community Foundations*. New York: Foundation Center.

Rudney, G. (1987). Creation of foundations and their wealth. In T. Odendahl (Ed.), *America's Wealthy and the Future of Foundations* (pp. 179–202). New York: Foundation Center.

Salamon, L. M., & Anheier, H. K. (1996). *The Emerging Nonprofit Sector: An Overview*. Manchester, UK: Manchester University Press.

Salamon, L. M. (1992a). *America's Nonprofit Sector: A Primer*. New York: Foundation Center.

Salamon, L. M. (1992b). Foundations as investment managers: Part I. The process. *Nonprofit Management and Leadership, 3*(2), 117–137.

Schiller, T. (1969). *Stiftungen im gesellschaftlichen Prozeß*. Baden-Baden: Nomos.

Statistisches Bundesamt. (1992, 1997). *Statistisches Jahrbuch für die Bundesrepublik Deutschland*. Stuttgart: Metzler-Poeschl.

Strachwitz, R. (1994). Stiftungen—nutzen, führen und errichten: Ein Handbuch. Frankfurt: Campus.

Strachwitz, R. (1998). Operative and fördernde Stiftungen: Anmerkungen zur Typologie. In Bertelsmann Stiftung (Ed.), *Handbuch des Stiftungsmanagements* (pp. 675–698). Wiesbaden, Germany: Gabler.

Strachwitz, R., & Toepler, S. (1996). Traditional methods of funding: Endowments and foundations. In L. Doyle (Ed.), *Funding Europe's Solidarity* (pp. 100–108). Brussels: AICE.

Toepler, S. (1996). *Das gemeinnützige Stiftungswesen in der modernen demokratischen Gesellschaft*. Munich: Maecenata.

Toepler, S. (1998). Foundations and their institutional context: Cross-evaluating evidence from Germany and the United States. *Voluntas, 9*(2), 153–170.

U.S. Bureau of the Census. (1996). *Statistical Abstract of the United States*. Washington, DC: Government Printing Office.

Wagner, A. (1997). Der Nonprofit Sektor in der Schweiz. In C. Badelt (Ed.). *Handbuch der Nonprofit Organisationen* (pp. 35–50). Stuttgart: Poeschl.

Weaver, W. (1967). *U.S. Philanthropic Foundations*. New York: Harper & Row.

Whitaker, B. (1974). *The Philanthropoids*. New York: William Morrow.

Workshop V: Community Foundations (1997). (Moderated by Shannon St. John). In Bertelsmann Stiftung (Ed.), *Operative Stiftungsarbeit: Strategien, Instrumente, Perspektiven* (pp. 131–142). Gütersloh, Germany: Verlag Bertelsmann Stiftung.

Ylvesaker, P. N. (1987). Foundations and nonprofit organizations. In W. W. Powell (Ed.), *The Nonprofit Sector: A Research Handbook* (pp. 360–379). New Haven: Yale University Press.

Part II

Comparative Studies

Systematic cross-national work on foundations has been notably absent from the bourgeoning research agenda of the nonprofit field both in the United States and abroad. This neglect stands in marked contrast to the increasingly international character of many foundations, and it is all the more surprising in the light of the contributions they are making to the design of a "New Europe," to the restructuring of Central and Eastern Europe, to developmental efforts in Africa, or to policy formulation at the international level.

While foundations are doubtlessly increasing both in numbers and in importance internationally, research has not kept up with these developments. Although much useful work has been carried out by historians and social scientists in the United States and, to a lesser extent, in some European countries, comparative issues have not been explored in any serious way. Accordingly, while there are a few basic statistics on the number and types of foundations in different countries, hardly any attempts have been made to examine more analytical problems. Included here are issues such as variations in the size, scope, and composition of foundation sectors cross-nationally; comparative analyses of the historical evolution of foundations in different national contexts; or the effects of different legal and policy environments on philanthropic foundations.

The three chapters in Part II constitute initial attempts to gauge the comparative dimensions of key aspects of the foundation world. From a historical point of view, Martin Bulmer charts the evolution of large philanthropic foundations in Great Britain and the United States around the turn of the century. Tymen van der Ploeg contrasts central aspects of the legal regulation of foundations in six countries, with a special emphasis on the issues of transparency and supervision. With the exception of the United States, Germany appears to be the only country so far to have produced a significant and fairly comprehensive body of data on the local foundation community. Drawing on these data, Helmut Anheier and Frank Romo present an extensive empirical comparison of grantmaking foundations in Germany and the United States.

All of these chapters testify to the usefulness of applying a comparative angle to the understanding of foundations. While the term *foundation* is in use in almost all countries, important historical, legal, and cultural differences exist that are in need of further cross-national exploration.

Chapter **2**

The History of Foundations in the United Kingdom and the United States

Philanthropic Foundations in Industrial Society

MARTIN BULMER

THE RELEVANCE OF HISTORY

Writing as a child in his autograph book in 1888, Seebohm Rowntree, son of the British Quaker chocolate manufacturer, noted Oliver Wendell Holmes's maxim: "Put not your trust in money, but your money in trust." It was a prescient remark bearing the influence of his father, who a few years later established three trusts. The Philanthropic Foundation is a distinctive twentieth-century social institution that has played a central role in charitable and voluntary support for a range of educational, medical, and scientific activities,

MARTIN BULMER • Professor of Sociology, University of Surrey, Guildford, Surrey GU2 5XH United Kingdom.

Private Funds, Public Purpose: Philanthropic Foundations in an International Perspective, edited by Helmut K. Anheier and Stefan Toepler. New York, Plenum Press, 1999.

which are not commonly identified with the voluntary sector today. The twelve years between 1901 and 1913 witnessed the emergence of this new form of philanthropy. Starting with the Rockefeller Institute of Medical Research and the Carnegie Institution of Washington, in 1901, there followed the establishment of the General Education Board in 1902, the three charitable trusts established by Joseph Rowntree in Britain in 1904, the Carnegie Foundation for the Advancement of Teaching in 1905, the Russell Sage Foundation in 1907, the Rockefeller Sanitary Commission in 1909, the Carnegie Corporation of New York in 1911, and the Rockefeller Foundation in 1913.

These foundations formed more than a new form of giving, for giving took on a new meaning. Rich American industrialists, and a small number elsewhere, set out to devote at least a part of their considerable personal wealth to broad philanthropic purposes. Other foundations followed in subsequent years, spread across many countries—Nuffield, Leverhulme, Gulbenkian, Agnelli, Körber, Thyssen, Ratan Tata and many others—but the basic pattern was established in the opening years of this century. What marks this period, in the United States in particular, is the appearance of a new and different source of support for public initiatives, mediating between the state and the citizen, but largely independent of the state. Moreover, the philanthropic foundation in the form it took is a social institution that defies easy classification. It is one that is to a considerable extent *sui generis* and has provoked considerable debate about its nature and its political and social significance.

The history of foundations opens up a number of themes relevant to this book. The character and purposes of foundations, as legally incorporated, are distinctive. Foundations represent a unique development in the organization of charitable giving, as a form of institution building in the transition from societies based on status to those based on contract, from community to association in Toennies's terms. The control of foundations is a central issue. On whose behalf is their power to influence social development exercised? To whom are foundations answerable? Foundations' place in the social structure is also a contested issue. At least since 1910, the activities of large foundations have been politically contentious, with critics charging that they are institutions designed to further the interests of elites and powerful class interests. These issues will be explored further here with particular reference to the period between 1870 and 1930, and with some emphasis on foundation involvement in the study of social conditions and social problems.

The cases discussed in this chapter are drawn mainly from the United States and the United Kingdom. Although insofar as major US foundations have throughout their history pursued international programs, the focus is wider than that. The history of foundations has been a growing field in recent years, but it is still not very well known.

THE CONCEPT OF THE FOUNDATION AND ITS LEGAL STATUS

The origins of institutions endowed with capital assets in perpetuity for charitable purposes is of course far older than the twentieth century (cf. Coing, 1981). In Britain, bodies as various as hospitals, private boarding schools, almshouses for the relief of the poor, and Oxford and Cambridge colleges were established in this way from the sixteenth century or earlier. Yet though one may talk of "the foundation" in relation to such bodies, they were not philanthropic foundations in the sense that we use the term in this volume. Such philanthropic foundations are distinguished by at least four characteristics:

1. Foundation objectives are the furtherance of some public purposes as defined in the establishing deed and interpreted by the trustees. The purposes are to be achieved indirectly by making grants to others, usually other organizations or institutions, rather than individuals, that actively pursue the desired philanthropic goals. Usually, these goals are of a very broad and multiple kind designed to benefit the public in some form, and are not limited to a particular place or a particular client group. Thus, Joseph Rowntree, in 1904, defined the aims of his three newly established trusts as religious, political, and social (each of which was further specified). Frederick Gates chose for the Rockefeller Foundation in 1913 the aim of "the well-being of mankind throughout the world," which when the Rockefeller Foundation was reorganized in 1929 became "the advancement of knowledge throughout the world." The trust deed of the U.K. Nuffield Foundation, set up by Lord Nuffield in 1943, speaks of "the advancement of social well-being."

2. The establishment of foundations has happened hand in hand with the advancement of science and the application of scientific method to human affairs—interpreting "science" in a broad way. Foundations departed from a model of charity in terms of giving to individuals, or even to classes of individuals, in favor of an attempt to identify and influence or control more fundamental processes in nature and society (Karl & Katz, 1981). Relief of the needy was not their purpose; their instrument was the furtherance and harnessing of research. In programs such as those for the eradication of hookworm in the American South or the establishment of public libraries, foundations aimed to achieve major social transformations. Joseph Rowntree wrote in his original trust deed that much current philanthropic effort was "directed to remedying the more superficial manifestations of weakness or evil, while little thought is directed to search out their underlying causes" (Rowntree, 1904, p. xiv). He criticized the alleviation of Indian famines without examining their

causes, and directed that none of his three trusts should support hospitals, almshouses, or similar institutions.

3. The great foundations enjoy very large endowments, mainly derived from industrial wealth that enable them to operate on a scale quite different from individual philanthropy. Historically, foundations (such as the General Education Board and the Carnegie Foundation for the Advancement of Teaching) have undertaken responsibilities (especially in the field of higher education) that were subsequently assumed by governments.

4. Foundations are legally incorporated bodies whose charitable public purposes are thereby publicly recognized. This also implies public acceptability. The bill to establish the Rockefeller Foundation running into political opposition in Congress after 1910, the Foundation was incorporated in the state of New York by the state legislature in 1913. Foundations are managed by professional staff who operate the programs of the foundation and are influential in shaping them. In some respects, they are more similar to business enterprises than to individual charitable activity or small, voluntary associations. When contemplating foundations as a way to manage the distribution of his wealth, John D. Rockefeller, Sr. spoke of "the business of benevolence." Many other founders also sought to apply business methods to the running of their operations. They employed rationality, organization, and efficiency in giving as in commercial activity.

THE PHILANTHROPIC FOUNDATION AS THE INSTITUTIONALIZATION OF KNOWLEDGE-BASED SOCIAL ENGINEERING: A GRADUAL EVOLUTION

Over a period of sixty years, between approximately 1870 and 1930, the development of the foundation as a major social institution may be traced. This evolution has to be seen in the wider context of the increasing industrialization and urbanization of North America and parts of Western Europe, the ensuing social problems, and the attempt to frame an institutional response capable of tackling them. For all that, the aims of foundations were expressed in general terms such as the advancement of knowledge and the improvement of human welfare. Foundations were part of a broader process involving the growth of government, greater government intervention in more areas of social life, and the erosion of personal relationships as the basis of social cohesion. The German sociologist Ferdinand Toennies conceptualized this change as one from *Gemeinschaft* to *Gesellschaft,* usually, but not quite accurately, translated as from community to association. Foundations evolved in a world where different routes were being sought to the solution of social problems through the various civic and voluntary reform movements of the latter nineteenth century. Not only did they tend to operate with different models of the relationship between the individual, society, and social agencies, but also the role of the state was ambivalent, and foundations evolved at some distance from it.

Charity Organization

Britain and the United States had very different political systems, and the history of foundations in each society is somewhat different. Nevertheless, in the field of social welfare, there was much interchange of ideas and institutions between the two, and in our period a reasonable awareness of developments in the other country. With the move of large, migrant populations into urban areas, how to contain, control, and tackle the problems of the greater visibility of poor health and housing, poverty, vice, and crime was the question posed in the middle and late nineteenth century in the field of charitable activity. Elites and members of the upper middle class, who acknowledged a responsibility to the working classes, adopted these issues. In an age that did not believe in government involvement, the main sources of assistance were private individuals organized into voluntary bodies. With the advent of foundations, the responses remained individual ones, but on more systematic principles. The scale of the problems and the limitations of individual philanthropy required more systematic organization of giving. Something more was needed than soup or alms for the poor.

The London Charity Organisation Society, established in 1869 for the relief of poverty, ushered in an era of "scientific philanthropy." Better organization of relief with less duplication, more discrimination in the giving of assistance, and more individual attention to those in need was required. "Friendly visiting" of the poor in their homes by charity organization workers was the core activity, reflecting the belief that the reform of the individual was the key to improvement. By 1930, charity organization work had evolved into social work, become more professionalized and bureaucratized, and its connection to charitable effort considerably attenuated. "Scientific philanthropy," however, still relied heavily upon an individualistic model of social intervention.

Settlement Houses

A more organized and collective type of response was through the Settlement House movement. The original settlement, Toynbee Hall in the east end of London, was set up in 1884 by Canon Samuel Barnett, an Anglican clergyman influenced by John Ruskin, William Morris, and early Christian socialism. Its objectives were to "bridge the gulf that industrialism has created between rich and poor, to reduce the mutual suspicion and ignorance of one class for the other, and to do something more than give charity." This was to be achieved by the establishment of a voluntary association with residential premises located in an urban, working-class area, an institutional intermediary between different geographical and social worlds. Its practical aims were threefold: (1) to spread education and culture, (2) to enable middle-class people to form personal relationships with members of the working class, and (3) to discover facts about social problems (Briggs & Macartney, 1984). By 1911, forty-six such settlements had been founded in Britain. In the United States, growth was even faster, as young Americans such as Jane Addams visited Toynbee Hall and returned to found settlements like Hull-House in Chicago, the University Settlement, and Henry Street in New York. By 1910, there were more than 400 American settlements.

The significance of the Settlement House as a training ground for socially concerned young people was considerable. Although Canon Barnett at first espoused a person-centered explanation of social pathology, between 1880 and 1900, he moved sharply away from such a Charity Organisation Society view of the world toward economic explanations for the causes of social distress and a growing belief in state intervention to provide for the destitute, pensions for the elderly, and training schemes for the unemployed.

Canon Barnett was by 1900 one of Britain's most highly regarded authorities on the causes and remedies of poverty. He was critical of the ideas of the Charity Organisation Society (see McBriar, 1987, pp. 61–65) and favored centralization and a greater role for the state in social welfare. He took an active part in the debates about Poor Law reform that followed the appointment of the Royal Commission on the Poor Laws in 1905. He generally supported the views put forward by Sidney and Beatrice Webb in favor of larger, more disinterested units of organization and control, and the rationalization of administration in the hands of officials, rather than boards of guardians. He wrote, "The same . . . body, which is responsible for the health, for the education, and for the industrial fitness of some members of the community should be responsible in like manner for all the members, whatever their position" (quoted in Meacham, 1987, p. 112).

It is easy in retrospect to poke fun at settlements for their high-flown aspirations juxtaposed to the reality of "slumming," for the social distance between their residents and their working-class neighbors, and for their relative ineffectiveness in making an impact upon social conditions in the locality. Toynbee Hall, indeed, was built as a "manorial residence," in nineteenth-century Elizabethan style more characteristic of Oxford than the East End. Yet this urban echo of collegiate life—and its later British and American followers—helped to form the worldviews of a number of influential figures in public life. Canon Barnett's protégés included Alfred Milner, Robert Morant,

Arthur Salter, and William Beveridge, Beveridge indeed being brought in as subwarden in 1903 specifically to sharpen Toynbee Hall's attack on social problems (Harris, 1977, pp. 48–49). R. H. Tawney, challenged by the Master of Balliol, Edward Caird, to go and find out why England had poverty alongside riches and do something about it, lived there for over four years beginning in 1903, at the same time as Beveridge (Terrill, 1974, pp. 31–35).

The most striking American example of the influence of settlements upon developing social ideas was Hull-House in Chicago. Among its leading residents, in addition to Jane Addams, at the start of our period were Julia Lathrop, later first head of the U.S. Children's Bureau; Florence Kelley, pioneer social investigator and later head of the National Consumer's League; and Edith Abbott, pioneer in social service education. John Dewey and George Herbert Mead of the University of Chicago were friends of Addams. The residents were young (in their twenties), thoughtful, and socially committed. Unlike Toynbee Hall, Hull-House was nonsectarian and more explicitly committed to tackling social problems. One historian has called such settlements "ad hoc graduate schools," and it is indeed realistic to see Hull-House (and Toynbee Hall for some of its residents) as a kind of graduate school in social policy before such opportunities existed in universities.

Settlements provided an institutional base from which problems of poverty could be tackled. It is salutary to remember that in the period before 1914, Jane Addams was America's best-known and most admired woman in public life, possibly even the most respected public figure. When she seconded Theodore Roosevelt's nomination as Progressive Party candidate for the presidency in 1912, she received as great an ovation as Roosevelt himself. Addams, Lathrop, and Kelley gave the Settlement House movement leadership and visibility, and a more immediate public impact, than the residents of Toynbee Hall.

Studies of Social Conditions

One means by which they made their impact was through studies of social conditions. The main social investigations of poverty at this period were undertaken by private individuals from their own resources and the results addressed to a general, educated public. Charles Booth, the pioneer social surveyor, was a Liverpool businessman, Seebohm Rowntree, the son of a Quaker chocolate manufacturer. They undertook their studies in London and York (Booth, 1889–1903; Rowntree, 1901), using their own family wealth, and in both cases combined active social investigation with the continuing pursuit of business interests. The importance of these studies lay first in giving some precision to estimates of the extent of poverty. In Booth's case, he used an arbitrary poverty standard, but Rowntree based his standard upon calorific requirements derived from the American nutritionist Atwater to lend the measure a more objective standing. Both agreed closely that approximately three-tenths of the population of the cities studied were living in poverty.

Second, they went some considerable way to illuminating the dynamics of poverty and its underlying causes, through Rowntree's analysis of the cycle of poverty and Booth's investigations of the relation between low wages, unemployment, and poverty. Third, they provided a standard to emulate in other studies, subsequently in Britain and in the United States, initiating a movement of thought about social problems that had far reaching effects. One U.S. study modeled on Booth, throwing important light on social conditions among blacks, was W. E. B. Du Bois's study *The Philadelphia Negro* (1899). Other studies bore clear signs of his influence, such as Robert Hunter's *Tenement Conditions in Chicago* (1901), and the latter's *Poverty* (1904) also drew upon Rowntree. As Allen Davis has observed, many early settlement workers were influenced by Booth "and set out to emulate his painstaking research and to gather statistics about urban life, first in their neighborhood then in the city. They investigated child labor, tenement houses and tuberculosis, and they were interested in studying the problems of the city in all its aspects" (1967, pp. 171–172).

Social inquiry was a prominent element in the American Settlement House ethos. Charles Booth's studies of poverty in London provided the inspiration for the Hull-House Maps and Papers (1895), the first American social survey. Florence Kelley convinced Jane Addams that investigations at Hull-House would result in a survey on a par with Booth's work (Sklar, 1992). It was shortly followed by *The City Wilderness* in 1899, edited by Robert Woods and written by settlement workers attached to Boston's South End House. The role of settlements was to try to reintegrate the city wilderness of isolation and congestion, responding to both the dynamism of city life and the social distance between classes, the corruption and the poverty that they saw around them. A more specific focus upon poverty was provided in Robert Hunter's 1904 study, *Poverty*. A resident of Hull-House after graduating from the University of Illinois in 1896, he was influenced by Booth and Rowntree as well as by Riis's *How the Other Half Lives* (1890). Hunter attempted to place the study of the phenomenon on an objective basis by adopting a Rowntree-style absolute definition of poverty. On this basis, he estimated that 12 percent of the American population (10 million out of 82 million) were poor. This was concentrated in Northern industrial areas where 6.6 million, or 20 percent of the population, were poor. Only about 4 million out of America's 10 million poor received any public relief. Like Booth, Hunter focused upon the structural conditions producing poverty, particularly low wages and unemployment. From the 1900 census, he estimated that 22 percent of the labor force were unemployed at some point during the year, over half of them for more than four months out of twelve. None of them received unemployment insurance, which had almost no public support at the time.

The role of the Settlement House movement in publicizing social conditions was not confined to poverty. Issues such as child labor, the treatment of juveniles in the court system, sweated labor, and poor housing conditions loomed as large, if not larger, in their concerns. Jane Addam's first book, *Democracy and Social Ethics* (1902), painted the issues on an even broader canvas, reaching a wide audience. Her book, wrote Oliver Wendell Holmes, "gives me more insight into the point of view of the working man and the poor than I had before." In the United States, the Settlement House movement exercised an influence upon city and state governments. Though cities, notably Chicago, were often unresponsive due to their control by political machines, at the state level, some notable innovations were effected, for example, the establishment of the Illinois Juvenile Court in 1899 (Mennel, 1973). Such instances of legislative influence were typically a result of reformers' efforts to add new responsibilities to government.

The Social Survey Movement

One means of increasing social awareness of poverty in the United States took the form of a Movement, underpinned by support from the Russell Sage Foundation, one of the earliest foundations to concern itself with social conditions. When Mrs. Russell Sage sought advice in 1906 on the disposition of her husband's fortune, her lawyer Robert W. Forest, president of the Charity Organization Society of New York City since 1888, suggested the establishment of the "Sage Foundation for Social Betterment," having as its object "the permanent improvement of social conditions." Its role would be to investigate the causes of adverse social conditions, to suggest how these conditions might be remedied or ameliorated, and to take action to that end. When the Russell Sage Foundation was incorporated in New York in 1907, one of the first projects it supported was the Pittsburgh Survey, with a grant of $27,000 for "a careful and fairly comprehensive study of the conditions under which working people live and labor in a great industrial city" (Glenn, Brandt, & Andrews, 1947, pp. 210–211).

The Pittsburgh Survey had its roots in social work and philanthropy rather than the settlement houses. Its prime movers belonged to the world of organized philanthropy, and its director was Paul U. Kellogg, managing editor of *Charities and the Commons,* the leading social work magazine. Kellogg and his staff published six stout volumes between 1909 and 1914, presenting the results of their work. In a later volume (1915, p. iii) Kellogg drew an explicit comparison between their study and that of Booth. In fact, though Booth was certainly an inspiration of the study, the methods used were more those of investigative journalism rather than social measurement. The approach was descriptive rather than analytical, with quite strong overtones of muckraking (for a full discussion, see Greenwald & Anderson, 1996).

Following the publication of the Pittsburgh Survey, requests for "surveys" began to come to the Foundation from various parts of the country. The Director considered that it was worth fostering "the spirit of inquiry into local conditions by the people of localities and to advise as to methods of procedure in order that serious mistakes may be avoided." The Foundation seemed "the best, if not the only, agency that can give the proper guidance and control to local surveys." Thus, in 1912, the Department of Surveys and Exhibits was established, headed by Shelby M. Harrison, who had worked on the Pittsburgh Survey, as a clearing house for advice and field assistance in the conduct of surveys and organization of local exhibits. The department's peak of activity was reached by 1920. The most significant study undertaken was the Spring-field Survey.

The Social Survey Movement, which flourished between 1912 and 1930, was sustained by the support of the Russell Sage Foundation, losing its impe-tus in the latter 1920s and having virtually disappeared by the mid-1930s. An important element lay in the fact that it was a social movement. The notions of publicity and community self-study were an integral part of the Movement, articulated by Shelby M. Harrison as director of the department of surveys and exhibits at the Russell Sage Foundation. Russell Sage's funding of the Pitts-burgh Survey and subsequently of many major surveys, including the Spring-field Survey, which Harrison directed, was the first major example of large-scale philanthropic funding of social inquiry, of which more later.

PHILANTHROPIC FOUNDATIONS

The wealthy American industrialists who established foundations did not move in the circles of charity organization work or early social investigation. They came from the world of business and industry, though they were not all of a pattern. John D. Rockefeller Sr. was a devout Baptist. Andrew Carnegie had risen from humble Scottish origins and retained an acute awareness of class differences and cultural disadvantage among the working classes on both sides of the Atlantic, but particularly in Britain. Mrs. Russell Sage inherited the wealth of her unpleasant husband and was more closely connected to the world of charity than her male counterparts.

One interpretation of foundations' emergence is practical. To give away the wealth which John D. Rockefeller Sr. had derived from cornering the oil market, required entirely new institutions. During the 1880s, he hired Freder-ick Gates to help him deal with requests for charitable assistance. As a matter of policy, Gates rapidly made the transition from retail to wholesale philanthropy, from dealing with individuals to dealing with institutions. This, however, was not enough to absorb the wealth that Rockefeller had accumulated, and even large endowments to new institutions such as the University of Chicago in the 1890s did not absorb more than a fraction of the surplus. So starting in 1901, a whole swathe of foundations was created, with grand objectives reflecting the faith that scientific knowledge was the key to social improvement. Many of them reflected Gates's strong belief in the value of supporting medicine and public health as a means of increasing human welfare. They included the Rockefeller Institute for Medical Research, the China Medical Board, the Rockefeller Sanitary Commission (later the International Health Board) and the Division of Medical Education. All but the first were brought together in the Rockefeller Foundation when it was incorporated in 1913. It was "a mosaic consisting of its various organizations in medicine and public health, thrown together without thought of integration and without central control" (Kohler, 1978). The General Education Board was created in 1902 to support American colleges, and the International Education Board was added in 1923.

The international significance of these activities should also be underlined. The Carnegie Corporation pursued an active policy of supporting activities in Britain, reflecting its founder's Scottish origins. The (Rockefeller) International Health Board had divided the world up into sectors and saw London as the capital of the British empire, the ideal place to create strategically placed centers of medical education, endowing the London School of Hygiene and Tropical Medicine in 1922. Donald Fisher (1978) considers it unlikely that this institution would have come into existence without the support of the Rockefeller Foundation. In the social sciences, developments in Britain were heavily dependent upon American philanthropic support, though whether this influence was for good or ill is strongly contested among those who have studied the subject. (See, for example, the debate between Bulmer [1984] and Fisher [1984].) What is significant is the wider international perspective that it introduced, which developed particularly strongly in medicine and science.

Apart from the war period, there was little government funding available between the wars that was earmarked for social science. U.S. foundations played a particularly important role in providing "core" funding at leading private universities, although from the mid-1930s onward, such support was cut back in favor of program and project grants for more specific proposals, as the foundations made clear that they could no longer continue to underwrite basic development of the higher education system outside the state universities. Support in Britain was more modest and devoted mainly to direct welfare intervention (cf. Mess & Braithwaite, 1947).

This feature of the interwar period necessitates some revision of the view taken of state structures and social knowledge production. There is continuing controversy about the significance of the social role played by foundations and their degree of disinterestedness in providing support (contrast Arnove, 1980, with Karl & Katz, 1981 and 1987). During this period, foundations were more and more controlled by their professional staff, rather than trustees, who were inclined to take a more detached and long-term view of the social contribution that philanthropic giving might make. Thus Beardsley Ruml at the Memorial staunchly defended a policy of underwriting social science research at selected centers, leaving disbursement of the grants within the university to social science staff at the institution. Studies of this process need to progress beyond arguments about whether foundations were the tools of capitalism to understand to what extent they reflected and to what extent they influenced contemporary developments, and in what ways they shaped the development of the social sciences. In particular, what aspirations did they embody as to the application of social science to social problems, and how far was such an emphasis significant in shaping the form of later developments after World War II? Whom did the trustees and staff of philanthropic bodies represent, and what was their relationship to academic experts? Sealander (1997) has made a start in relation to the development of American social policy.

The Laura Spelman Rockefeller Memorial

The evolution from charity to knowledge-based social engineering may be shown by considering briefly the history of the Laura Spelman Rockefeller Memorial (the Memorial), created by John D. Rockefeller Sr. in memory of his wife in 1918, with a capital of $74 million, and its successor after 1929, the Social Science Division of the Rockefeller Foundation (Bulmer & Bulmer, 1981). Initially, the Memorial supported work in areas in which Mrs. Rockefeller had been particularly interested, mostly concerning women and children. In the first four years, to 1922, over four-fifths of its income was devoted to social welfare or religious organizations such as the YMCA and YWCA, Scouts, the Salvation Army and the Baptist church, and for emergency relief in Russia and China. Its aims were little different from many upper- and middle-class charitable activities on behalf of the "lower orders."

Then, in 1922, Raymond Fosdick persuaded Rockefeller Jr. to appoint as full-time director the young Beardsley Ruml, trained as a psychologist, who had worked as an applied psychologist developing occupational tests in the War Department in 1917–1918, and who had recently been assistant to the head of the Carnegie Corporation. Ruml was committed to the development of the social sciences as a means of tackling social problems. The development of the social sciences was essential for the furtherance of human welfare. He very rapidly brought about a fundamental change in Memorial policy, from social amelioration to supporting basic but practically useful social science research. The parallel with fundamental knowledge underlying medical practice was emphasized. Among other issues for attention he identified children, the elderly, the poor, problems affecting the immigrant, the character of neighborhoods. A very important principle was that the program should be advanced by supporting research in universities, which was the optimum location for such inquiries.

In the next seven years, Ruml developed a major program of basic research in the social sciences, located in major American and European universities such as the University of Chicago, the London School of Economics, Columbia University, Harvard University, the Universities of Minnesota, Iowa State, Yale, North Carolina, California, Cambridge and Texas, in addition to the (U.S.) Social Science Research Council, the National Bureau of Economic Research in New York, and a scheme for fellowships for young social scientists. In this period, about $25 million was allocated to basic social science research, a very large sum indeed for the period, and one that was a major stimulus for empirical social research in economics, political science, psychology, sociology, anthropology, and international relations. Although some research in social work and welfare was supported, the main thrust of the program was for basic disciplinary work.

At the same time, partly based on his experience as an applied psychologist, Ruml argued that basic social science would help to produce applied results that would assist in the solution of social problems. He particularly favored interdisciplinary work and sought to break down barriers that separated the different disciplines. Several other features of the program were distinctive. Ruml formed close links with leading social scientists on both sides of the Atlantic, such as Chicago political scientist Charles Merriam and social economist William Beveridge, the director of the London School of Economics. Grants were given not only for research programs but also for academic infrastructure: research buildings, libraries, and, in some cases, endowed chairs. The Memorial had a small staff of its own and provided support in the form of block grants to institutions, which were expected to create their own internal organization to administer and distribute the grant. The Memorial did not seek publicity; indeed, it actively discouraged recipients of its grants from revealing the source of their support.

In 1929, the Memorial became the Social Science Division of the Rockefeller Foundation, and Ruml moved on to other things (including, during World War II, the invention of Pay-as-You-Go income tax). The activities of the Memorial contributed to fundamental changes in the kind of social science research being done in certain departments at leading universities. It marked the beginning of a modern phase in the organization of social science, which took it well beyond the lone scholar working upon documents and books in a library, supervising a few Ph.D. students using similar methods, and favoring impressionistic analysis. It helped to move some departments in some disciplines in the social sciences toward more systematic, extensive, and often quantitative analyses, and to lay the foundations of the research-oriented graduate schools, drawing heavily on external funding, which became more characteristic of the postwar academic scene. The Memorial was a major source of patronage in the social sciences, and considerably influenced their development around the world in the 1920s and afterward.

The wider significance of this example of a foundation program lies in several directions. It encouraged and created the necessary conditions for a major change taking place in the orientation of a group of academic disciplines and the way in which they regarded the world. It thus contributed to a major change in the external environment, which one foundation official judged, and the trustees were persuaded, was desirable and right. The Memorial pursued a policy to promote change that it judged the correct one. This policy was pursued entirely through other institutions, most of them preexisting (the universities) but a few, such as the SSRC and the National Bureau, having come into existence specifically to meet certain objectives that the Memorial endorsed. The program reflected the belief that science offered solutions to the problems facing industrial societies, and that supporting fundamental research and talented individuals was the best way in which to advance the well-being of mankind. The Memorial's work was carried out in secret, without publicity, and although its role was known in the research community, no external discussion or announcement of its role was encouraged. And the program was the creation of one man, Beardsley Ruml, with support from key trustees such as Raymond Fosdick and Arthur Woods. It was further evidence, already apparent for science in the work of Wickliffe Rose and in medicine of Abraham Flexner (cf. Wheatley, 1988) of the emergence of the foundation official as one of the key actors in the work of large foundations. Trustees were the formal source of authority, but to an increasing extent, they acted upon the recommendations of their staff, who formulated the policy and conducted the detailed negotiations with grant recipients.

POWER AND RESPONSIBILITY

The Implications of Being "Private" Bodies

Foundations are private philanthropic bodies run by small groups of trustees and officials. There are at least two senses in which they are "private." As this volume testifies, foundations are part of the third sector and are neither part of the state apparatus nor commercial undertakings. Foundations themselves and many of the institutions that they support were and are "intermediary institutions" between the state and its citizens. Particularly in the United States, federal and state governments did not consider it their responsibility to get involved in many of the areas in which foundations interested themselves. In the first forty years of the twentieth century, various forms of voluntary action and private initiative were highly significant—and in many cases, more significant than state action—both in social welfare delivery and in studies of social conditions. In the United States, many leading universities were and remain private universities. Foundations worked in close association with these bodies and saw themselves as being outside the sphere of government. During the early 1930s, when newly elected President Herbert Hoover established a committee to study and report on *Recent Social Trends,* this presidential commission was funded not from Congress but from the Rockefeller Foundation, which contributed $0.5 million for its inquiries (Fisher, 1993).

Foundations, moreover, also drew sharp distinctions. Until the late 1920s, it was a fixed Rockefeller policy, first articulated by Gates, that grants would only be given for programs at private and not state universities. Some private universities such as Johns Hopkins, Stanford, and Clark were indeed the result of individual benefactions in the late nineteenth century. The University of Chicago was founded in 1891 by Rockefeller, Sr. U.S. foundations played a particularly important role in providing "core" funding at leading private universities for scientific, medical, and social science research. Although, from the mid-1930s onward, such support was cut back in favor of program and project grants for more specific proposals, as the foundations made clear that they could no longer continue to underwrite basic development of the higher education system outside the state universities. Support in Britain was much more modest and devoted mainly to direct welfare intervention (cf. Mess & Braithwaite, 1947).

The history of foundations sharply highlights the controversial role they have played since their inception, but the extent to which they were truly "private" has been the subject of sharp disagreement ever since their establishment (Karl & Katz, 1981). One of the central issues of controversy is that closed and private institutions have sought to address public issues, and increase the public welfare, without acknowledging public responsibility for the policies that they were pursuing. The types of criticism that have been leveled at foundations have changed relatively little over the last eighty years. Criticisms had a populistic tinge and were based on the assumption that foundations represented the investment of ill-gotten gains in a way that threatened to subvert the democratic process by giving philanthropists a determining role in the conduct of public life. From the protest against congressional incorporation of the Rockefeller Foundation and the Walsh Commission hearings on industrial relations of 1915–1916, in the bitter attacks of Harold Laski and others in the late 1920s and early 1930s, to the twin attacks of conservative

Congressmen and political radicals in the 1950s and 1960s, similar themes recur:

> money which ought to be in the hands of the public is being retained by aristocrats for purposes beyond the control of democratic institutions; the academic freedom of universities is being subverted by control of academic budgets by the foundations; public policy is being determined by private groups; the scientific and scholarly research and artistic creativity of individuals are being subverted by the emphasis of foundations on group-research; smallness and individual effort are thwarted by materialistic and business-oriented demands of foundation management; foundations are bastions of an elite of white, Anglo-Saxon, Protestant managers holding out against the normal development of a pluralistic and ethnic society; and so on. (Karl & Katz, 1981, pp. 248–249)

These criticisms have been articulated particularly strongly in the United States, where the disjunction between the large wealth of rather secretive foundations and the democratic ethos of the society has been particularly sharp, but they have been present in all societies in which foundations are set up. On the other side of the Atlantic, European socialism has been rather distrustful of foundations, established by rich persons, which seek actively to promote the public welfare; socialists repose more confidence in the state (Coing, 1981). The debate has not been quite so pointed, however, because foundations have not been so wealthy as their great American counterparts, and have played a smaller role in the pursuit of public policy.

The Critique of Foundations

Among the criticisms directed at foundations have been the following. Early Congressional critics of the Rockefeller philanthropies argued that they were sophisticated vehicles for tax avoidance. The Ford Foundation was set up in 1937 for tax purposes but did not become active as a donor until about 1950. Nielsen (1985) lists a few very large U.S. foundations of recent origin where family interests and foundation interests seem very close together. Whatever the motives, moreover, charitable status confers considerable tax advantages upon the donor and his or her bequest. Thus, one consideration influencing Lord Nuffield to establish the Nuffield Foundation was the potential burden of death duties (inheritance tax) upon his estate in the event of his sudden death. A continuing justification for legislative scrutiny of foundations has been the need to see that they are doing what they claim to be doing and are not merely avoiding tax. The vast majority of foundations are in the clear, but the need to demonstrate probity is a continuing and perpetual one.

Another early and persistent criticism of foundations is that they are set up by wealthy industrialists to put a more favorable gloss on their activities as industrialists and to present themselves in a better light or as a means of retaining control of the industrial enterprise whence the endowment derives. "Tainted money," the Trojan Horse, and the Kiss of Judas were all accusations made against the Rockefeller incorporation. The usual defense of this has been the gradual separation of personal affairs from those of the Foundation. Thus, in 1915, Rockefeller, Jr. was stung by questioning by the Walsh commission, which pointed out that at that time, the Foundation and the family concerns shared offices at 26 Broadway and were more or less indistinguishable. Shortly afterward, he relinquished the management of the Rockefeller Foundation and separated the two sets of offices. In later years, the direct criticism of donors such as Nuffield or Wellcome has been less sharp, but the obloquy of "tainted money" remains one of the bases of distrust of foundations. And indeed, one motive of establishing the Nuffield Foundation was to enable control of Morris Motors to be retained (Clark, 1972, p. 6).

Almost always, the appointment of trustees is a private matter, in many cases lying in the hands of the existing trustees. Foundations are thus not responsible to anyone for whomever they appoint and may often be a self-perpetuating body. This is usually justified in terms of the benevolent intentions of the foundation, but contrasts with the position vis-à-vis public joint stock companies, where members of the board are subject to public election and periodic reelection. On occasion, an outside body may be asked to nominate trustees. Half of the Trustees of Joseph Rowntree's major trust are nominated by the Religious Society of Friends.

The unrepresentativeness of trustees is a continuing complaint against foundations. The initial trustees were usually associates or friends, occasionally relatives, of the benefactor, and subsequent trustees have very commonly been chosen from among those with similar backgrounds and positions. This is made increasingly likely by the method of appointment. Writing in 1936, Eduard C. Lindemann charged that trustees represented "social prestige, financial success and middle-aged respectability" (p. 161). These were exemplary attributes, but he asked if they were the most appropriate for people charged with pioneering new ways of improving the welfare of mankind. British foundations have perhaps been less likely to appoint the financially successful as trustees. The initial trustees of the Wellcome Trust, for example (established in 1936 by the will of the founder of the drug company and with a medical focus), were two solicitors, an accountant, and two distinguished academic physiologists with medical backgrounds. The first trustees of the Nuffield Foundation were Lord Nuffield's first bank manager, who had become a public figure; a distinguished lady doctor; the professor agriculture at the University of Cambridge; the Master of Magdalene College, Oxford, a distinguished scientist; the Vice Chancellors (heads) of the Universities of Manchester and Glasgow; and a banker.If one compares the Rockefeller philanthropies with those of Wellcome and Nuffield in Britain, all of which have taken a particular interest in aspects of science and medicine, in the American case, the foundation officials are more likely to have had academic backgrounds and to possess expert knowledge or the necessary connections to expertise, while the trustees were laymen and laywomen, whereas in the British case, the trustees included a number of practicing scientists who were able to make expert judgments themselves on applications being considered. This suggests possibly a somewhat different role for the trustees in these two cases, both in the backgrounds from which they are drawn and in the function they performed.

One response to the criticism of the narrowness of the social backgrounds of American foundation trustees has been to argue that foundation officials became increasingly important over time. Certainly, in both the Rockefeller philanthropies and the Carnegie Corporation it was the officials who directed affairs, as is clear from the discussion of the Memorial earlier. In Rockefeller circles, many of the officials came from academic backgrounds, and there was some interchange with academia, Ruml himself becoming Dean of Social Sciences for three years at the University of Chicago after he left New York. The process by which foundation officials became professionalized was a gradual one but is distinctly visible. In general, they were inclined to take a more detached and long-term view of the social contribution that philanthropic giving might make. A countercriticism of this trend, voiced in the 1920s by no less a person than Frederick Gates, was that officials could tend to usurp the functions of the trustees and accumulate too much power into their own hands. Again, this was apparent from the way in which Ruml operated in the 1920s or an architect of science such as Warren Weaver with the Rockefeller Foundation in the 1930s (Kohler, 1991).

Whether controlled by officials or trustees, foundations have also been criticized for timidity. If interpreted as organizations that will promote social innovation, many foundations have showed themselves rather conformist in the policies that they have pursued. Even as relatively radical an operator as Ruml put limits on the kinds of research that the Memorial could support. Research into government structure and municipal reform was a particularly sensitive area in this regard (because of its political connotations in early twentieth-century America), and he ruled it out as an area in which research could be funded. Unusually among founders, Joseph Rowntree recognized that some purposes that his trusts might wish to pursue fell outside the definition of the strictly charitable, and he therefore established the Joseph Rowntree Social Service Trust Ltd., which was permitted to support activities, for example, of a political kind, which went beyond the normal remit of philanthropic foundations. As an example, he gave approval to the idea that this trust might purchase a newspaper.

Furthermore, there is continuing controversy, and some variation between countries, in the external checks and constraints operating on foundations to control their activities. The preference of foundations for discretion or outright secrecy about their subventions (as with the Memorial) adds further point to this sensitivity. One of the principal criticisms of foundations as a social institution for the advancement of public welfare has been that foundations are answerable to no one for their actions apart from their trustees, other than legislative and legal regulation to ensure that they do what is set out in their trust deed. This regulation has been undertaken by tax authorities, by bodies that police the voluntary sector such as the (British) Charities Commission, a statutory body that can grant, withhold, or rescind charitable status, and by occasional hearings by the legislature inquire into the status of foundations.

Unlike most voluntary bodies, foundations have no members or supporters to whom an annual report is rendered, nor in the nature of the case (as with religious charities) an ultimate sponsor (such as the church), since the rules for the establishment of foundations require a clear line to be drawn between the founder and the foundation. During the founder's life, this was not always possible to do sharply, but after death, it usually came about. So the issue of ultimate responsibility remains a moot point, which puts foundations on the defensive and gives added ammunition to their critics. This final lack of legitimacy, because foundations in effect legitimize themselves, or do so in terms of the founder's intentions, is at the root of their peculiarity as institutions.

Foundations as Pillars of the Ruling Class

These specific criticisms of the powers, privileges, and lack of accountability of foundations are capped by more thoroughgoing critiques of the place of foundations in the social structure, which postulate that foundations are a mechanism whereby the ruling class in industrial societies maintains its cultural hegemony and limits the nature of challenges that can be posed to the fabric of society. This view is represented, for example, in the critique of the Rockefeller Hookworm eradication program by Brown (1979), the papers in the Arnove collection (1980), and in Fisher's study of the American Social Science Research Council (1993). Arnove, for example, argues that foundations have played the role of unofficial planning agencies for both a national American society and an increasingly interconnected world system with the United States at its center. Foundations, he argues, represent a sophisticated conservatism. I have criticized this theory previously (Bulmer, 1984, 1987) and do not propose to repeat myself here, except to observe that many of the individual founders and officials of foundations did not conform to the stereotype of ruling-class member that these works portray.

Andrew Carnegie was a hard-nosed businessman, but he held somewhat unconventional social ideas for his class and in the 1880s entered British political journalism briefly as a newspaper owner, advocating Gladstonian Liberalism plus the abolition of the monarchy, the House of Lords, and the Church of England (Lagemann, 1989, pp. 14–15). Joseph Rowntree was a committed Liberal and social reformer, espousing issues such as land reform and temperance, as well as being deeply religious. Frederick Gates was a Baptist minister prior to working for Rockefeller, Sr., and the religious element in the establishment of philanthropic foundations has been quite ignored by the ruling-class critique. Beardsley Ruml was the grandson of a Czech laborer who had migrated from Bohemia to Iowa, and was someone who had achieved his position by sheer academic ability and connections plus some luck, rather than being born into the Eastern Establishment.

Studies of foundation influence need to progress beyond arguments about whether foundations were the tools of capitalism to understand to what extent they reflected and to what extent they independently influenced contemporary developments. Is there any necessary connection between the origins of wealth and the activities that foundations undertake? It was not obvious in 1900 that the Rockefeller interests would, through Ruml, become a mainstay of the social sciences in the 1930s. How did the rather conformist Carnegie Corporation come to support the greatest liberal critique of the position of black Americans in the first half of the twentieth century, Gunnar Myrdal's *An American Dilemma* (Lagemann, 1989, pp. 123–146)? To what extent did foundations shape provision independently (as the theorists of cultural hegemony would maintain) or respond to perceived needs on the part of those whom they funded? Whom did the trustees and officials of philanthropic bodies consult, and what was their relationship to such lay and expert advisers, some of whom were also recipients of support? In particular, what aspirations did both parties embody as to the application of fundamental knowledge to tackling social problems? To what extent was there an elective affinity between foundations and those in the field who sit on their boards and whom they consult?

CONCLUSION: THE INSTITUTIONALIZATION OF KNOWLEDGE-BASED SOCIAL ENGINEERING BY PECULIAR INSTITUTIONS?

Philanthropic foundations are peculiar institutions that continue to arouse controversy. Increasingly in the twentieth century, they have been concerned with knowledge-based social engineering. This chapter has concentrated on a particular period and a particular set of issues, the development of the social sciences and social investigation, which was only one part of a wide variety of philanthropic activity.

The development of the application and use of scientific research—including natural science, medicine, and social science—in relation to government and policymaking is a twentieth-century phenomenon. It has occurred alongside a massive expansion in the scope of governmental activity, a vast increase in the size of public bureaucracies, and an extension of the authority and involvement of the state into areas that in the nineteenth century were treated as a matter of individual and private responsibility. Nowhere is this more evident than in the field of social policy, where nation-states in the industrial world now assume responsibilities inconceivable a century ago. In the fields of health, housing, income maintenance, the personal social services, and education, the activities of governments are extensive, in many cases dominating provision. There are different mixes in the different countries, with varying degrees of dominance, but the general trend is unmistakable. In many areas, there is also a marked international dimension. Since 1945, an entire field of international policy, practice, and academic research, that of "development," has emerged as centrally concerned with the international dimension.

This chapter has not discussed the extent to which foundations have been involved in social experiment and trial social interventions, which has been characteristic in the post-1945 period. Many of the programs of the Ford Foundation are excellent examples of this mode of operation. Such programs, however, usually rest upon some analysis of the underlying issues and do not modify the generalization that foundations seek to promote knowledge-based social engineering.

"Intermediary Institutions"

How can one conceptualize the philanthropic foundation? It is a very different type of animal from the small charitable organization, which is frequently found in the voluntary sector. Yet philanthropic foundations, for all their peculiarities, are clearly central institutions in the voluntary spectrum, albeit often large and wealthy ones. In the U.S. context, they are clearly major actors in the nonprofit sector, even if their capital was ultimately derived from profits in most cases. Left-wing critics have in effect consistently argued through this century that they are mechanisms for laundering or legitimating profits, but this is an inadequate characterization of their significance.

The term "intermediary institution." may be introduced in an attempt to refine our understanding of state activity in the period covered. *Intermediary institutions* are more or less organized collectivities, formally independent of the state on the one hand, and being more than the vehicle of a particularly influential person on the other, which contribute to the process of policy formulation. There are affinities between this conception and Peter Berger's concept of "mediating structures" (1977), which refers to collectivities that lie between, and mediate between, the "megastructures" of the state and private industry on the one hand and the private worlds of home and family on the other. Some of the institutions considered in this chapter, such as settlement houses, social networks linking academics and politicians, and nongovernmental think-tanks clearly fall within this term, but others, such as philanthropic foundations or university departments, are much more part of the world of "megastructures," though not part of the state.

In the international field, where one is dealing with activities spanning a number of national societies, the term is also applicable but in a slightly different sense. Where one is dealing with relations between nation-states, with their own clear boundaries, various institutions may develop, including institutions of international government such as the League of Nations, which seek to coordinate activity and mediate between the different national entities. Some of these are institutions of international government, such as the International Court of Justice; others, such as the International Red Cross or the Save the Children Fund International Union, are "intermediary institutions" seeking to mediate between national states at a level other than that of international government.

The influence of intermediary institutions may be exercised through the creation and dissemination of ideas, practical research activity, institutional support for social inquiry, or involvement as collective actors in politics. An understanding of the part played by such collective actors can illuminate the relationship between social science knowledge and state activity at a time when such activity was limited or nonexistent. They bridge the academic and policy worlds. Study of them can reveal "the full array of interconnections between behavioral and social sciences findings and policy making over considerable periods of time" (Gerstein, Luce, Smelser, & Sperlich, 1988, p. 148).

The Role of the State

The part played by the state in shaping the agendas of these intermediary institutions was not as great prior to World War II as it subsequently became. These patterns of mutual influence require further study, for, certainly, the interaction later in the twentieth century as well as earlier has been in both directions. Just as social science does not feed smoothly into the decision-making process but is one competing input among many, societal developments impinge unevenly upon the preoccupations of social scientists. More knowledge does not mean better decision making. This is evident in the ambivalence that government and social science display to one another, summed up in the phrases "the uneasy relationship" and "the uncertain connection" (Lyons, 1969; Lynn, 1978; Bulmer, 1987).

One may indeed go further and emphasize what Barry Karl has called "the uneasy state". There is a particular danger in extrapolating from the British Liberal government of 1906–1914 or a few years of the New Deal, in neglecting the fact that the nature of the "state" and "government" was rather different at this period. The United States in the interwar period, as well as having a more diversified system of higher education, was also a more localized and regionalized society than it later became (Karl, 1983). For the majority of the population, the main frame of reference was not a national one; the federal government was weak, and moves to extend the authority of the center were slow, cautious and contested. The speed with which the wartime apparatus in Washington was dissolved in 1918 was one sign; the argument over the scope for planning in the New Deal was another. Up until at least the middle of the twentieth century, Robert Wiebe has observed that "the most useful image of (American) government was that of an empty vessel, a container into which power flowed and formed but which provided nothing of its own. Always an exaggeration . . . the image nevertheless expressed an approximate truth of high importance" (1975, p. 132). Britain possessed a more centralized system of governance, but prevailing conceptions of the proper scope for state activity remained very conservative. Many of the social investigators discussed earlier addressed themselves at least as much to arguments about the need to extend state activity as to the conditions that gave rise to the necessity for that extension. The tendency for the history of British social policy to be written in Whiggish terms has obscured this resistance to assuming new responsibilities. Throughout the 1930s, for example, the attempts by Keynes to influence Treasury management of the economy turned on the appropriateness of various forms of government intervention. State structures thus made use of the knowledge produced by social scientists but did not actively promote its production. Nor did the state, directly or indirectly, provide employment for social scientists at this period. Much more influential as agenda setters were those working in a variety of intermediary institutions. The significance of these national developments in the United States and Britain for international activity is that they convey a number of the features of the international scene within national developments.

Charity, Knowledge, and Public Policy

This transmutation of what in the nineteenth century was deemed charitable activity via the medium of the foundation into initiatives much more central to public policy has gone furthest in the United States, notwithstanding the ambivalent relationship throughout between foundations and the state. In part, this is due to the sheer scale of the great American foundations, both domestically and abroad. Their international programs alone sought worldwide influence, in Europe in the interwar period, postwar, particularly in the Third World in the case of the Rockefeller Foundation. British foundations are much more modestly funded, providing support to a greater extent at the margins rather than in the center, and only venturing overseas to a limited extent. Arguably their founders—men such as Joseph Rowntree and William Morris (Lord Nuffield)—were different sorts of men than Andrew Carnegie and John D. Rockefeller, Sr.

Anglo-American differences also reflect different political histories and structures, and a different role for the state, leaving much greater scope in the past for American foundations to take up issues, such as the development of higher education, which government did not regard at the time as its responsibility. From the United States, too, has stemmed the faith that knowledge is a source of insight and power over the natural and social world and should be systematically fostered in order to control and change that world. The intimate relationship that developed between the great foundations and higher education is quite distinctive, being somewhat less marked in Britain, though support for particular areas of academic work in science, medicine, and social science by particular foundations is notable. Although in many respects the scope of the voluntary or nonprofit sector has expanded over the last half century—for example, in the United States as a provider of public welfare—in other respects, it has shrunk somewhat as the state has taken over functions hitherto partially supported by foundations, such as parts of higher education.

Yet much about foundations remains to be explored. To what extent do foundations exercise power at the societal level? What kinds of influence do they exert? What effect do different legal systems have on their operation? How does the character of national elites, and national political structure, condition the operation of foundations in particular countries? How far are they constrained by lacking full legitimacy, as organizations responsible only to themselves, while claiming to contribute to the welfare of all?

REFERENCES

Addams, J. (1902). *Democracy and Social Ethics*. New York: Macmillan.
Arnove, R. F. (Ed.). (1980). *Philanthropy and Cultural Imperialism*. Bloomington: Indiana University Press.
Berger, P. (1977). In praise of particularity: The concept of mediating structures. In P. Berger (Ed.), *Facing Up to Modernity: Excursions in Society, Politics and Religion* (pp. 130–141). New York: Basic Books.
Booth, C. (1889–1903). *Life and Labour of the People of London* (17 vols.). London: Macmillan.
Bremner, R. H. (1988). *American Philanthropy*. Chicago: University of Chicago Press.

Briggs, A. (1961). *Social Thought and Social Action: A Study of the Work of Seebohm Rowntree 1871–1954*. London: Longman.

Briggs, A., & Macartney, A. (1984). *Toynbee Hall: The First Hundred Years*. London: Routledge & Kegan Paul.

Brown, E. R. (1979). *Rockefeller Medicine Men: Medicine and Capitalism in America*. Berkeley: University of California Press.

Bulmer, M. (1980). The early institutional establishment of social science research: The Local Community Research Committee at the University of Chicago, 1923–1930. *Minerva, 18*(Spring), 51–110.

Bulmer, M. (1981). Sociology and political science at Cambridge in the 1920's: An opportunity missed and an opportunity taken. *Cambridge Review, CII*(2262), 156–159.

Bulmer, M. (1984). Philanthropic foundations and the development of the social sciences in the early twentieth century: A reply to Donald Fisher. *Sociology, 18*(4), 572–579.

Bulmer, M. (1987). The rise of the academic as expert. *Minerva, 25*(3), 362–374.

Bulmer, M. (Ed.). (1987). *Social Science Research and Government: Comparative Essays on Britain and the United States*. Cambridge, UK: Cambridge University Press.

Bulmer, M., & Bulmer, J. (1981). Philanthropy and social science in the 1920's: Beardsley Ruml and the Laura Spelman Rockefeller Memorial, 1922–1929. *Minerva, 19*(Autumn), 347–407.

Bulmer, M., Bales, K., & Sklar, K. K. (Eds.). (1992). *The Social Survey in Historical Perspective, 1880–1940*. Cambridge, UK: Cambridge University Press.

Chambers, C. A. (1971). *Paul U. Kellogg and "The Survey."* Minneapolis: University of Minnesota Press.

Clark, R. W. (1972). *A Biography of the Nuffield Foundation*. London: Longman.

Coing, H. (1981). Remarks on the history of foundations and their role in the promotion of learning. *Minerva, 19*(2), 271–281.

Critchlow, D. T. (1985). *The Brookings Institution, 1916–1952: Expertise and the Public Interest in a Democratic Society*. DeKalb: Northern Illinois University Press.

Davis, A. F. (1967). *Spearheads for Reform: The Social Settlements and the Progressive Movement 1890–1914*. New York: Oxford University Press.

Du Bois, W. E. B. (1899). *The Philadephia Negro: A Social Study*. Philadelphia: University of Pennsylvania Press.

Fisher, D. (1978). The Rockefeller Foundation and the development of scientific medicine in Great Britain. *Minerva, 16,* 20–41.

Fisher, D. (1984). Philanthropic foundations and the development of the social sciences: A response to Martin Bulmer. *Sociology, 18*(4), 580–587.

Fisher, D. (1993). *Fundamental Development of the Social Sciences: Rockefeller philanthropy and the United States Social Science Research Council*. Ann Arbor: University of Michigan Press.

Flexner, A. (1930). *Universities: American, English, German*. New York: Oxford University Press.

Geiger, R. (1986). *To Advance Knowledge: The Growth of American Research Universities in the Twentieth Century, 1900–1940*. New York: Oxford University Press.

Gerstein, D. R., Luce, R. D., Smelser, N. J., & Sperlich, S. (Eds.). (1988). *The Behavioral and Social Sciences: Achievements and Opportunities: A Report to the National Research Council*. Washington, DC: National Academy Press.

Glenn, J. M., Brandt, L., & Andrews, F. E. (1947). *Russell Sage Foundation 1907–1946*. New York: Russell Sage Foundation.

Greenwald, M. W., & Anderson, M. (Eds.). (1996). *Pittsburgh Surveyed: Social Science and Social Reform in the Early Twentieth Century*. Pittsburgh: University of Pittsburgh Press.

Hall, A. R., & Bainbridge, B. A. (1986). *Physic and Philanthropy: A History of the Wellcome Trust 1936–1986*. Cambridge, UK: Cambridge University Press.

Harris, J. (1977). *William Beveridge: A Biography*. Oxford: Clarendon Press.

Hunter, R. (1901). *Tenement Conditions in Chicago*. Chicago: City Homes Association.

Hunter, R. (1904). *Poverty*. New York: Macmillan.

Karl, B. D. (1974). *Charles E. Merriam and the Study of Politics*. Chicago: University of Chicago Press.

Karl, B. D. (1983). *The Uneasy State: The United States from 1914 to 1945*. Chicago: University of Chicago Press.

Karl, B. D., & Katz, S. N. (1981). The American private philanthropic foundation and the public sphere, 1890–1930. *Minerva, 19*, 236–270.

Karl, B. D., & Katz, S. N. (1987). Foundations and ruling class elites. *Daedalus, 116*(1), 1–40.

Kellogg, P. U. (Ed.). (1909–1915). *The Pittsburgh Survey: Findings in Six Volumes*. New York: Charities Publication Committee.

Kohler, R. E. (1978). A policy for the advancement of science: The Rockefeller Foundation 1924–1929. *Minerva, 16*, 480–515.

Kohler, R. E. (1991). *Partners in Science: Foundations and Natural Scientists 1900–1945*. Chicago: University of Chicago Press.

Lagemann, E. C. (1989). *The Politics of Knowledge: The Carnegie Corporation, Philanthropy and Public Policy*. Middletown, CT: Wesleyan University Press.

Laski, H. (1930). Foundations, universities and research. In *The Dangers of Obedience and Other Essays*, Ch. 6. New York: Harper.

Lindemann, E. C. (1936). *Wealth and Culture: A Study of 100 Foundations during the Decade 1921–1930*. New York: Harcourt Brace.

Lynn, L. E., Jr. (Ed.). (1978). *Knowledge and Policy: The Uncertain Connection*. Washington, DC: National Academy of Sciences.

Lyons, G. M. (1969). *The Uneasy Partnership: Social Science and the Federal Government in the Twentieth Century*. New York: Russell Sage Foundation.

McBriar, A. M. (1987). *An Edwardian Mixed Doubles: The Bosanquets versus the Webbs: A study in British Social Policy 1890–1929*. Oxford, UK: Clarendon Press.

Meacham, S. (1987). *Toynbee Hall and Social Reform 1880–1914: The Search for Community*. New Haven, CT: Yale University Press.

Mennel, R. M. (1973). *Thorns and Thistles: Juvenile Delinquents in the United States 1825–1940*. Hanover, NH: University Press of New England.

Mess, H. A., & Braithwaite, C. (1947). The great philanthropic trusts. In H. A. Mess et al., (Eds.), *Voluntary Social Services since 1918* (pp. 172–187). London: Kegan Paul, Trench, Trubner.

Nielsen, A. (1985). *The Golden Donors*. New York: Dutton.

President's Research Committee on Social Trends. (1933). *Recent Social Trends in the United States*. New York: McGraw-Hill.

Riis, J. (1890). *How the Other Half Lives*. New York: Scribner.

Rowntree, B. S. (1901). *Poverty: A Study in Town Life*. London: Macmillan.

Rowntree, J. (1904). The founder's memorandum. Reprinted in L. E. Waddilove, (1983). *Private Philanthropy and Public Welfare* (pp. xiii–xviii). London: Allen & Unwin.

Sealander, J. (1997). *Public Wealth and Private Life: Foundations, Philanthropy and the Reshaping of Social Policy from the Progressive Era to the New Deal America*. Baltimore: Johns Hopkins University Press.

Shils, E. (1979). The order of learning in the United States from 1865 to 1920: The ascendancy of the universities. In A. Oleson & J. Voss (Eds.), *The Organization of Knowledge in Modern America* (pp. 19–47). Baltimore: Johns Hopkins University Press.

Sklar, K. K. (1992). Hull-House maps and papers as women's work in the 1890s. In M. Bulmer, K. Bales, & K. K. Sklar (Eds.), *The Social Survey in Historical Perspective* (pp. 111–147). Cambridge, UK: Cambridge University Press.

Terrill, R. (1974). *R. H. Tawney and His Times: Socialism as Fellowship*. London: Andre Deutsch.

Veysey, L. R. (1965). *The Emergence of the American University*. Chicago: University of Chicago Press.

Waddilove, L. E. (1983). *Private Philanthropy and Public Welfare: The Joseph Rowntree Memorial Trust, 1954–1979*. London: Allen & Unwin.

Weibe, R. H. (1975). *The Segmented Society: An Introduction to the Meaning of America*. New York: Oxford University Press.

Wheatley, S. C. (1988). *The Politics of Philanthropy: Abraham Flexner and Medical Education*. Madison: University of Wisconsin Press.

Woods, R. (Ed.). (1899). *The City Wilderness: A Settlement Study by Residents of the South End House*. Boston: Houghton Mifflin.

Chapter **3**

A Comparative Legal Analysis of Foundations

Aspects of Supervision and Transparency

TYMEN J. VAN DER PLOEG

INTRODUCTION

A legal approach to the cross-national study of foundations depends on many factors: different legal systems, the varying roles of government in society, historical aspects, as well as the level of economic and social development. Generally, the existence of foundations can be considered a sign of civil freedom: Private organizations for the general interest are recognized or, at least, accepted. Moreover, according to international treaties concerning human rights, the freedom of association (which applies to other voluntary organizations as well as foundations) may only be restricted by two types of rules: to protect public order and public safety in a broad sense; and to protect the liberty and interests of others.[1] In this chapter, I take the freedom of association and the restrictions formulated in these treaties as a starting point to evaluate the legal requirements for the establishment and supervision of foundations. For this purpose, I examine the rules that regulate the establishment of foundations, the accountability of the directors or trustees, and the regulatory powers of government, judiciary, and other interested parties.[2]

TYMEN J. VAN DER PLOEG • Faculty of Law, Vrije Universiteit, De Boelelaan 1105, 1081HV, Amsterdam, the Netherlands.

Private Funds, Public Purpose: Philanthropic Foundations in an International Perspective, edited by Helmut K. Anheier and Stefan Toepler. New York, Plenum Press, 1999.

The countries included in this study are the United States, England (and Whales),[3] Germany, Austria, France, and the Netherlands. These countries have in common that they are developed market economies. They differ, however, in other aspects that informed my choice for including them: First, two important legal systems are represented—the common law tradition (United States and England) and the civil law tradition (France, Germany, Austria, and the Netherlands). Second, they show different approaches to the involvement of government with the establishment of foundations. Third, they represent different ways of organizing the supervision of foundations.

It is a very delicate matter to compare legal regulations across civil law and common law countries, because definitions and concepts are frequently different. This is also true for the comparison of foundation law. The term *foundation* and its equivalents in other languages and cultures does not have a universally accepted legal meaning. To facilitate the comparison, I use a sociological description and definition of *foundations as nongovernmental, nonmembership organizations that are recognized as a legal category and serve a purpose in the general public interest.* This definition needs some further explanation:

• *Nongovernmental* means that the foundation is neither established by a public agency or administrative body nor regulated by public law.

• *Nonmembership* means that the foundation has no members who can vote in general meetings and appoint the board members. In civil law, membership organizations have the association form, nonmembership organizations the foundation form. In countries with common law tradition this distinction is not made in this way,[4] and the internal organization of foundations is frequently left open.

• *Recognized as a legal category* means in this context that the law either recognizes the foundation as a special type of legal person or regulates it independent of its legal form in special statutes.[5]

• *The purpose in the general interest* is the purpose that the directors or trustees have to pursue in managing/governing the property and operations of the foundation. General interest is to be contrasted to self-interest and also to the common interest of the founders and contributors. The general interest purpose makes foundations suitable for tax benefits.

The first section of this chapter explores the differences in the common law and the civil law approach to foundation law. The next section deals with the characteristics of a supervisory or regulatory system for foundations. After that, I present a country-by-country overview of aspects of supervision, concerning establishment, registration, accountability, sanctions, and appeals. This is followed by an analysis of the options interested parties have to get access to information and to request sanctions against foundations. The article concludes with an evaluation of the various regulatory systems in terms of the freedom of association and the protection of the interests of donors and creditors.

COMMON LAW VERSUS CIVIL LAW

In the Western World, there are two major legal approaches to the regulation of foundations. One is the charity law approach of the common law system. Common law originated in England and has been adopted by many English speaking countries. The other is the civil law system. Civil law includes a variety of legal systems with a civil code, based on principles of Roman law. Civil Codes developed in the nineteenth century in different parts of continental Europe (France, Austria, the Netherlands, Germany). Apart from Scandinavia, all continental European countries belong to it, as do other countries that have either been colonies of civil law countries or voluntarily adopted this system, such as Japan and Turkey.

Common Law

In the common law family, foundation law has as its starting point the recognition of benevolent action of people for the public interest. Its legal development originated in the Middle Ages. In England, this has led to "charity law," while later, in the United States, it led to the law on tax-exempt organizations.[6] Although English and American law on foundations differ in several aspects, they have in common a focus on the charitable or tax-exempt status. The actual legal form of charities varies but often takes the forms of charitable trust, unincorporated association, or charitable corporation.

Charitable trusts are characterized by the entrusting of a certain property—in legal terms the *trust res*—to one or more trustees.[7] The trustees must administer the property for the benefit of the beneficiaries. However, unlike private trusts, a charitable trust has no specific beneficiaries with beneficiary rights. The establisher of the trust—the settlor—has given to the trustees a set of binding rules, the trust instrument. By entrusting his property to the trustee, the settlor effectively gives up ownership. The trustees in turn do not assume ownership of the trust property but have fiduciary rights to it. The charitable trust is not fixed to a certain period, differing from private trusts for which the "rule against perpetuities" is in force. In addition, the court has under certain circumstances the power to adapt the purpose of the trust according to the *cy-près* rule (see below).

A charity may be incorporated according to the Companies Act in England (which rarely occurs) and according to comparable state laws in the United States. The incorporation is dependent on the recognition of the government. The incorporated form is dominant only in America. If incorporated, the corporation is owner of the property and the trustees have become the board (directors) of the corporation.

Being a foundation in common law countries has generally fiscal implications. The most prominent ones in this sphere are exemption from company or corporation tax and tax deductibility related to the income tax for donors to foundations. In addition, a specific characteristic of English and American charity law is the restrictions for charities regarding political activities.[8]

Civil Law

In civil law countries, such as Austria, France, Germany, and the Netherlands, a foundation is in the first place a type of legal personality. In law, a "legal person" is treated in the same way as a private individual. Civil law is systematically based on the concept of the person, the subject in law, with his or her subjective rights and obligations. Not only private individuals but also legal entities can act and be treated as persons. A legal person may own property and can be held liable. The board members act on behalf of the legal person and are in principle not liable to its creditors. Civil law countries distinguish between different types of legal persons with different organizational and financial characteristics. As legal persons that further the general interest, both associations and foundations can be considered.

Foundations are typically organizations to administer property that a founder sets apart for a special public-interest purpose. Regarding foundations, the wishes of the founders that have attributed property to the foundation play generally an important role, contrary to associations in which the wish of the members is directive.[9] Since foundations are legal persons without a necessary internal controlling body, external control is desirable and in the general interest. However, as will be shown in the next section, there are considerable differences in the foundation laws of civil law countries, which means that a civil law approach only exists at the level of the concept of legal personality.

Theoretically, the distinction between associations and foundations is clear; in practice, however, associations and foundations can be rather similar. In reality, the legal form chosen often reflects either tradition or a preference for the form that is least regulated. Unlike common law countries, the establishment of a foundation as a legal person does not necessarily lead to fiscal benefits, but foundations, as defined in the first section of this chapter, are normally tax-exempt and their donors enjoy tax deductions (McLean, Kluger, & Henrey, 1990). In the civil law countries considered here, no restrictions on political activities exist. Foundations in the general interest are, without penalties, allowed to be involved in advocacy activities (Randon and 6, 1994).

ESTABLISHMENT AND SUPERVISION OF FOUNDATIONS

As mentioned before, according to international law, the rules on the establishment and supervision of foundations have to protect the public order and safety, as well as the liberty and interests of others. In the next paragraphs, I analyze the foundation laws on these points. The protection of public order and safety is in any case a matter of criminal law, but I only focus on the administrative and private legislation concerned. The protection of the liberty and interests of others has different implications. Legislation should safeguard the interests of the founders, donors, and the general public in the pursuit of the stated purpose of the foundation. As an internal control of trustees or the board is often lacking in foundations due to their nature, an external supervisory system seems necessary to verify the execution of the stated purpose of the foundation. One purpose of this chapter is to see if a supervisory system exists in the first place. The term *supervisory system* refers to one or more official agencies to which foundations must report; that have the power to request additional information from the trustees or the board; and that have the competence to take legal measures themselves or request for such measures to be taken up by the courts. In addition, a comparative analysis of supervisory systems also sheds light on the way in which the autonomy of the board and therewith the freedom of foundations is taken into account.

The United States

In the United States, foundations are regulated by federal tax law as well as state law, which generally governs the establishment of organizations (Hopkins & Moore, 1992). Both levels of law are applicable to tax-exempt organizations. Regarding the regulation of foundations, the federal tax law is both more developed and more specific than the laws on establishment and supervision at the state level. Foundations, like other nonprofit organizations, can either be incorporated or take the trust form. For the establishment of charitable *corporations*, state laws require a charter between the corporation and the state government. Although this charter is considered to be a contract, it does not empower the state to control the corporation.[10] State control at the time of establishment is a control of legitimacy to ensure conformity of the purpose and bylaws with the law, with the intent of preventing the incorporation of unlawful organizations.[11] Generally, there are only very few acts that specifically address charitable corporations, which led the American Bar Association (ABA) to draft a revised model Nonprofit Corporation Act in 1988. The states maintain their own register of corporations, but they seldom collect information from nonprofit organizations and foundations. Besides incorporation, foundations may also take the trust form. The establishment of a *trust* is an act of private matter, by which assets are set apart for a specific purpose under the trusteeship of others than the settlors. Regulated by common law, the states do not interfere or register trusts.[12]

Whether in trust or corporate form, foundations need to *register* with the Internal Revenue Service (IRS), the federal tax authority, in order to obtain tax-exempt status. The IRS annually collects detailed financial information to ascertain that tax-exempt organizations remain within the boundaries of their exempt status. Although federal tax law and several state laws have different types of rules restricting the disposal or the ownership of property in general and assets in particular (Fremont-Smith, 1965, pp. 98ff., 123ff.), the IRS has largely taken the initiative concerning the issue of accountability of foundations by issuing detailed regulations regarding the financial activities of private foundations. More specifically, the Federal Tax code imposes a number of "first-tier" taxes on violations of regulations concerning self-dealing (section 4941), failure to distribute (section 4942), excess business holdings (section 4943), jeopardizing investments (section 4944), and nonconforming expenditures (section 4945). Foundations in trust form are also subject to trust law. However, under trust law, trustees manage the foundation at their own discretion but are subject to control by the court in case of abuse (American Law Institute, 1959, section 382). Generally, the courts do not interfere with financial management, as long as trustees follow the "prudent man rule" (Fremont-Smith, 1965, pp. 97–98).

Since effective supervision requires enforcement, federal and state law hold specific rules on *sanctions*. At the *federal level*, the IRS, based on the detailed information it collects, may take measures in the form of fiscal penalties in cases of noncompliance with the tax rules. As mentioned before, private foundations are subject to a number of specific "first-tier" taxes. The IRS may also impose a "second-tier" tax if the conditions leading the "first-tier" tax are not remedied.[13] IRS decisions can be appealed in Tax Court or in the Court of Claims (to which any claim against the Government can be brought). Appeal against decisions of these courts may be made in the U.S. Circuit Courts.

At the *state level*, the attorneys general have the right to request information from both charitable corporations and trusts to ensure compliance with the law, but have also access to the information collected by the IRS (Office of the Ohio Attorney General, 1977, Table 7). In most cases, failure to submit a financial report to the attorney general upon request may result in involuntary dissolution of the organization (Edie, 1987, p. 54). In cases of mismanagement or violations of the law, the attorney general may request the court, on behalf of the general public, to order officers to pay damages or to cancel the transfer of property, and to order the dismissal of board members or trustees (Conviser, 1964, pp. 98ff.) or even the winding up of the corporation.[14] The parties involved may appeal the decision to a higher state judiciary.

Another case involving external supervision relates to situations where the original purpose of a trust, as stipulated by the founder, can no longer be reasonably accomplished. In such cases, the courts can, at the request of the trustees or the attorney general, apply *cy-près* rule and change a trust's purpose to a different purpose, which, however, must be close to the original. In some states, the impossibility of accomplishing the original purpose is the only ground for an alternation of purpose, whereas in other states, the *cy-près* rule may also be applied when carrying out the original purpose appears impracticable.[15] This lack of unity raises practical problems, especially for charitable trusts operating in more than one state.

To summarize, in the United States, the federal fiscal regulation forms a supervisory system in which foundations are monitored financially in detail by the IRS. These tax rules, through their emphasis on accountability, seem to have a positive effect on the management of foundations, even if unintentionally. At the state level, regulations in general do not require charitable organizations to provide regular information. Thus, an explicit supervisory system does accordingly not exist.

England

The establishment of a charitable trust or an unincorporated association is a private matter, regulated by common law. Governmental recognition is only required for the establishment of a company limited by guarantee according to the Companies Act 1985. Foundations[16] may take either of these legal forms. As far as foundations are registered charities, the Charities Acts of 1993[17] provides for a special supervisory system with the Charity Commission, which registers and supervises most[18] charities, including foundations. As an independent body, whose members are appointed by the government, the Charity Commission decides whether the purposes of an organization fall within the four heads of charity and whether the organization therefore qualifies for charitable status. This decision is recognized by the Inland Revenue (Hopkins & Moore, 1992, pp. 197–201). The control exercised by the Charity Commission at registration only concerns the conformity with the law, but not the social or political desirability of a foundation. However, as trusts have positively to fall under one of the four heads, the Charity Commission's view of what is in line with contemporary public policy may play a role.[19]

More specific regulation on the *accountability* of board and trustees of a foundation are stipulated by the various Charities acts in force. Charities have to submit their annual accounts to the Charity Commission.[20] In addition, the Charity Commissioners, as supervisors, may also request other information as they think fit.[21] The Charity Commission has also the power to institute inquiries with regard to charities and may publish the report of such an inquiry.[22] The Charity Commission may also get directly involved in the operations of a charity by advising trustees and ordering a scheme of administration.[23] There are also rather detailed restrictions concerning the transfer and mortgaging of charity land, to which the court or the Charity Commission have to give consent.[24] Concerning investments, the Charity Commission has arbitrary control under the Trustee Act 1925, the Settled Land Act 1925, and the Trustee Investment Act 1961. However, the Charities Act 1992 granted the Secretary of State the power to suspend some investment categories from these rules.

The Charity Commission can take *measures* to ensure the fulfillment of the law and good management practice under the authority of the High Court (Chancery division), and lately, the Commission has seen it as part of its duties to make charities more effective and efficient.[25] In case of mismanagement, the Commission can generally dismiss trustees or board members and appoint new ones,[26] vest property in the official custodian, restrict transactions, and appoint a receiver and manager.[27] The Commission also has the power to remove a charity from the register if it concludes that the object of the organization is no longer charitable,[28] to change the purpose of a trust, and to transfer trust property under the *cy-près* rule if the original purpose can no longer be accomplished.[29] The parties concerned can appeal decisions of the Charity Commission to the High Court, while appeals of high Court decisions can be brought to the Court of Appeal.

Since the Charity Commission has sufficient information and powers to make inquiries, as far as charities are registered, a true supervisory system is in place. Somewhat questionable, however, is whether the broad regulatory authorities of the Charity Commission respect the autonomy of trustees, although changes in the Charities Act 1992 have brought some improvements in this respect. Apparently, the protection of trust property and other parties is considered more important than the freedom of founders or trustees. Outside charity law, there is no apparent supervisory system for voluntary organizations, including foundations. Noncharitable foundations are accordingly not subject to control by the Charity Commission and enjoy more freedom with respect to their internal governance. The interests of third parties are protected by the courts when lawsuits concerning damages are brought before them.

Germany

German regulations of foundations have a dual character. The Civil Code contains a limited number of general articles about foundations as legal persons, while rules for the establishment of foundations are considered to be a matter of state (*Länder*) administrative law. According to paragraphs 80–88 of the German Civil Code (*Bürgerliches Gesetzbuch,* or BGB), a written document (such as a notarized deed or testament), governmental consent (*Genehmigung*), and the entrusting of an endowment are necessary prerequisites for a foundation (*Stiftung*) to obtain legal personality. Rules concerning, *inter alia,* the required content of the statutes (bylaws), the administrative consent, the management and procedures for the appointment and dismissal of board members, and governmental supervision, are laid down in the Foundation Acts of the different *Länder.*[30] In theory, the concerned governmental agency (*Genehmigungsbehörde*) has more or less discretionary power regarding its consent, but in practice, this appears to be generally restricted to a control of legitimacy (conformity with the law). Where a more discretionary control on efficiency is executed, it aims at preventing the use of (inherited) property for purposes not in the public interest.[31]

According to German doctrine, the state shares a general responsibility for the accomplishment of the purpose of the *Stiftung* or the will of the founder, respectively, since there is no internal supervision inherent to the foundation form.[32] This serves to justify a state supervisory system, which in some states takes the form of control of efficiency of foundations' operations, but is restricted to a control of legitimacy in other states.[33] Some *Stiftungen* Acts also require the registration after governmental consent is granted, although this has no bearing for the establishment of a foundation.

With regard to accountability issues, the *Stiftungen* Acts of the *Länder* contain for the most part general rules aimed at preserving and protecting foundation endowments and other property. In Bavaria and Rheinland-Pfalz, foundation boards need consent of the governmental supervisory agency (*Aufsichtsbehörde*) for certain transactions,[34] and foundations are required to submit annual accounts to this agency. The *Aufsichtsbehörde* has the power to declare decisions of a foundation board void if such decisions violate either the statutes or the law in general. Under most *Stiftungen* Acts, supervisory agencies can take direct measures in case of mismanagement and may dismiss board members on "important grounds" (Soergel-Neuhoff, 1978, pp. 28ff). Important grounds usually imply unlawful activities or transactions. Under Baden-Württemberg law, the *Aufsichtsbehörde* can furthermore order the board to perform activities required by law. When the board fails to do so, the agency can act itself substituting the board.[35] In some circumstances, the agency may sue board members for damages on behalf of the foundation.

Across all states, Art. 87 BGB grants supervisory agencies the right to change the purpose of, or even to dissolve, a foundation where execution of the purpose is either impossible or detrimental to public welfare. In principle, the intentions of the founder are nevertheless to be respected. In some cases, foundation statutes may grant internal bodies, such as the board, the authority to amend the statutes. Such amendments, however, require consent of the *Aufsichtsbehörde*. Decisions of supervisory agencies may be appealed in administrative court by either the *Stiftung* itself, its board members, or interested parties.[36] Only public, but not private, interest conflicts constitute a reason for appeal.[37]

In summary, the German foundation law provides for a supervisory system in which governmental authorities supervise the establishment and, with different intensity, the financial operations of foundations and have the power to takes measures in case of mismanagement. Considerations concerning the protection of foundation endowments and property in the interest of founders and the public at large appear to limit somewhat the autonomy of foundation management. Interested third parties can only indirectly challenge the management by appealing supervisory agency actions towards it.

Austria

Austrian law provides two types of foundations, the *Stiftung* (regular foundation) and the *Privatstiftung,* or private foundation.[38] Unlike some other civil law countries, neither the Austrian Civil Code nor state laws hold specific provisions concerning foundations. Instead, both types were introduced in two separate federal acts: the Act on Foundations and Temporary Funds (*Stiftungen und Fondsgesetz*) of 1974, which is a combination of civil and public law rules governing regular foundations,[39] and the Civil Law Act on *Privatstiftungen* of 1993.[40] The legal treatment of both types of foundations is significantly different. Whereas the 1974 Act prescribes general interest purposes for regular foundations, the 1993 Act allows private foundations to pursue non-charitable purposes and largely exempts them from governmental intervention, but minimum assets of one million *Schilling* (approximately US$ 45,000) are required.

Regular Foundations

The Foundation Act[41] of 1974 contains both the civil law requirements and public law rules on supervision. Generally, a written document, such as a notarized deed or testament, an endowment dedicated by the founder(s) to a stated purpose of public interest or of charitable character, and the admission (*Zulassung*) by the respective supervising authority (*Stiftungsbehörde*) are prerequisites for the establishment of a foundation under this Act.[42] Foundations are admitted and supervised by the Office of the President of the State, except if the statutes specifically entrust the supervision to a federal ministry.[43] Admission is dependent on the lawfulness of the founding act, the public-interest or charitable character of the proposed purpose, and on whether the endowment is considered to be sufficient to execute the purpose.[44] The federal Minister of Interior keeps a register of admitted foundations.[45]

Foundations must annually submit financial reports to the *Stiftungsbehörde* as supervisory agency. To protect and preserve foundation endowments, the board is under the fiduciary obligation to treat the endowment like the property of a person under guardianship.[46] Alterations of the level of the endowment in any way require approval of the *Stiftungsbehörde*.[47]

The law also imposes a number of sanctions. More specifically, if the requirements of law and statutes are not met, the *Stiftungsbehörde* has to instruct the board to fulfill its obligations within a period of four weeks.[48] In case of noncompliance, board members must be dismissed by the authorities. Where board vacancies or mismanagement put the operations of a foundation at risk, the *Stiftungsbehörde* can appoint a foundation governor (*Stiftungskommissar*),[49] who must propose a new management to be appointed by the governmental authority within eight weeks.[50] At the time of the governor's appointment, the existing officers lose their powers. When the execution of the purpose becomes impossible or would endanger the charitable or public-interest character of the foundation, a change of purpose is possible, subject to approval of the *Stiftungsbehörde*.[51] Foundations and board members can appeal decisions of the *Stiftungsbehörde* to the federal Minister competent in the foundation's field or, for foundations not falling under any specific Ministry, to the Minister of the Interior.

Private Foundations

In contrast to regular foundations, private foundations are not subject to any kind of control by governmental authorities, as the supervision of this type of foundation is completely left to civil law regulation. For the establishment of a *Privatstiftung*, an authorized written document is required spelling out the purpose, the endowment, a list of beneficiaries, and other general conditions. Legal personality is obtained by registration in the firm's register without further governmental consent or admission.[52] For registration, a bank declaration verifying the availability of the endowment capital is needed.[53]

In terms of internal governance, the law stipulates that the board has to consist of at least three members, who may not be beneficiaries or family members of beneficiaries, and that legal transactions must be signed by all board members. Board members have the duty to act economically on behalf of the foundation and to take into account the obligations to creditors.[54] The foundation must draw up annual accounts according to the stipulations of the commercial code,[55] which are to be audited by a special examiner on court order or on request of any internal supervisory body. Members of such an internal body may also request the court to order a special audit if unreasonable or imprudent actions, or severe violations of the law or the statutes have taken place (para. 31). Disputes about financial matters are decided by the courts.

The imposition of sanctions in case of mismanagement is also in the competence of the courts. The court can dismiss board members (para. 27) and take measures to protect the purpose of the foundation (para. 31.5). If the purpose can no longer be executed, the board has to dissolve the foundation. If the board fails to take this decision, the court has the power to dissolve the foundation on request of any member of an internal body of the foundation or of beneficiaries (para. 35).

The conclusion concerning the foundation law in Austria is twofold. For *Stiftungen,* a clear supervisory system on the basis of legitimacy control exists, executed by the concerned supervising authority (Stiftungsbehörde). By the same token, the government has extensive powers to safeguard the proper management of the foundation in case of mismanagement. In the case of *Privatstiftungen,* the supervision is left to examiners or auditors and then the courts, which will act on the request of interested parties, such as members of internal bodies or beneficiaries. This arrangement seems to leave the autonomy of the board intact while safeguarding the proper management of private foundations.

France

Until 1987, the regulation of foundations in France was entirely in the administrative discretion of the government. Foundations obtained legal personality by applying for a "declaration of public utility" to the State Council (*Conseil d'État*), as the competent administrative agency under the authority of the central government. With a legal basis for the establishment of foundations missing until that point, the *Conseil d'État* has issued standards for drawing up statutes, spelling out its expectations in this respect. With the passing of the Act on the Development of Philanthropy (*mécénat*) in 1987,[56] the establishment and regulation of foundations are now based on a statute rather than administrative practice. According to the Act, the requirements for the establishment of foundations as legal persons include an irrevocable endowment for a purpose of general, but not commercial, interest and the governmental recognition of its public benefit character.

Generally, a real supervisory system does not exist. Although the *Conseil d' État* is involved in the establishment, there is no obligation for foundations to submit annual accounts. Indeed, bookkeeping and the preparation of annual accounts are only mandatory for organizations ruled by the Commercial Code. However, foundations need the consent of the *Conseil d' État* for certain transactions, which are void without this consent. In practice, these administrative powers are executed by local authorities and the Ministry of Interior with the possibility of appeal to the *Conseil d'État* (Pomey, 1980, pp. 61, 210). The board has to use the endowment for the purpose stated by the donor but may request the court for adaptation in case the circumstances make the execution of the purpose is extremely difficult or damaging (Art. 900.2–900.8, Civil Code). Remarkably, according to the standard statutes of the State Council, the members of the board of a foundation should consist of representatives of the relevant ministries and, if possible, of independent experts. So, in general, there is much government involvement in foundations (see Encyclopédie Dalloz, no. 61–96). Nevertheless, the only sanctions the *Conseil d' État* can impose against unlawful behavior or mismanagement are to dismiss government-appointed board members and to revoke the declaration of public utility, which leads to its dissolution (cf. Pomey, 1980, pp. 214ff.). In conclusion, French foundation law does not provide for a truly autonomous and independent board. With the high degree of discretionary powers that government authorities maintain, foundations work more or less within the public sphere.

The Netherlands

The regulation of the establishment of foundations (*stichting*) in the Netherlands is the most liberal of the countries in this comparison. The government is not involved in the establishment of foundations at all, but they have to be established by notarized deed (Art. 2:286, Dutch Civil Code). Art. 2:285 of the Civil Code defines a foundation as a legal person "created by a legal act that has no members and whose purpose is to realize an object stated in its statutes using capital (property) allocated to such purpose." The donation of an endowment at the establishment is not required. Although without property a foundation's purpose cannot be executed, it is up to the founders to decide when and how to obtain the necessary means. The public notary is responsible for ensuring that the establishment and the statutes of the *stichting* comply with the law. Board members have the duty to ensure registration with the regional chambers of commerce (Art. 2:289, Dutch Civil Code). Registration is not a requirement for obtaining legal personality. However, if not registered, board members are liable for the debts of the foundation.

Apart from requirements concerning bookkeeping and the preparation of annual accounts, there are no general mandatory rules concerning the financial management, and foundation boards face no other restrictions relating to the administration. Accordingly, the board is not obliged to submit annual accounts to the register at the chamber of commerce or elsewhere.[57] A few exceptions exist, however. More specifically, the board may only enter into agreements to purchase, dispose of, or encumber registered property, or agreements under which the foundation serves as a guarantor for others, if explicitly authorized to do so in the statutes (Art. 2:291.2, Civil Code). When the board fails to properly manage the foundation's operations, its members can be held liable for the damages to the foundation.

The public prosecutor has no direct power to obtain information from a foundation but may examine the books and other documents with the consent of the court if serious doubts have arisen about the financial management of a foundation. Furthermore, the prosecutor is barred from imposing sanctions in cases of unlawful behavior or mismanagement, or if a foundation fails to disclose its books,[58] but, on his or her request, the courts can dismiss board members.[59] As a minor sanction, he or she might petition the courts to declare void decisions of the foundation that are inconsistent with the law or its statutes.[60] In some circumstances, the courts can decide to dissolve a foundation on request of the public prosecutor.

The statutes of the foundation may declare an internal body of the foundation competent to change the statutes, but they may also limit this or forbid it. The founder, the board, or the public prosecutor can, however, eventually apply to the courts for changes to the purpose when it becomes necessary.[61] The courts will then determine a new purpose that is closely related to the original, not necessarily the purpose suggested by the applicant. The courts may also change the purpose to avoid dissolution when the purpose is not in accordance with the legal definition of *stichting* or when there is lack of sufficient property (Art. 2:294, Dutch Civil Code). Parties involved in the original procedure may appeal judicial decisions of the district courts in the Netherlands to the Court of Appeal.

Foundations operating an enterprise and having an obligatory works council (required if there are fifty or more employees) may also be subject to sanctions imposed on the basis of an inquiry procedure. An inquiry procedure is initiated through the enterprise division of the Court of Appeal of Amsterdam in cases of mismanagement by the foundation's board. Generally, the Advocate General of the Court of Appeal of Amsterdam,[62] trade unions, and individuals or groups authorized by the statutes have the right to initiate such a procedure. After mismanagement has been proven, the court can also declare decisions void, change the statutes, dismiss the board members, appoint temporary board members, and eventually dissolve the *stichting* (Art. 2:356, Civil Code).[63] In summary, since public prosecutors have no direct access to annual accounts of foundations, which would be a necessary precondition to supervise foundations effectively and to request the court for sanctions in case of malpractice, the Netherlands do not have a real supervisory system.

PUBLIC DISCLOSURE

Except for France and some German states, a public register of foundations is kept in most countries studied in this chapter. The degree of information that the registers provide, and the persons that have access to this information, however, vary between the countries. Foundation registers generally contain information about the purpose, articles of association (statutes), and actual board members and the respective capacities of board members. This information is generally open to the public. The public disclosure of annual accounts and other documents is less common, although the involvement of foundations in matters of public benefit could provide a rationale for it.

In the United States, interested parties, in their capacity as taxpayers, have access to the annual tax returns collected by the IRS, but not to additional, more detailed information. The public has in principle no access to any information collected by the attorneys general. The register of the Charity Commission in England contains annual accounts and other relevant documents that are open for public inspection.[64] The financial information that foundations must submit to the government authorities in Germany, Austria (only regular foundations), and France is as such not open to the public.[65] Conceivably, laws on "administrative transparency" may serve as a gateway for interested parties to access this information, with some limitations based on, f.i., privacy concerns. This would, of course, not be applicable in situations without administrative involvement in the supervision of foundations, such as private foundations in Austria and foundations generally in the Netherlands. The Austrian Act on *Privatstiftungen* nevertheless provides for a right of beneficiaries to obtain information about the way a foundation pursues its purpose, including the annual accounts and the accountants' reports. In case of noncompliance, the courts can enforce access to such documents by an auditor.[66] In the Netherlands, foundations currently have no obligation whatsoever to make annual accounts public.[67] The information contained in the public registers, held by the chambers of commerce, is only intended to allow parties entering into contracts with a foundation to check the purpose and any restrictions on the capacity of agents to represent the foundation.[68] Interested parties, on the other hand, have no right to petition the court for disclosure. Only through the inquiry procedure, the enterprise division of the Court of Appeal of Amsterdam can empower an investigator to examine the books.

SANCTIONS AGAINST FOUNDATIONS ON REQUEST
OF INTERESTED PARTIES

In some countries, the state is regarded as the only institution empowered to care for and protect the general interest and to oversee the functioning of foundations in the interest of all parties involved. This view is strongly held in France and in the United States. In France, it seems like the State is considered to be the only party with a legitimate interest in foundations.[69] In the United States, individuals or groups other than the competent state or federal authorities have generally no possibilities to request sanctions against foundations or their boards. No one can force the attorney general to take action, but attorneys general often rely on the public and the media to bring possible misconduct to their attention (Fremont-Smith 1965, pp. 200ff.). In principle, third parties "have standing" against foundations, only based on contractual rights or personal injuries. The state corporation acts do not grant "standing" to "interested parties" in cases of statute violations by the board. The statutes are considered a contract in which outsiders are not taking part and therefore cannot derive a right from it. Only at the federal level can interested parties sue a foundation on the grounds of damages suffered as a taxpayer or a citizen. Actions in these cases have to be based on violations of federal laws or the constitution and it is necessary to prove that there is both an injury and a concrete complaint.[70]

In England, parties interested in charities whose income does not exceed 500 pounds, and—in case of local charities—two or more inhabitants of the area must petition the Charity Commission if they believe that actions inconsistent with the foundation's purpose are being pursued.[71] For other charities, a "charity proceeding" in the courts may be initiated, which must be authorized by the Charity Commission. However, the Commission can take it on itself if, in the Commission's opinion, the involvement of the courts is not necessary.[72]

The German approach of providing "standing" to interested parties is rather limited, as there is no right to petition the *Aufsichtsbehörde* to take measures. The only right interested parties have is to request a review of this agency's decisions toward a foundation on the basis of the general interest, if a personal interest that is affected by that decision can be proven.[73] A lawsuit in the civil courts against the foundation is only possible on the basis of damages for a personal injury.

Austria has similar arrangements concerning regular foundations: The supervisory system regarding these foundations is a public system, and interested parties can only contest the decisions of the supervising agency under certain conditions. A civil lawsuit against the foundation or its board can only be based on injury. As far as *Privatstiftungen* are concerned, the only interested parties able to petition the courts are the members of internal bodies of the foundation and the beneficiaries.

By contrast, the situation in the Netherlands seems rather liberal. An important difference with the other continental countries is that the supervisory regulation is not of public but of civil character.[74] Interested parties may sue the foundation for dismissal of board members and dissolution, in the same way as the public prosecutor. In addition, they may request decisions of the board (or other internal bodies of the foundation) to be declared void. When such decisions are contrary to mandatory law or the statutes of the foundation, it is deemed to be inherently void and everyone can ask the court to declare that to be the case. At the request of any person with a specific interest, board decisions can be overturned by the courts in cases where procedural rules, bylaws or the dictates of "reasonableness and fairness" within the organization are violated.[75] Legally, the circle of interested parties is restricted to persons who either belong to the organization or can show a specific and concrete injury to themselves in their relation to the foundation.[76] In a remarkable decision, the Court of Appeal of Amsterdam decided that groups of beneficiaries targeted by the foundation, although they have no direct right to a grant, could under certain circumstances also have a tort claim against the foundation.[77]

DISCUSSION AND CONCLUSION

Summarizing the discussion, the countries studied here can be classified as follows: France is an example of a country with little legislation on foundations, but a high degree of discretionary government powers relating to the establishment and operation of foundations.

The United States (at federal and state level), and Germany and Austria (only regular foundations) are examples of countries with substantive legislation on foundations, in which—primarily—legitimacy control is exercised by the government; and England, Austria (*Privatstiftungen*), and the Netherlands are examples of countries with substantive legislation on foundations, in which legitimacy control is exercised by the judiciary or an independent agency.

Table 3.1 shows this in tabular form. Generally, supervision of foundations can be linked to (1) the establishment, (2) the registration, (3) their operations later on, or to a combination thereof. Governmental agencies, or a semigovernmental agency in the case of the Charity Commission in England, are involved with the establishment of the foundation in all countries included in this comparison, with the exception of the Netherlands. The desirability of governmental intervention in relation to the establishment of foundations is

Table 3.1. Establishment, Transparency, and Supervision of Foundations

	United States	England	Germany	Austria	France	Netherlands
Establishment						
Government discretionary control	–	–	–	–	+	–
Government legitimacy control	+	–	+	+a	–	–
Legitimacy control by independent agency/judiciary	–	+	–	+b	–	–
Public registration	+	+	–/+	+	+	+
Transparency and Supervision of Activities						
Consent for certain financial transactions by government or independent agency	–	+	–/+	+/–	+	–
Financial report to government	+c	–	+	+a	–	–
Financial report to independent agency/judiciary	–	+	–	–	–	–
Reports open to interested parties	+	+	–	–/+b	–	–
Measures taken by government	–	–	+	+a	+/–	–
Measures taken by independent agency	–	+	–	–	–	–
Judicial Involvement						
Appeal against governmental decisions to administrative court	–	–	+	–d	–	–
Appeal against decisions of independent agency to court	–	+	–	–	–	–
Measures at request of government or independent agency	+	+	–	–	–	+
Measurements on request of interested parties	–	+	–	+b	–	+

Note. + indicates present; – indicates absent; a, Stiftung; b, Privatstiftung; c, Internal Revenue Service; d, Appeal against government control decisions concerning regular foundations in Austria is only to the relevant minister.

usually considered a political and not a legal question. Indeed, the political–historical traditions of a country are often primarily responsible for decisions on how much freedom to give to voluntary organizations. From a legal point of view, arguments for governmental interference, especially relating to the concession system, are not convincing.

The advantage of serious involvement by the government, or an independent body such as the Charity Commission, in the establishment of a foundation is that there is some degree of "quality control" in terms of purposes that foundations pursue. Supervision at the establishment level has the further advantage that the supervisory agency has the ability to collect information about existing foundations as a starting point for the development of an effective supervisory system. Such a system exists, at least theoretically, in the United States with the IRS, in England, Germany, and in Austria for regular foundations. On the other hand, government involvement can also easily limit choices. Thus, the autonomy of donors to establish foundations for whatever purposes they consider useful or necessary is best preserved when there is only a passive role, or no role at all, for the government or any other approving authority in the establishment process (cf. Kübler, 1981, p. 138).

With regard to accountability issues, the analysis suggests the importance of clear rules on accounting practices, the preparation of annual accounts, and, in the case of foundations above a certain size, mandatory auditing requirements. An obligation to submit annual accounts to the government or an independent agency provides a useful means of supervision, although budgetary constraints often prevent systematic monitoring of financial data.[78] The same is true for the preventive control of significant financial transactions of foundations by supervisory agencies. The question that arises here is whether it might be sufficient to subject such transactions to mandatory disclosure in the annual accounts[79] in combination with specific sanctions on board members and trustees in case of mismanagement.

On the issues of public disclosure, the conclusion that flows from the comparison is that foundation laws in general do not take into account the interest of third parties, especially potential grantseekers and donors of foundations. The implication would be that such interests are not a public-interest concern. However, relevant information for such parties is relatively easily available in England. In the United States, at least financial information is available through the tax system. In continental European countries with public supervision of foundations, the availability of financial information on foundations depends on the existence of administrative transparency regulations and privacy laws. On a most general level, however, public disclosure laws, where they exist, are not specifically tailored to the interests of donors and grantees, which provides an opening for self-regulatory activities.[80]

Finally, from the point of view of organizational freedom and board autonomy, judicial control of foundation activities is preferable to administrative control, since the judiciary system is less prone to intermingle the supervisory function with current governmental policy concerns. Although foundations usually can appeal administrative decisions concerning different aspects of governmental supervision, the process is more protracted and burdensome than direct supervision by the courts.[81] Delegating the supervisory function to an independent body of mixed judicial and administrative character, like the Charity Commission in England, has the advantage of impartiality toward foundations,[82] but there might be problems in clearly defining the powers of such a body.[83] The disadvantage of supervision by the judiciary is that this function is not performed in a continuous and systematic way, since the courts can only react to actual violations brought to them. This problem could, however, be solved by granting the public prosecutor and interested third parties access to registration details and financial accounts. Conceivably, the risk that misuse and mismanagement of foundations under this scenario go undetected and unsanctioned is probably as low as in theoretical case of continuous supervision by a governmental or quasigovernmental agency, which, as indicated earlier, is in practice often limited by fiscal constraints.

NOTES

1. Treaty Protecting Human Rights and Fundamental Liberties (1950), Art. 11, and the International Treaty on Civil and Political Rights (1996), Art. 22.
2. However, this chapter does not deal with the practical support and cooperation that governments give foundations. As a legal comparison, only the norms, but not necessarily the facts, of the supervisory systems are covered.
3. In what follows, "England" is used as a shorthand for "England and Wales;" English law applied in both countries.
4. The New York not-for-profit corporation law of 1969, for instance, leaves the internal organization more or less open.
5. In the United States, a further distinction is made between public and private foundations; see Simon, 1995.
6. For a discussion of the differences in approach between the United States and England, see Hopkins and Moore, 1992, pp. 196–197.
7. On trusts in general, see Riddall, 1982; Martin, 1985; American Law Institute, 1959.
8. For the United States, see Chisholm, 1987–1988; for England, Picarda, 1995, pp. 151–168. Foundations that are political are legally permissible, but they cannot be charities and do not qualify for a number of important tax benefits. As they are atypical, I have not taken them into account in this comparison.
9. The basic principle of associations is that the members form a body. At the minimum, the general meeting has the right to appoint and dismiss board members and to amend the statutes and to dissolve the association.
10. See Ludes and Gilbert, 1985, Corporations, sections 17–18.

11. See Fremont-Smith, 1965, p. 112ff. For a survey of the legal requirements for charitable corporations of all states of the United States, ibid., p. 479. Karpen's view (1980, p. 53) that the United States has a concession system seems to be disputable, since the only control is the control of legitimacy of especially the purpose.
12. On trust law generally, see American Law Institute, 1959, section 382.
13. For a critical review of this tax approach to the regulation of private foundations, see Simon, 1995.
14. See New York not-for-profit corporation law 1969, section 1101: Attorney's General Action for Judicial Dissolution. A practical example is the dissolution of a charity running bingo games in Missouri (see *the Chronicle of Philanthropy*, September 5, 1989).
15. See Fremont-Smith, 1965, p. 76. On the use of the *cy-près* rule in the famous "Bucks' case," see Simon, 1987, pp. 641–648.
16. The term *foundation* is used here as defined in the introduction.
17. A recent commentary on this act is Pettit, 1993. For a very comprehensive discussion, see Picarda, 1995.
18. There are, however, many charities that are exempt or except and are not registered or supervised by the Charity Commission.
19. See Picarda, 1995, p. 10–11.
20. See Charities Act 1993, section 41ff. The Deregulation and Contracting Out Act of 1994 (1994 c 40) has abolished this rule for charities with an annual turnover of less than 10,000 English pounds (amending section 45, Charities Act 1993).
21. Section 9, Charities Act 1993.
22. Section 8, Charities Act 1993.
23. Section 20.5, Charities Act 1993. These schemes are announced a month before and are published.
24. Section 36 (1), Charities Act 1993. On the disposition of charity land, see Pettit, 1993, p. 216.
25. Guthrie, 1988, pp. 9ff.
26. Section 18, Charities Act 1993.
27. Sections 18–19, Charities Act 1993.
28. Section 3, subsection 4, Charities Act 1993.
29. Sections 13–14, Charities Act 1993.
30. On German foundation law in general, see Münchener Kommentar zum BGB, I (Reuter), paras. 80–9; Seifart, 1987; Ebersbach & Strickrodt, 1972; Soergel-Neuhoff, 1978, Palandt, 1995; Rawert, 1995.
31. For advantages and disadvantages of the German pluriform foundation law, see Kübler, 1981, p. 138.
32. This is explicitly stated by the Oberverwaltungsgerichtshof (Administrative Court of Appeal) of Lüneburg in its judgement of September 18, 1984, *Neue Juristische Wochenschrift* (NJW), 1985, p. 1572.
33. For more details, see Rawert, 1995, pp. 392ff.
34. However, this is not generally the case in other state foundation laws and remains a contested issue; see Soergel-Neuhoff, 1978, p. 31.
35. Section 11, Stiftungsgesetz Baden-Würtemberg of October 4, 1977.
36. Section 40, Verwaltungsgerichtsordnung.
37. See, for instance, Verwaltungsgerichthof Mannheim, September 17, 1974, NJW, 1975, p. 1573; and Oberverwaltungsgerichtshof Lüneburg, September 18, 1984, NJW, 1985, p. 1572.
38. The private foundation under Austrian law is not to be mistaken with the "private independent foundation" concept in the United States.
39. Federal Act of November 27, 1974, Bundesgesetzblatt, 1975, no. 11.

40. Act of October 14, 1993, Bundesgesetzblatt 1993, p. 694.
41. *Fonds* (temporary funds)—although also eligible for legal personality—are a rather atypical form and will not further be taken into account.
42. Paras. 1 to 6, Foundation Act 1974.
43. Para. 39, Foundation Act 1974.
44. See paras. 5–6 Foundation Act 1974. According to para. 5, sec. 2 of the Act, admission is to be refused if sufficient means to execute the purpose are not expected. On behalf of the state, the Ministry of Finance (*Finanzprokurator*) is involved in the evaluation of the application.
45. Para. 40, Foundation Act 1974.
46. Para. 14, Foundation Act 1974.
47. Para. 14, Foundation Act, Stammer, 1975, p. 104.
48. Para. 15, subs. 5, Foundation Act 1974.
49. Para. 16, Foundation Act 1974.
50. See Stammer, 1975, p. 108ff.
51. Para. 18, subs. 3, Foundation Act 1974.
52. Para. 7, Act on Private Foundations 1993.
53. For cases in which foreign money is included, see paras. 11 and 12, Act on Private Foundations 1993.
54. Paras. 15–17, Act on Private Foundations 1993.
55. See Para. 18, Act on Private Foundations 1993.
56. Act of July 23, 1987, Act (*Loi*) no. 87-571. A second Act on Corporate Foundations was passed in 1990. However, since corporate foundations constitute a special form and are still insignificant in numbers, I concentrate on the regulation of regular foundations. For a discussion of corporate foundations in France and the 1990 Act, see Chapter 9 by Archambault et al.
57. However, the recent law of January 30, 1997 (*State Gazette,* 1997, p. 53) requires that foundations carrying on an enterprise with an annual turnover of Dfl. 6 million ($3 million), from January 1, 1998 on, prepare annual accounts according to the regulations for companies (Articles 2:360ff. Dutch Civil Code) and deposit them at the chamber of commerce.
58. In a judgment of December 22, 1989, NJ 1990, 512, the Supreme Court found it within the bounds of legality for foundations to disclose financial information in a chaotic, disorderly form. This can be interpreted as an invitation to the legislation to set rules for financial reporting for foundations.
59. For more detail, see Articles 297–298, Dutch Civil Code.
60. Art. 2:14–15, Civil Code.
61. According to section 1 of Article 2:294, Civil Code, this is the case "when under the existing circumstances the original statutes would lead to consequences that reasonably would not have been wished by the founders."
62. The Advocate General may only request an inquiry on grounds of a public interest violation.
63. Recently, the chambers of commerce have acquired an independent right to dissolve foundations that failed to pay registration fees to the chamber.
64. See Section 3 (1) and (8), Charities Act 1993.
65. The Stiftungen und Fondsgesetz (Foundation Act) of Austria, para. 40.1, explicitly declares the right of everyone to have access to the information contained in the register. This does not include, however, the annual accounts submitted to governmental authorities.
66. Para. 30, Law on Private Foundations 1993.
67. The foundations mentioned in footnote 57 require publicity of the annual accounts.
68. The contracting parties may rely on the published data, even if they appear to be not correct.

69. See Pomey, 1980, p. 103. On the French approach toward foundations in general, see Raynaud, 1989, and Chapter 9 by Archambault et al.
70. See *McGlotten v. Connally* (338F Suppl. 448 DDC "72"); Bittker & Kaufman, 1972.
71. Section 16.5, Charities Act 1993.
72. Section 33, Charities Act 1993.
73. Stelkens–Bonk–Leonhardt 1983, para. 13.
74. With the exception of the regulation concerning private foundations in Austria as noted earlier.
75. Outsiders cannot refer to this last criterion.
76. See the decision of the Dutch Supreme Court of October 25, 1991, NJ 1992, 149, with my critical comment (van der Ploeg, 1992, p. 105).
77. Not published, see van der Ploeg, 1986, p. 158. An example would be if the distribution of grants is deemed discriminatory.
78. The value of generating information on foundations thus involves cost–benefit considerations. The maintainance of appropriate registers is usually a costly task, especially if access to information is only necessary to investigate concrete cases of mismanagement or violations of the law; a more cost-effective way would be to grant supervisory agencies the right to request pertinent information as needed on a case-by-case basis.
79. An obligatory consent of an internal supervising body could also be a helpful.
80. A prime example for such self-regulatory activities is the Foundation Center in New York.
81. In appealing a decision by an administrative supervisory agency, the court or higher administrative body evaluates whether the governmental agency has stayed within the limits of its competence. The acts of the board of the foundation are only indirectly evaluated. In the case of court supervision, the judge evaluates directly the lawfulness of the acts of the foundation's board. Governmental policies do thus not play a role.
82. Hopkins and Moore (1992, p. 209) also prefer an independent agency to a governmental (tax) agency.
83. For a discussion of the desirability of creating an independent agency instead of the IRS in the United States, see Ginsburg, Marks, and Wertheim, 1977, pp. 2640–2643.

REFERENCES

American Law Institute (1959). *Restatement of the Law (Second), Trusts.* Philadelphia: Author.

Bittker, B., & Kaufman, K. (1972). Taxes and civil right: "Constitutionalizing" the Internal Revenue Code. *Yale Law Journal, 82,* 51ff.

Chisholm, L. (1987–1988). Exempt organization advocacy: Matching the rules to the rationales. *Indiana Law Journal, 63,* 201–299.

Conviser, R. (1964). *The modern philanthropic foundation in American and Germany.* Doctoral dissertation, University of Cologne.

Ebersbach, H., & Strickrodt, H. (1972). *Handbuch des deutschen Stiftungsrecht.* Göttingen: Vandenhoeck & Ruprecht.

Edie, J. (1987). *First Steps in Starting a Foundation.* Washington, DC: Council on Foundations.

Encyclopédie Dalloz. (1992). "Foundation" by C. Debbasch. Paris: Dalloz.

Fremont-Smith, M. (1965). *Foundations and Government, State and Federal Law and Supervision.* New York: Russell Sage Foundation.

Ginsburg, D., Marks, L., & Wertheim, R. (1977). Federal Oversight of Private Philanthropy. In *Research Papers Sponsored By The Commission on Private Philanthropy and Public Needs,* Vol. 5, Part 1 (pp. 2575–2696). Washington, DC: Department of the Treasury.

Guthrie, R. (1988). *Charity and the Nation*. Fifth Arnold Goodman Charity lecture. Tonbridge, UK: Charity Aid Foundation.

Hopkins, B. & Moore, C. (1992). Using the lessons learned from English and U.S. law to create a regulatory framework for charities in evolving democracies. *Voluntas, 2,* 194–214.

Karpen, U. (1980). *Gemeinnützige Stiftungen im pluralistischen Rechtsstaat; Neuere Entwicklungen des amerikanischen und deutschen Stiftungs-(steuer-)rechtes.* Frankfurt am Main: Metzner.

Kübler, F. (1981). *Gesellschaftsrecht.* Heidelberg-Karlsruhe: Müller.

Ludes, F. J., & Gilbert, H. J. (1985). *Corpus Iuris Secundum: A Complete Restatement of the Entire American Law.* West St. Paul, Mn.

McLean, S., Kluger, R., & Henrey, R. (1990). *Charitable contributions in the OECD, a tax study.* Geneva: Interphil.

Martin, J. E. (1985). *Hanbury & Maudsley, Modern Equity,* 12th ed. London: Stevens.

Münchener Kommentar zum BGB, 1 (Reuter), paras. 80–88. Munich: Beck.

Office of the Ohio Attorney General. (1977). The Status of State Regulation of Chartiabel Trusts, Foundations, and Solicitations. In *Research Papers Sponsored By the Commission on Private Philanthropy and Public Needs,* Vol. 5, Part 1 (pp. 2705–2780). Washington, DC: Department of the Treasury.

Palandt (1995). *Bürgerliches Gesetzbuch,* 54th ed. Munich: Beck.

Pettit, P. H. (1993). Charities. *Halsbury's Laws of England,* 4th ed., Vol. 5(2), London: Buttersworth.

Picarda, H. (1995). *The Law and Practice Relating to Charities,* 2nd ed. London: Butterworths.

Pomey, M. (1980). *Traité des foundations d'utilite publique.* Paris: PUF.

Randon, A. & 6, P. (1994). Constraining campaigning: The legal treatment of nonprofit policy advocacy across 24 countries. *Voluntas, 5,* 25–58.

Rawert, P. (1995). *J. von Staudingers Kommentar zum Bürgerlichen Gesetzbuch mit Einführungsgesetz und Nebengesetzen,* Vol. 1, 13th ed., Stiftungen (pp. 363–495). Berlin: Selier–de Gruyter.

Raynaud, P. (1989). Les fondations, problèmes de droit civil. In R. J. Dupuy (Ed.), *Le droit des fondations en France et à l' étranger* (pp. 41–46). Paris: La Documentation Francaise.

Riddall, J. G. (1982). *The Law of Trusts,* 2nd ed. London: Butterworths.

Simon, J. (1995). The regulation of American foundations: Looking backward at the Tax Reform Act of 1969. *Voluntas, 6,* 243–254.

Soergel-Neuhoff (1978). *Stiftungen,* §§80–88 BGB. Essen, Germany: Stifterverband fur die Deutsche Wissenschaft.

Stammer, O. (1975). *Das Östereichische Bundes-Stiftungs and Fondsgesetz mit Erläuterungen.* Vienna: Juridica Verlag.

Stelkens-Bonk-Leonhardt (1983). *Verwaltungsverfahrensgesetz,* 2nd ed. Munich: Beck.

Seifart, W. (1987). *Handbuch des Stiftungsrechts.* Munich: Beck.

van der Ploeg, T.J. (1986). *Preadvies Nederlandse vereninging voor rechtsvergelijking nr. 37, Stichtingen en trusts in het algemeen belang,* pp. 103–185. Deventer, the Netherlands: Kluwer.

van der Ploeg, T. J. (1990). *Law and the Freedom to Do Good.* Research Report, International Fellows in Philanthropy Program. Baltimore: Johns Hopkins Institute for Policy Studies.

van der Ploeg, T. J. (1992). Annotation of HR 25 Oktober 1991, NJ 1992, 1992 149. *TVVS, Tijdschrift voor Ondernemingsrecht,* 105–108.

Chapter 4

Foundations in Germany and the United States

A Comparative Analysis

HELMUT K. ANHEIER AND FRANK P. ROMO

INTRODUCTION[1]

Philanthropic foundations are a rare species. Ylvesaker (1987, p. 360) remarked that they are a "mere speck on the canvas of American society,"
accounting for only approximately 3 percent of the over 1 million tax-exempt
organizations. In Germany, where their number amounts to about 2 percent of
the 280,000 registered associations, they are almost as rare as stock corporations, which number less than four thousand. Like in the United States, German foundations are among the most infrequent organizational forms. In
other countries as well, grantmaking foundations are few, both in absolute
numbers and in relative terms, when compared either to the total number of
organizations in society or viewed as a proportion of the nonprofit entities (see
Chapter 1, this volume, Renz & Lawrence, 1993, pp. 7–9). Nonetheless,
foundations are increasing in number; and in many countries, we are experi-

HELMUT K. ANHEIER • Director, Centre for Voluntary Organisation, London School of Economics, London WC2A 2AE, United Kingdom.   FRANK P. ROMO • Associate Professor, Department of Sociology, State University of New York at Stony Brook, Stony Brook, New York 11794-
4356.

Private Funds, Public Purpose: Philanthropic Foundations in an International Perspective, edited by
Helmut K. Anheier and Stefan Toepler. New York, Plenum Press, 1999.

encing a kind of foundation renaissance. Some observers such as Berkel et al. (1989) go as far and speak of a new, third "foundation wave," after a first growth period in the late Middle Ages, alongside the rise of commerce and finance, and a second one in the late nineteenth century, following the industrial revolution.

In the introductory chapter to this book, Anheier and Toepler suggest that knowing how many foundations exist where, of what size, and for what purpose tells us much about the countries and the times in which foundations operate. Foundations offer indications, perhaps more than other types of nonprofit organization, about long-term directions and shifts in the relationship between public and private responsibilities, and changes in the relationship between private wealth and public goods. In short, the behavior of foundations may be "seismographic" of these important and often indiscernible features of society. They owe this ability to their *built-in ambivalence* in a number of important organizational components: asset preservation versus grant promotion in economic terms (Salamon, 1992, p. 118); expressing the will of the donor versus broad-based participation in social terms (Neuhoff, 1992, p. 1972); and finally, ambivalence in political terms because, as private endowments for public purposes, they operate outside the direct majoritarian public control; foundations represent private agendas in public arenas (see Karl & Katz, 1987; Nielsen, 1972).

In this context, we examine the foundation sectors in the United States and (West) Germany in terms of their size and scope. Although other countries such as the United Kingdom, Italy, Spain, or Japan have relatively large and diverse foundation sectors, those of the United States and Germany are the largest in terms of numbers and assets. And, as we will see shortly, they tell a story of remarkable similarities and differences.

A Terminological Note

For the purposes of comparative analysis, it is useful to clarify a number of conceptual issues. The term *foundation,* particularly in Europe, applies to a variety of institutions, including operating foundations such as hospitals, grantmaking intermediaries financed by public budget allocations, and numerous hybrid forms between grantmaking and operating, as well as public and private, institutions. The term *foundation,* as used in this study, refers primarily to private, grantmaking foundations that disburse grants, originating from some form of endowment, to third parties for purposes stipulated in the foundation's charter or constitution. Such a minimal definition excludes operating foundations, and public foundations and trusts that are fully part of government. Specifically, in the United States, we include independent foundations, corporate foundations, and community foundations; in Germany, civil law foundations, independent public law foundations, independent foundations established under church law, and several of the special legal substitute forms available to foundations in civil law systems. For reasons of convenience, we exclude the approximately 60,000 church foundations, most of which represent church-related endowments to support the salary of the clergy or to maintain church property such as the parish church or a monastery.

While such a minimal definition encounters undoubtedly many difficulties at the borders between the foundation world and the state (e.g., public trusts or public law foundations), business (e.g., company foundations; foundations as the governing body of corporations as in Italy and Germany), religion (e.g., ecclesiastical foundations), and the family (e.g., family trusts and foundations), it has nonetheless the significant advantage that the two major data sources on foundations in Germany and the United States are based on a similar terminology and organized accordingly. For inclusion in its database, the Foundation Center defines *foundation* as a "nongovernmental, nonprofit organization with its own funds and program managed by its own trustees and directors, established to maintain or aid educational, social, charitable, religious, or other activities serving the common welfare, primarily by making grants" (Foundation Center, 1993; Renz & Lawrence, 1993, p. 87).

In the German case, the *Bundesverband Deutscher Siftungen* (1991, p. xvi) did not employ a general definition but listed ten legal forms or types of foundations for inclusion (see Table 4.1), while excluding church foundations

Table 4.1. Legal Status of German and U.S. Foundations, 1990–1992

	Germany			United States		
Legal status	Number	%	%	Foundation type	Number	%
Civil law foundation	2,636	77.8	81.5	Independent	29,476	88.4
Public law foundation	163	4.8	5.0	Corporate	1,775	5.3
Limited liability company	23	0.7	0.7	Community	335	1.0
Registered association	29	0.9	0.9	Operating	1,770	5.3
Dependent civil law foundation	139	4.1	4.3	TOTAL	33,356	100
Dependent public law foundation	147	4.3	4.5			
Dependent church foundations	9	0.3	0.3			
Public law church foundation	34	1.0	1.1			
Civil law church foundation	40	1.2	1.2			
Other legal forms	14	0.4	0.4			
Unknown	155	4.6	—			
TOTAL	3,389	100	100			

serving internal church matters only. Taken together, the various legal types come very close to the definition used by the Foundation Center. With the data at hand, it is, however, not possible to exclude all public foundations and trusts that are fully part of government. As a consequence, the German data contain a small number of *de facto* and *de jure* governmental institutions. Since both the German Foundation Directory and the U.S. Directory identify operating from primarily grantmaking foundations, we were able to exclude the former from the analysis. Nonetheless, both the German and the U.S. data sources include grantmaking foundations that also operate institutions or organizations.

Data Sources

Because the Foundation Center and the Bundesverband employ near identical operational definitions of what constitutes a grantmaking foundation, we have, for the first time, comparable data sources available that allow us to explore the size and scope of the foundation sector in two countries.

1. *The Foundation Center's Database.* The U.S. database includes the 33,356 grantmaking foundations that made grants of at least one dollar between 1989 and 1992. The Foundation Center complies the actual data from four sources:

- The annual tax return forms (PF 990) filed by foundations with the Internal Revenue Service (IRS). These forms are prepared and made available to the Foundation Center as "yearly transaction tapes" and updated in monthly "aperture cards."
- The financial and program information provided by the foundations themselves in annual reports and similar publication.
- Questionnaires mailed to nearly 9,000 larger foundations asking information about employment, size of assets, grants, investments, and areas of activities among other items.
- Survey of community foundations. Since this type of foundation is not included in the information provided by the IRS, the Foundation Center surveys community foundations with the help of a questionnaire.

The various data collection efforts from different sources are necessary because the IRS tax form does not include information on important variables such as staffing. Because of the way the data have been collected over time, the amount of information we have on the United States varies by the size and the establishment year of foundations. Coverage is better for larger foundations than for smaller ones. Moreover, since the mid-1980s, the Foundation Center has significantly broadened its efforts to improve data coverage to the effect that information on recently established foundations is better than for those created prior to 1987. This applies to key variables such as staffing and year of establishment.

2. *The Verzeichnis der Deutschen Stiftungen* (Inventory of German Founda-tions) is based on data collected by the Munich-based MAECENATA, a con-sulting firm for foundations, for the *Bundesverband Deutscher Stiftungen,* the Federal Association of German Foundations (1991, 1992). This effort marks the first time that systematic data have been gathered on German foundations, with the notable exception of the *Stiftungshandbuch* (Foundation Handbook), a compendium that reports primarily on some 350–400 larger foundations in the fields of research, education and culture (Berkel et al., 1989).

Between 1989 and 1991, a basic questionnaire was sent out to nearly 6,000 foundations that had been identified by contacting numerous federal and state agencies, municipalities, churches, and universities in an effort to update the inventory of foundations maintained by Federal Association of German Foundations. About 50 percent of the questionnaires were returned in time for the publication of the *Verzeichnis Deutscher Stiftungen* in October 1991. Since then, more have been returned, in addition to new foundations that were either created or identified after 1991. As Table 4.2 shows, the total number of known and active foundations in West Germany amounts to 5,394.

The database includes information on 3,313 foundations, which indicates an overall response rate of 0.61 or slightly over 60 percent. An analysis of missing cases is impossible given the data available to us, and we cannot say with any degree of certainty how representative the data are for German foundations as a whole. Nonetheless, since most of larger and more established

Table 4.2. Number of Foundations and Response Ratios by State, 1990–1992

State/Land	Total number of known foundations	Percent of total	Number of foundations in database	Percent of total	Response ratio
Baden-Württemberg	785	14.55	525	15.85	0.67
Bayern	1,424	26.4	976	29.46	0.69
Berlin	221	4.1	168	5.07	0.76
Bremen	40	0.74	21	0.63	0.53
Hamburg	525	9.73	327	9.87	0.62
Hessen	530	9.83	282	8.51	0.53
Niedersachsen	529	9.81	359	10.84	0.68
Nordrhein–Westfalen	961	17.82	447	13.49	0.47
Rheinland-Pfalz	139	2.58	82	2.48	0.59
Saarland	42	0.78	32	0.97	0.76
Schleswig–Holstein	198	3.67	94	2.84	0.47
TOTAL	5,394	100.00	3,313	100	0.61

foundations are included in the database, it is probably fair to assume a high degree of representativeness in terms of asset size, grants, and employment for fully operational foundations.[2] As Table 4.2 shows, response rates differ some- what by state (*Land*). The lower-than-average rate for the states of Nordrhein– Westfalia and Hesse indicate the weakest areas in terms of geographical cover- age. As we will see, both states contain among the highest shares of founda- tions established after World War II, which indicates a slight bias in favor of older foundations in the data. However, since larger and established founda- tions are generally well represented, we are most likely underreporting smaller, less than fully operational foundation from these two states (see note 3).

A Cautionary Note

Because the German Foundation Directory was compiled for the first time, it will not be possible, with few exceptions, to explore in a systematic way trends and changes in the size and scope of the foundation sectors over time. For this reason, the following study is largely restricted to a cross- sectional analysis of the foundation sector in the two countries. We should keep in mind that while the German data are based on one data source (i.e., a questionnaire), the U.S. data combine information obtained from IRS sources with data collected by means of survey forms. As a result, the numerical base for U.S. information varies between 33,000 for the entire database to about 9,000 for those foundations with assets over $1 million or $100,000 in grants made. Finally, we should recall that neither the German nor the U.S. data represent probability samples; rather, both are attempts to collect information on the universe of foundations that exist in each country. In neither case, however, do we know how representative the directories are of the total set of foundations in each country. Therefore tests of statistical significance are inap- propriate both within and between "samples," and readers are advised to interpret differences between and among the separate U.S. and German foun- dation data sets with great caution.

Finally, we should mention that the German data reported here refer to the western part of the country prior to unification in 1990. Given the fluidity and complexity of the legal situation in East Germany between 1989 and 1992, we decided to exclude approximately 100 foundations that had responded to the questionnaire. More recent data reported in Anheier (1998) and Brummer (1996) show that 317 foundations existed in East Germany as of 1996. With over 7,200 foundations estimated to exist in Germany in the mid-1990s, these 317 East German foundations amount to less than 5 percent of the total, suggesting that the German foundation sector remains primarily a "Western" phenomenon.

A COMPARATIVE ANALYSIS

In this section, we present an analysis of foundations in Germany and the United States by looking at three major areas: first, size of the foundation sector in terms of number of organizations, assets, grantmaking and employment; second, the scope of foundation activities according to various grantmaking domains; and finally, regional and over-time variations in terms of development and growth.

Before entering into such analysis, however, it will be useful to point out the various types and frequencies of foundations operating in each country. As Table 4.1 shows, the U.S. foundation world consists of four major types: independent, corporate, community, and operating (or grantmaking). Independent foundations account for about 9 out of 10 foundations (88.4 percent), whereas corporate and grantmaking foundations are much less frequent (5.3 percent each, and almost 11 percent taken together). Finally, community foundations represent about one in one hundred foundations (i.e., 1 percent). There is little differentiation in legal forms, and foundations are typically established and operated as corporations or trusts according to state law.

By comparison, the German foundation sector is more varied, reflecting in large measure the complex morphology of association and corporation law in civil law countries (Table 4.1). Nonetheless, the field is clearly dominated by one legal form, that is, civil law foundation (77.8 percent), and together with dependent civil law foundations (4.1 percent), accounts for about the same share as independent foundations in the U.S. (83 percent). Thus, the legal complexity of the sector is introduced at the margins, where most of the diversity in types is represented in little more than 17 percent of all German foundations.

While the organizational setup and purpose of these special types of foundations may not be very different from civil law foundations, they differ in terms of founder and governance: The tripartite distinction between civil, public, and ecclesiastical law implies that foundations may be established by quite different types of founders (e.g., private individuals and corporations, government and public authorities, and the churches). It also implies that different types of foundations are regulated by distinct legal systems. Since ecclesiastical law is constitutionally equivalent to public law, churches, as legal personalities *sui generis*, can establish foundations on their own and are exempt from reporting requirement vis-à-vis secular authorities. Relatively rare are foundations in corporate form, either in form of a limited liability company or as a registered association.

How has the composition of foundation types evolved over recent decades? In the United States, we find that the corporate foundation is a relatively recent development, having achieved some critical mass only since the 1950s. Community foundations, which were first established in the 1920s at more frequent rates, have become somewhat more numerous since the 1970s, although they continue to account for the smallest share of foundations (see also Renz & Lawrence, 1993, p. 25). In Germany, the data also portrays relative stability in the share of legal forms.[3] Civil law foundations represent 80.7 percent of the foundations established before 1919, 81 percent for those created after World War II until 1969, and 84.8 percent for the 1980s. Foundations as limited liability companies represent the only innovation in the German foundation sector. There is also a slight increase in the establishment of dependent foundations. In the latter case, foundations are legally administered and represented by third parties, such as a corporation, university, or municipality. Church foundations and public law foundations, however, show a slightly downward trend. Whereas they respectively represent 3.4 percent and 8.2 percent of the pre-1919 cohort, their share is now down to 1 percent and 4 percent, respectively. Thus, for Germany, we observe slight increases in commercial forms (corporate foundations and limited liability companies) and a relative decline of public legal forms in Germany. Nonetheless, in both countries we find relative stability in basic legal types.

Size

How many foundations are there? As Table 4.3 shows, the Foundation Center lists well over 33,300 grantmaking foundations, and the German Foundation Directory reports almost 5,400 organizations (excluding the foundations operating in eastern Germany at that time).[4] For 1991, the total assets of

Table 4.3. Foundation Sector in the United States and Germany, 1990–1992

	United States	Germany	United States: Germany	Germany: United States
Number	33,356	5,394	6.18	0.16
Employment	9,230	2,536	3.64	0.27
Assets (billions)	162.90	21	7.76	0.13
Grants (billions)	9.20	3.50	2.63	0.38
Foundations per 1 billion GDP	6.46	1.39	1.80	0.55
Foundations per 1 million employment	266.14	194.42	1.37	0.73
Foundations per 1 million population	134.09	86.14	1.56	0.64
Foundation assets in % of GDP	3.16	1.39	2.28	0.44

the U.S. foundations amount to $162.9 billion, with a total of $9.2 billion in grants. In Germany, data on total assets are incomplete,[5] but can be estimated, however crudely, to range between $14.5 and $28.8 billion (with $21 billion as the midpoint).[6] In 1991, U.S. foundations paid out a total of $9.2 billion in grants, compared to $1.9 billion in Germany. In the same year, U.S. foundations employed over 9,000 people, including program officers and support staff, whereas German foundations employed a little over 2,000 individuals. Based on these data, the U.S. foundation sector is about six times larger than the German one in terms of size, four times larger in terms of employment, nearly eight times larger in assets, and about five times larger in relation to the sum of grants paid. Stated the other way around, the German foundation sector is about 13 to 25 percent of its U.S. counterpart.

Relative and Absolute Size

Yet which foundation sector is larger in relative terms? Since the U.S. economy is larger than the German one, it may come as no surprise that its foundation sector is larger as well. To take into account such differences, we relate the total number of foundations to gross national product (GNP), total employment, and population size (Table 4.3). We find that in relative terms, the U.S. foundation sector is between 1.4 and 1.8 times larger than the German foundation sector, which, in turn, represents between 55 percent and 73 percent of that of the U.S. foundation sector. Per $1 billion in gross domestic product (GDP), there are 6.4 foundations in the United States, and 3.6 in Germany; per 1 million employees, there are 266 foundations in the United States, and 194 in Germany; and finally, per 1 million inhabitants, the United States counts 134 foundations and Germany 86.

Thus, we find that in terms of absolute and relative frequency, the U.S. has a higher propensity to create foundations. As Table 4.3 shows, this tendency is even more pronounced when we take total assets into account. Related to GDP, foundations assets account for about 3.2 percent of the U.S. GDP and about 1.4 percent of the German GDP. In relative terms, total assets of German foundations represent less than half (44 percent) of those of the United States. In summary, foundations in Germany are less frequent and smaller compared to foundations in the United States.

Foundations Large and Small

Foundations range in size from very small organizations like the Johann–Berend–Stiftung, established in 1960, with total assets of DM 32,699 ($20,000) to support the education of "girls born out of wedlock" in the north-German city of Kiel, to large foundations like the Fritz Thyssen Stiftung, with DM 84 million in assets and over DM 20 million in annual grants and expenditures for research purposes. In the United States, we find a similar range, perhaps well exemplified by the Sabbah Family Foundation in Greenboro, NC, with assets of about $100,000 to support religious and charitable organizations, to the Duke Endowment for health and medical research, with $1.2 billion in assets.

Table 4.4. The Fifteen Largest Foundations in the United States
and Germany, 1990–1992

Name	Field	Assets in millions of dollars
Germany		
1 Volkswagen Stiftung	Education and research	1,709
2 Deutsche Bundesstiftung Umwelt	Environment	1,574
3 Bayerische Landesstiftung	Multipurpose	478
4 Robert–Bosch–Stiftung	Health	446
5 Alfred–Krupp–von Bohlen u. Halbach–Stiftung	Research	348
6 Carl–Zeiss–Stiftung	Research	313
7 Oberfrankenstiftung	Art and culture	234
8 Gemeinnützige Hertle-Stiftung	Research	199
9 Hilfswerk für Behinderte Kinder	Social services	140
10 Stiftung F.V.S.	Art and culture	119
11 Körber-Stiftung	Research and art	125
12 Dr. Mildred Scheel-Stiftung für Krebsforschung	Health research	96
13 Fritz Thyssen–Stiftung	Research	84
14 Zeppelin–Stiftung	Social services	80
15 Stiftung Stahlanwendungsforschung	Applied research	71
TOTAL ASSETS (millions)		6,016
United States		
1 Ford Foundation	Multipurpose	6,253
2 Kellogg Foundation	Multipurpose	5,397
3 Robert Wood Johnson Foundation	Health	4,085
4 Lilly Endowment	Education	3,593
5 John D. and C. T. MacArthur Foundation	Research	3,393
6 Pew Charitable Trust	Multipurpose	3,338
7 Rockefeller Foundation	Multipurpose	2,172
8 Andrew W. Mellon Foundation	Arts and research	1,203
9 Robert W. Woodruff Foundation	Health and education	1,495
10 Annenberg Foundation	Education	1,477
11 Kresge Foundation	Education and research	1,422
12 Duke Endowment	Health	1,212
13 Charles Stewart Mott Foundation	Education	1,095
14 DeWitt Wallace–Reader's Digest Fund	Education	1,088
15 McKnight Foundation	Social services	1,067
TOTAL ASSETS (millions)		39,190

The foundation sector in both countries appears highly concentrated, whereby a relatively small number of foundations accounts for most of the financial weight in the sector. In the United States, only about one in four (8,500) of the total number of grantmaking foundations held assets of $1 million or more. Together, the assets of these 8,500 foundations constitute nearly 97 percent of total foundation assets in 1991. Moreover, the 418 foundations with assets of $50 million represent 1.3 percent of all foundations, yet maintain 67.2 percent of all foundation assets. In Germany, 30 percent of foundations have DM 100,000 ($62,500) or less in assets, and about three in four have less than DM 1 million. Using the same range as in the United States, we find that 20.6 percent of the German foundations have assets of $1 million or higher. This set of foundations accounts for 94.9 percent of all assets held. In addition, the fifteen largest foundations represent close to one in three dollars held by German foundations in assets, compared to one in four in the United States. Thus, while both foundation sectors are highly concentrated and dominated in size by a relatively small number of organizations, the German foundation sector, while smaller in size, appears even more concentrated than the U.S. sector.

Table 4.4 lists the largest foundations in the two countries. The asset distribution underscores the pronounced size differential between German and U.S. foundations. The largest German foundation, Volkswagen–Stiftung, would rank ninth in the United States, the second largest tenth, and the third largest in Germany would no longer appear on the U.S. list. Both the Stiftung Stahlanwendungsforschung (Foundation for Steel Application Research) and the McKnight Foundation rank fifteenth, yet the assets of the former amount to only 6.7 percent of the latter. The ratio between rank one and rank fifteen is twenty-four in Germany, indicating that the Volkswagen–Stiftung is twenty-four times the size of the foundation ranked fifteenth on the list. In the United States, the comparable measure is 5.9, implying that the Ford Foundation is about six times the size of the McKnight Foundation. These data point to the fact that the German foundation sector is more concentrated at the top than the U.S. sector. In other words, the size of the Volkswagen–Stiftung and the Deutsche Bundesstiftung Umwelt stands out far more in Germany than the Ford and Kellog Foundation do in the United States.

Grants[7]

U.S. foundations paid out a total of $9.2 billion in grants during 1992, whereas German foundations made grants totaling between $1.9 and $5.3 billion (with a midpoint value of $3.5 billion). This means that the ratio of assets to grants is 0.056 or 5.6 percent in the United States and 0.09 or 9 percent in Germany (assuming a grant total of $1.9 billion). This implies that both overall, and relative to their total assets, German foundations paid out more than U.S. foundations. While a fuller portfolio analysis (see Salamon, 1992) would be needed to support such comparisons, nonetheless our crude figures correspond to provisions in tax laws. According to the 1969 Tax Reform Act in the United States, foundations must pay out as grants the higher of a minimum portion of their assets or the total value of their investment earning. This proportion, initially 6 percent, was later reduced to 5 percent, which is close to the ratio of 0.056 reported by U.S. foundations. In Germany, tax law regulations do not stipulate floor values for payout rates relative to the value of assets. In principle, the balance of revenue over administrative expenditure must be dedicated to the explicit purpose of the foundation in a timely, direct, and selfless manner. Up to one-fourth of this balance can, however, be used as a capital reserve to safeguard against the relative loss of asset values due to inflationary pressure. Because the "default settings" in the tax regime for German and U.S. foundations are different, one demanding minimum performance, the other a general disbursement of revenues combined (after a long legal battle with a reluctant legislature) with asset preservation, there are indications that German foundations seem to have developed, on average, higher payout rates than their U.S. counterparts.

Table 4.5 supports this general trend. The overall distribution of grant payments is closer to held assets in German foundations than it is in U.S. foundations. In Germany, the top 1.4 percent of foundations accounts for two out of three dollars made in grants, and three out of four dollars in assets. In the United States, the largest foundations pay out 48 percent of total grant sums, or one out of two grant dollars, while those with assets of less than $1 million accounted for 12 percent (Renz & Lawrence, 1993, p. 10). Moreover, as Table 4.5 shows, three out of four foundations pay grant sums less than $100,000, representing 6.5 percent of total grant disbursements. In Germany, three out of four foundations, while in the same grants range, account for only 2 percent. Among the top U.S. foundations, in turn, we find that they pay out

Table 4.5. Comparison of Foundation Grants Ranges,
United States and Germany, 1990–1992

Grants range	% United States foundations	% of grant disbursements	% Germany foundations	% of grant disbursements
$10 Million +	0.4	38.0	1.4	66.5
$1 Million–10 Million	3.7	35.9	4.8	24.2
$100,000–$1 Million	18.1	19.6	18.6	7.3
Under $100,000	77.9	6.5	75.2	2
TOTAL	100.0	100.0	100.0	100.0
	N = 33,356	$9.2 billion	N = 987	$.6 billion

only 38 percent of the total grants as compared to 66 percent in Germany. These figures imply that relative to their assets, smaller U.S. foundations pay out more and larger U.S. foundations less.

Employment

In terms of employment, we find that the great majority of foundations in both countries retain neither full-time nor part-time staff (Table 4.6). The proportion of foundations in Germany with employees is around 10 percent, which is 12 percent lower than in the United States, where 22.7 percent of foundations report staff members.[8] For foundations in both countries with employees, the modal value is one, and the mean number of employees is 4.5 persons per foundation. There are some differences in the distribution of employment insofar as U.S. foundations tend to be more frequent in the middle categories (two to twenty people), whereas the German foundations tend to be more frequently in the lowest categories. Among the largest employers in both countries, the Volkswagen–Stiftung (Germany's largest) has a staff of 180, compared to the Ford Foundation (largest in the United States), which has with 227 full-time professionals and 331 full-time support staff (558 in total). The nine German foundations with more than fifty staff account for 44 percent of employment as reported in the *Stiftungsverzeichnis*; and the six U.S.

Table 4.6. Foundation Staffing, United States
and Germany, 1990–1992

Number of staff	United States (%)	Germany (%)
50+	0.7	2.1
20–49	2.4	1.5
10–19	4.8	1.9
5–9	12.0	9.4
4	6.1	5.7
3	13.4	9.2
2	26.7	15.5
1	33.9	54.7
	100.0	100.0
	N = 2,039	N = 381
% with no staff	77.3	88.80
TOTAL	N = 8,971	N = 3,389
Number of staff positions	9,230	1,724
Average per foundation	4.53	4.5
Modal employment	1	1

foundations with more than 100 staff represent nearly 15 percent of total staff positions reported in a 1992 Foundation Center Survey.

Thus, we conclude that, in terms of labor inputs, the operation of foundations relies typically on voluntary boards (and in Germany additionally on often municipal administrations), and in only about one in ten cases in Germany, and one in five in the United States, do foundations employ staff. In this sense, the "volunteering" component is more pronounced in Germany. In addition, over half of the German foundations with employees report only one staff position. By contrast, the U.S. foundation sector, largely due to its greater size, seems more professional in the sense that more foundations have more staff. Overall, however, foundation employment is minuscule in both countries: We can estimate that German foundations add between 2,300 and 2,800 jobs to the economy, and their U.S. counterparts between 9,200 and 10,000 jobs. In both countries, foundation employment represents between 0.007 percent and 0.008 percent of total employment.

Scope

Having looked at the size of the foundation sectors in Germany and the United States, we now examine how they differ in their scope of purposes and activities in terms of major grantmaking areas or domains.[9] Table 4.7 offers a comparison of grant categories for the United States and Germany. We see that the category "social services," which includes social assistance grants, represents the most prominent area, with 31.1 percent of a total of 6,000 grants mentioned by the 3,400 German foundations that provided such information. This is followed by the field of education (21.8 percent), research (12.6 percent), and finally arts and culture (9.6%). The fields of health, family, environment, international support, and religion are all very small, ranging between 2 percent and 5 percent of all grantmaking activities. The magnitude of grants provided for political and economic issues indicates that they are clearly tiny specialty areas (together attracting less than 2 percent of all grantmaking activities). Thus, German foundations show a pronounced social service and educational orientation, followed by the support of research, arts, and culture. This result is also highlighted when we consider that 55.5 percent of all German foundations support the social service field, four out of ten (38.9 percent) fund education, one in five (22.5 percent) support research, and 17.1 percent support arts and culture.

In the United States, we find a different emphasis in terms of funding domains. The distribution of grantmaking activities is less concentrated than in Germany, as exemplified by the field of social services. For U.S. foundations, social services, education, health, and arts and culture represent the major funding domains. About one in three U.S. foundations support activities in

Table 4.7. Grant-Making Domains for German and U.S. Foundations, 1990–1992

Germany				United States			
Domain	Count	% of responses	% of cases	Domain	Count	% of responses	% of cases
Social services	1,867	31.1	55.5	Social services	5,425	18.1	33.4
Politics	30	0.5	0.9	Politics	1,158	3.8	7.1
Economy	35	0.6	1.0	Economy	222	0.7	1.4
Education	1,307	21.8	38.9	Education	5,394	18.0	33.3
Religion	180	3.0	5.4	Religion	2,955	9.9	18.2
Family	256	4.3	7.6	Family	572	1.9	3.5
Research	758	12.6	22.5	Research	2.798	9.3	17.2
Health	301	5.0	9.0	Health	5,028	16.8	31.0
Environment	180	3.0	5.4	Environment	931	3.1	5.7
International	128	2.1	3.8	International	444	1.4	2.7
Arts and culture	575	9.6	17.1	Arts and culture	4.332	14.5	26.7
Other	383	6.4	11.4	Other	578	1.9	3.6
TOTAL	6,000	100.0	N = 3363	TOTAL	29,837	100.0	N = 1,6222

social services, education, and health, and one in four provides support for arts and culture. Like the German foundation sector, U.S. foundations show a pronounced social service, educational, and cultural orientation. Unlike the German case, health emerges as a major area of interest to foundations, perhaps reflecting the absence of broad-based public health insurance systems in this country. Another striking difference between the United States and Germany is the importance of grantmaking for religious activities. In the German data, religion plays only a minor role. Not so in the United States: Here we find that almost one in five foundations (18.2 percent) support religious programs, compared to one in twenty in Germany (5.4 percent). In this sense, the U.S. foundation sector appears more religiously motivated and less secular.

Do domain clusters into broader funding categories? Do foundations that support health activities also make grants in social services or in research domains? And to what extent is religious giving by foundations tied into other funding domains? To answer these questions, we performed a K-Means cluster analysis. For Germany, results indicate a four-cluster model (Table 4.8a). The first cluster combines 443 foundations that are active in the field of culture and arts. The second cluster combines a large group of 1,563 foundations that work almost exclusively in the field of social services and assistance. There is a significant segmentation between foundations in the first and the second cluster, and little overlap between in funding domains. The

Table 4.8a. The Structure of Grantmaking Activities among German Foundations

	Social service	Political interests	Economy	Education	Religion	Family services	Research	Health	Environment	International	Art and culture	Other	Size
Cluster 1:	0.08	0.01	0.02	0.03	0.03	0.01	0.28	0.02	0.17	0.06	0.73	0.37	442
Cluster 2:	1.00	0.00	0.00	0.23	0.03	0.09	0.03	0.04	0.01	0.01	0.03	0.04	1,563
Cluster 3:	0.00	0.01	0.02	0.57	0.06	0.10	0.47	0.13	0.03	0.03	0.03	0.07	1,044
Cluster 4:	0.79	0.01	0.01	0.99	0.18	0.02	0.28	0.27	0.16	0.16	0.54	0.25	339
TOTAL													3,388

Table 4.8b. The Structure of Grantmaking Activities among U.S. Foundations

	Social service	Political interests	Economy	Education	Religion	Family services	Research	Health	Environment	International	Art and culture	Other	Size
Cluster 1:	0.11	0.02	0.00	0.05	0.09	0.01	0.02	0.00	0.02	0.01	0.07	0.01	8,509
Cluster 2:	0.47	0.07	0.01	0.00	0.29	0.04	0.16	1.00	0.06	0.03	0.33	0.05	2,062
Cluster 3:	0.73	0.19	0.05	0.75	0.19	0.12	1.00	0.57	0.15	0.05	0.58	0.08	2,268
Cluster 4:	0.55	0.12	0.01	0.96	0.33	0.05	0.00	0.50	0.10	0.05	0.51	0.05	3,383
TOTAL													16,222

third and fourth clusters combine domains. Just over 1,000 foundations in the third cluster serve both education and research. Finally, the fourth cluster of 339 foundations is largely devoted to the three domains of social services, education, and culture.

The results of the cluster analysis indicate that the four fields of social services, arts and culture, education, and research dominate foundation giving, whereby all other areas tend to be secondary. Political, religious, international, and environmental interests do not emerge as separate fields independent of other grantmaking activities; rather, they tend to be tied to dominant clusters, particularly to the multipurpose cluster 4. For example, religious purposes are not pursued alone but in some form of combination with social services, education, and arts and culture.

The four German foundation clusters carry unequal financial weights. Since data on actual grant disbursements are incomplete, we use asset size as a proxy to explore how the various domains differ in terms of funding support by private foundations. The field of social services is the smallest financially; foundations operating in this domain, while most numerous (46.1 percent), represent only 18.8 percent of total assets, with an average of about $335,000 dollars. In contrast, foundations in the domain of research and education have average total assets of $1.26 million. While accounting for one in three foundations, organizations in the education and research cluster represent one out of every two dollars (54 percent) in assets in Germany's foundation sector. The cultural domain ranks second in terms of its financial weight, followed by the mixed domain populated by foundations that combine social service, educational, and cultural support. Thus, while the social service domain is the most frequent funding activity for German foundations, it is, in financial terms, the relatively least important. Education, research, and the support of culture and the arts emerge as the dominant fields of foundation funding in Germany.

For U.S. foundations, we find a more complex structure among the over 16,000 foundations for which such information was available (Table 4.8b). As in the German case, results suggest a four-cluster model, whereby the first cluster, with about 50 percent of all foundations, represents a truly multipurpose group. With no loading higher than 0.11, this seems to suggest that foundations in this group spread their grantmaking to any of the various activity domains, *with the exception of health*. Health funding turns out to be the exemplar in second cluster. All of the 2,062 foundations in this cluster fund health activities, and just under half (47 percent) support social service activities. Whereas the second funding cluster suggests a health–social service group, the third cluster, with almost 2,300 foundations, tend to focus on research and education programs, with tertiary interests involving social service, health, and the arts. While *all* foundations in this cluster fund research, between 50 percent and 75 percent also work in the other domains just mentioned. The final cluster is primarily made up of foundations that fund educational and social service activities, but no research.

As in Germany, political, religious, international, and environmental interests do not emerge as separate fields independent of other grantmaking activities, and tend to be linked to dominant activities. While religious purposes were largely part of multipurpose group (cluster 4), it tends to be most closely associated with the second and third cluster in the United States. Every third foundation in the health domain also supports religious activities, as does every third foundation in the education–social service cluster. It seems that religious philanthropy is linked to specific funding domains in a much more pronounced way than is the case in Germany. In this sense, the U.S. foundation sector appears more religious and less secular, not only in terms of the frequency of the religious activities, but also in the terms of domain structures. A fuller analysis of these differences would require knowledge of the foundation's founder in order to take account of institutional versus individual, and religious versus secular backgrounds. Unfortunately, there is no systematic and comparative information on founders available.

Regional Variations

So far, we have examined the foundation sectors in their entirety, speaking of the German or U.S. foundation sector as if they represented solid entities. Yet much can be learned about the German and U.S. foundation sector by looking at internal regional variations and changes over time. Are foundations distributed equally across different regions and parts of the country? Table 4.9a examines the number of foundations in the ten West German states and West Berlin. In discerning the relationship size and geography, we use two measures: (1) the number of foundations per 1 million population; and (2) the number of foundations per DM 1 billion of GDP. Table 4.9a reveals significant variations in the relative frequency of foundation by state for each of these measures. Relative to population size, the frequency of foundations is lowest in the two westernmost states of Rheinland–Pfalz (37.5 per 1 million inhabitants [PMI]) and Saarland (39.4 PMI). The frequency is highest in the northern city–state of Hamburg (322.8 PMI), followed by Bavaria as a distant second (126.9 PMI), with other states ranking in between and ranging between 107 PMI (Berlin) and 56 PMI (Nordrhein–Westfalia). This ranking is largely preserved when we look at the frequency of foundations relative to GDP, with the exception of some interchanges of position in the middle ranks.

How can we explain these variations and what follows from them? Let us look at Hamburg and Bavaria first. Both rank high in the relative frequency of foundations, between one-half and one full standard deviation above the mean for Germany as a whole. Yet, they seem to embody two different foundation

Table 4.9a. Number of German Foundations by State Characteristics

State/land	Population in 1000 (1990)	Population % Catholic	Population % non-Christian	Foundations Per 1 million population	GDP in DM million (1990)	Foundations per GDP DM 1 billion	Employment (1990)	Foundations per 1 million jobs
Baden-Württemberg	9,619	45.3	1.4	81.61	389,277	2.02	4,447	176.52
Bayern	11,221	67.2	8.9	126.90	442,307	3.22	5,416	262.92
Berlin	2,068	12.8	38.9	106.87	91,363	2.42	995	222.11
Bremen	674	9.9	30.4	59.35	32,685	1.22	276	144.93
Hamburg	1,626	8.5	41.5	322.88	110,229	4.76	741	708.50
Hessen	5,661	30.4	17.9	93.62	249,809	2.12	2,561	206.95
Niedersachsen	7,284	19.6	15.2	72.62	236,823	2.23	3,112	169.99
Nordrhein–Westfalen	17,104	49.2	15.4	56.19	625,707	1.54	6,973	137.82
Rheinland-Pfalz	3,702	54.5	8.3	37.55	136,454	1.10	1,629	85.33
Saarland	1,065	72.7	5.4	39.44	35,385	1.19	428	94.13
Schleswig–Holstein	2,595	6.2	20.5	76.30	82,770	2.39	1,166	169.81
TOTAL	62,619	42.9	15.5	86.14	2,422,809	2.23	27,744	194.42

histories. Bavaria, with a predominantly Catholic population, and until the 1950s, mainly rural infrastructure, represents a foundation sector either linked directly to the church or rooted in eighteenth- and nineteenth-century Catholic society. As we will see further later, secular foundations have significantly increased in recent years, particularly in Munich, where every third foundation was established after 1983. Thus, the Bavarian foundation sector includes two developments: (1) a significant stock of foundations rooted in Catholicism and religious welfare efforts; and (2) an ever-increasing segment of secular foundations made possible by the wealth accumulated in the post–World War II era.

In historically predominantly Protestant Hamburg, we find a different development. Among larger German cities, Hamburg achieved the most pronounced expressions of liberal, bourgeois society, with a economy based on industry and international trade that could support a self-confident middle class. Here, foundations flourished along with industrialization and the expansion of commerce. They were related to civil society, and more independent from religious organizations than in other parts of the country.

To varying degrees, and with sometimes additional local influences—like the strong impact of the Napoleonic secularization of church property in the western parts of Germany or the recent growth of foundations in Bonn (all but three were established after World War II)—the relative strength of the church-related versus the civil society–related developments seems to account for the general composition and orientation of the foundation sector at the state level until 1933. After the Nazi period, and increasingly since the 1950s, German foundations are more and more part of secular culture and less rooted in religion. In this sense, regional differences among foundations established after World War II most likely reflect the preferences of the economic and political elites of an area and are less differentiated in terms of their religious or secular roots.

In the United States, the persistent tension between secular and religious powers that shaped Germany's foundation sector has been largely absent. Here, the Northeast has traditionally accounted for the relative and absolute largest share of foundations in terms of sheer number and assets (Table 4.9b). However, during the last two decades, several Southern and Western states—Texas and California in particular—have become more prominent. Nonetheless, New York in the East is still home to about one in six U.S. foundations and holds 21.8 percent of total assets. Renz and Lawrence (1993, p. 19) report that ten states (New York, California, Pennsylvania, Illinois, Michigan, Texas, Ohio, New Jersey, Minnesota, and Florida) are responsible for 71 percent of total foundation giving in the United States.

Table 4.9b relates the frequency of foundations to population size and GDP. Relative to GDP, we find that New York, Massachusetts, and Delaware show the highest propensity to create foundations per 1 billion gross state product, and the District of Columbia relative to population size. Delaware owes its prominence among foundations largely to favorable tax and incorporation laws, and Washington, D.C. owes its prominence to being the seat of the federal government. Most states in the Pacific, Mountain, and South-central regions of the country consistently show lower propensities to create foundations than the Midwest and Northeastern regions. Even California, where significant growth in the number of foundations occurred in recent years, still has a propensity that is about three times lower than that of New York or Massachusetts. Thus, whereas in Germany the regional difference in the frequency of foundations reflects the interplay between religious and political forces as well as the strength of civil society, differences in the United States appear to be related to time period of settlement and to major industrial and governmental sites.

Several other results emerge when we compare the United States and Germany in terms of regional variations. First, there is no equivalent of the centrality of New York City in the German foundation landscape. While Hamburg may represent, at least numerically, the foundation capital of Germany, it does not compare to the significance of New York City in terms of asset size and is generally not regarded as a central location for foundations. Moreover, the coincidence between the financial and industrial importance in the case of New York City and Boston, and of political centrality in the case of Washington, D.C. on one hand, and the frequency of foundations on the other, does not exist in Germany. The financial center, Frankfurt, accounts for only 5 percent of all German foundations. Moreover, industrial centers such as Essen account for only 3 percent of the foundations, and political centers such as Bonn and Berlin account for 1 percent and 5 percent, respectively.

Second, while foundations in Germany are less concentrated in one or two locations, they are at the same time more unevenly distributed across states and regions than U.S. foundations. Looking at the distribution of the number of foundations PMI, we find that this number ranges between 38 PMI and 323 PMI in Germany, with a mean of 86 PMI, and between 40 PMI and 426 PMI in the United States, with a mean of 134 PMI. The coefficient of variability is higher for Germany (92.3) than for the United States (55.4), which suggests that the relative frequency of foundations varies more in Germany than in the United States. The same holds for variations in the frequency of foundations relative to gross state product. The German coefficient of variability is with 47.9, and the United States figure is 37.8. We should keep in mind that even if the United States shows more geographic concentration than Germany, it maintains a consistently higher propensity to establish foundations than Germany.

Table 4.9b. Number of U.S. Foundations by State Characteristics

State	Number of foundations	Gross state product (in $billion)	Employment (in 1,000)	Population (in 1,000)	Foundations per 1 billion GSP	Foundations per 1 million employment	Foundations per 1 million population
New England							
Maine	228	23	647	1,228	9.91	352.40	185.67
New Hampshire	210	25	643	1,109	8.40	326.59	189.36
Vermont	86	12	311	563	7.17	276.53	152.75
Massachusetts	1,868	145	3,127	6,016	12.88	597.38	310.51
Rhode Island	158	19	513	1,003	8.32	307.99	157.53
Connecticut	827	89	1,801	3,287	9.29	459.19	251.60
Middle Atlantic							
New York	5,720	441	8,583	17,990	12.97	666.43	317.95
New Jersey	1,038	203	4,018	7,730	5.11	258.34	134.28
Pennsylvania	1,869	228	5,933	11,882	8.20	315.02	157.30
East North-Central							
Ohio	1,460	212	5,440	10,847	6.89	268.38	134.60
Indiana	681	105	2,798	5,544	6.49	234.39	122.84
Illinois	2,101	256	6,029	11,431	8.21	348.48	183.80
Michigan	975	182	4,543	9,295	5.36	214.62	104.90
Wisconsin	808	94	2,592	4,892	8.60	311.73	165.17
West North-Central							
Minnesota	616	94	2,431	4,375	6.55	253.39	140.80
Iowa	504	53	1,516	2,777	9.51	332.45	181.49
Missouri	757	100	2,689	5,117	7.57	281.52	147.94
North Dakota	62	11	317	639	5.64	195.58	97.03
South Dakota	58	11	361	696	5.27	160.66	83.33
Nebraska	226	31	857	1,578	7.29	263.71	143.22
Kansas	390	49	1,295	2,478	7.96	301.16	157.38
South Atlantic							
Delaware	161	15	364	666	10.73	442.31	241.74
Maryland	597	99	2,554	4,781	6.03	233.75	124.87

District of Columbia	233	35	262	667	0.04	918.44	420.69
Virginia	610	136	3,306	6,187	4.49	184.51	98.59
West Virginia	111	28	783	1,793	3.96	141.76	61.91
North Carolina	578	130	3,445	6,629	4.45	167.78	87.19
South Carolina	238	60	1,744	3,487	3.97	136.47	68.25
Georgia	563	130	3,166	6,478	4.33	177.83	86.91
Florida	1,367	227	6,431	12,938	6.02	212.56	105.66
East South-Central							
Kentucky	294	66	1,744	3,685	4.45	168.58	79.78
Tennessee	355	92	2,416	4,877	3.86	146.94	72.79
Alabama	325	68	1,894	4,041	4.78	171.59	80.43
Mississippi	130	38	1,183	2,573	3.42	109.89	50.52
West South-Central							
Arkansas	154	37	1,118	2,351	4.16	137.75	65.50
Louisiana	210	79	1,933	4,220	2.66	108.64	49.76
Oklahoma	264	52	1,517	3,146	5.08	174.03	83.92
Texas	1,531	340	8,555	16,987	4.50	178.96	90.13
Mountain							
Montana	90	13	403	799	6.92	233.33	112.64
Idaho	82	16	504	1,007	5.13	162.70	81.43
Wyoming	62	11	240	454	5.64	258.33	136.56
Colorado	419	66	1,755	3,294	6.35	238.75	127.20
New Mexico	71	25	715	1,515	2.84	99.30	48.86
Arizona	231	65	1,704	3,665	3.55	135.56	63.03
Utah	150	28	805	1,723	5.36	186.34	87.06
Nevada	94	28	649	1,202	3.36	144.84	78.20
Pacific							
Washington	575	96	2,498	4,867	5.99	230.18	118.14
Oregon	311	52	1,508	2,842	5.98	106.23	109.43
California	2,702	697	14,833	29,760	3.88	182.16	90.79
Alaska	22	20	258	550	1.10	85.27	40.00
Hawaii	152	26	561	1,108	5.85	270.94	137.08
TOTAL (N = 16,221)	33,350	5,162	125,312	248,709	50.3	266.14	130.09

Historical Variations

What is the relationship between the historical epoch in which foundations were established and other organizational characteristics? Are they primarily products of particular time periods rather than others? How do the two
countries differ in these respects?

The oldest foundations in Germany are hospital foundations established
to support patients in need and the poor in general, as well as the operation of
the hospital itself, such as living quarters for staff. They are typically both
"grantmaking" (i.e., alms-giving) and operative in nature—a distinction that
emerged much later—and they are often dedicated to serve those residing in
a particular town or area. Hospital foundations are a product of the high
Middle Ages, such as the Hospital–Stiftung in Wemding, established in 950, or
the Hospital–Stiftung St. Georg in Melsungen, established in 1300. In the
fifteenth century, the first foundations were established to support educational
activities. The Halepaghen–Stiftung of 1484 issued stipends for students to
study theology. The Fugger, a wealthy merchant family of Augsburg, Bavaria,
established nine foundations serving social welfare, religious, and health-
related purposes between 1521 and 1595. In relation to significant dates of
German history, we see that 3.9 percent of the foundations listed in the *Stiftungsverzeichnis* predate the end of the Thirty Year War in 1648; 8.2 percent
were established before the Vienna Congress; 10 percent were founded before
Revolution of 1848; 12.3 percent came into existence prior to the Franco–
Prussian War of 1870–1871; 20.7 percent were around to witness the outbreak
of World War I; and over 30 percent saw the defeat of the Nazis in 1945.[10]

While the longevity of these foundations is truly impressive, especially
considering the political and economic upheavals of this century alone, we
cannot say how representative they are of the foundations established during
the Reformation period or in the pre-March Era between 1830 and 1848. What
we can say, however, is that the present German foundations sector, despite the
fact that it can look back on 1,000 years of institutional history, is very much a
product of the twentieth century: Four out of five foundations were established after World War I. As Table 4.10a shows, it would be perhaps only a
slight overstatement to say that the German foundation sector is of a fairly
recent vintage in which two out of every three foundations were created after
1945. The time periods in Table 4.10a indicate that during the twenty-six years
between the creation of the Weimar Republic in 1919 and the Allied Victory in
1945, 11.2 percent of existing German foundations were created. We can also
assume that many fell victim to the inflationary period of 1923, and the
repressive Nazi policies and activities.

Figure 4.1 demonstrates the significant increase in the frequency of German foundations as their birth dates egress from 1945 and approach 1990.

Table 4.10a. Founding Periods of German Foundations by State

State/land	1070–1918	1919–1945	1946–1968	1969–1982	1983–1991	Total %	N
Baden-Württemberg	12.90	13.60	12.90	24.60	36.10	100	487
Bayern	30.60	12.10	16.10	16.00	25.20	100	944
Berlin	16.50	13.90	15.20	21.50	32.90	100	79
Bremen	19.00	19.00	9.50	28.60	23.80	100	21
Hamburg	22.70	15.60	25.20	18.10	18.40	100	326
Hessen	12.90	5.80	16.90	23.60	40.90	100	225
Niedersachsen	36.30	8.40	11.10	24.70	19.50	100	190
Nordrhein–Westfalen	16.00	5.40	17.70	26.90	34.00	100	350
Rheinland-Pfalz	17.80	8.20	15.10	19.20	39.70	100	73
Saarland	3.30	6.70	20.00	26.70	43.30	100	30
Schleswig–Holstein	17.60	18.60	12.20	21.60	29.70	100	74
TOTAL	22.10	11.20	16.30	20.70	29.70	100	2,799

Table 4.10b. Founding Periods of U.S. Foundations by State

State	−1918	1919–1945	1946–1968	1969–1982	1983–1992
New England					
Maine	0	1.7	23.3	6.6	68.3
New Hampshire	0	4.6	27.7	10.8	56.9
Vermont	10.7	3.6	3.6	7.1	75
Massachusetts	5.4	6.8	28.9	12.3	46.6
Rhode Island	6.6	5.3	39.5	9.2	39.5
Connecticut	2.8	9.4	24.9	14.7	48.2
Middle Atlantic					
New York	1.2	6.4	32.4	13.6	46.5
New Jersey	0.4	4.3	25.5	12.8	57
Pennsylvania	1.8	5.9	32.3	11.2	48.9
East North-Central					
Ohio	1.6	5.3	37.1	12.8	43.2
Indiana	0.7	5.9	25.1	15.1	53.1
Illinois	0.5	3.72	28.1	11.8	55.9
Michigan	0.6	7.2	30.3	12.2	49.7
Wisconsin	0.5	4.2	37.3	13.3	44.7
West North-Central					
Minnesota	0.6	7.2	30.3	12.2	49.7
Iowa	0	2.4	20.7	11.5	65.4
Missouri	0.6	7.2	30.3	12.2	49.7
North Dakoka	0	5.6	22.2	11.1	61.1
South Dakota	0	6.7	6.7	20	66.7
Nebraska	0.9	1.9	24.5	21.7	50.9
Kansas	0	0.7	27.6	14.5	57.2
South Atlantic					
Delaware	0	11.6	41.9	13.9	32.6
Maryland	1.7	4	25.8	12	56.5
District of Columbia	0	6.2	35.8	12.4	45.7
Virginia	0	3.3	32.7	16.4	47.6
West Virginia	0	8.7	34.8	8.7	47.8
North Carolina	0	9.4	30.2	15.6	44.8
South Carolina	0	10	32.2	12.2	45.6
Georgia	0.7	7.2	33.4	16.4	42.3
Florida	0.1	2.1	22.7	13.1	61.9
East South-Central					
Kentucky	1.9	4.8	19.1	12.4	61.9
Tennessee	0	6	28.6	10.4	54.9
Alabama	0	4.7	13.5	21.6	60.1
Mississippi	0	2.1	23.4	14.9	59.6
West South-Central					
Arkansas	0	1.7	34.5	18.9	44.8

(continued)

Table 4.10b. *Continued*

State	−1918	1919–1945	1946–1968	1969–1982	1983–1992
Louisiana	0	4.9	43.1	14.7	37.3
Oklahoma	0	8.7	34.1	17.4	39.9
Texas	0	4.5	37.8	17.2	40.7
Mountain					
Montana	0	3	15.2	6.1	75.8
Idaho	0	0	19.4	11.1	69.4
Wyoming	0	10.3	20.7	6.9	62.1
Colorado	0	8.1	18.1	16.7	57.1
New Mexico	0	2.6	7.7	17.9	71.8
Arizona	0	1	29.9	13.4	55.7
Utah	0	1.4	18.9	24.3	55.4
Nevada	0	5.7	11.3	15.1	67.9
Pacific					
Washington	0.8	3.3	24.3	14.4	57.2
Oregon	0	5.4	26.1	13.5	54.9
California	0.9	3.4	24.5	16.9	54.2
Alaska	0	0	17.7	23.5	58.8
Hawaii	6.9	9.3	19.8	10.5	53.5
TOTAL (N = 16,221)	1.1	5.2	29.5	13.9	50.3

There are only two foundations with birth dates of 1945; by 1950, this figure increases to thirteen, and then to twenty-four in 1954. Here, the frequency levels off to between twenty-five and thirty-five foundations established in each year for the next fourteen years, until 1968. This year signaled the end of what could be called the reconstruction era, and the beginning of the social democratic welfare state. The number of surviving foundations with birth dates between 1968 and 1982 continues to increase, averaging about forty-two each year. In our data, the mid-1970s show a decline in surviving foundations (averaging about twenty-six per year), but soon rebounds and reaches seventy-nine survivors per year at the end of the social democratic era.

The 1980s brings nothing less than a foundation boom as the upward trend that began in the mid-1970s increases in momentum. Nineteen eighty-five is the birth year of ninety-nine foundations in our data, 124 of the survivors were created 1986, 142 started in 1988, and 118 were born in 1990 (Figure 4.1a). In less than a decade, between 1983 and 1991, close to 30 percent of all existing foundations were established. Their number is close to that of the foundations established before 1945. In other words, the foundation sector appears to be experiencing not only a boom, but also perhaps, for the first time, a broad-based development independent of church, state, and

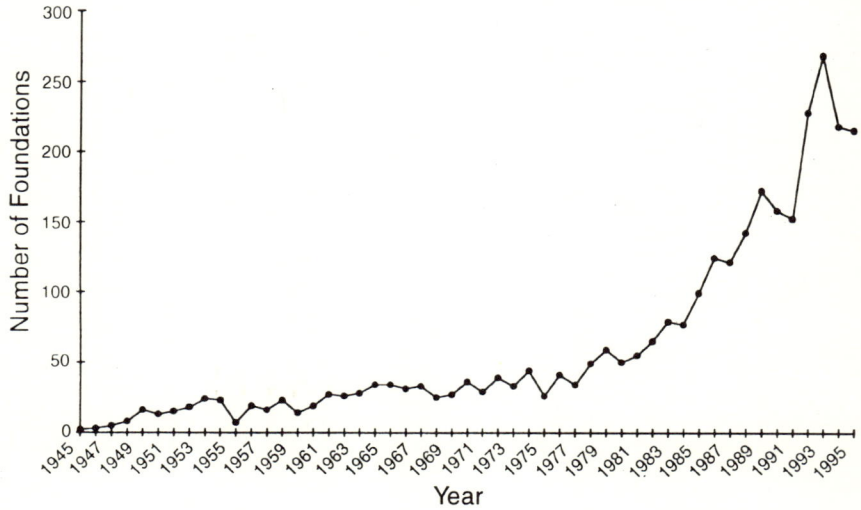

Figure 4.1. Number of German foundations established annually, 1945–1995.

economic elites. In other words, we believe the large number of foundations in our cross-sectional data that were established in the 1980s is *not* simply a product of temporal attenuation; it actually reflects changes in the political and legal environments of the country, which were favorable to the expansion of the foundation sector. What is more, the growth pattern for Germany is also present in the United States: Most foundations are of recent vintage (Figure 4.2).

How do the "new" foundations differ from "older" ones in terms of size, scope, and regional variations? Table 4.11a indicates that the German foundations established between 1983 and 1991 have, on average, fewer assets than those created between 1969 and 1982. At the same time, measures of dispersion (standard deviation, coefficient of variation) for the younger foundations are substantially lower as well. The quartile distributions for both cohorts, however, are similar, which implies that the difference between the 1969–1982 and the 1983–1991 cohort is primarily found in the relative absence of very large foundations among the latter. The same observation holds when we include the first post–World War II cohort. Together, these results point to a general trend whereby relatively fewer very large foundations are being established. In other words, it seems that the establishment of newer foundations is often predicated on smaller endowments.

Looking at differences in the scope of German foundation activities across cohorts, we see in Table 4.12 that the prominence of social services as a grantmaking area significantly declines from a high of 73.7 percent for the

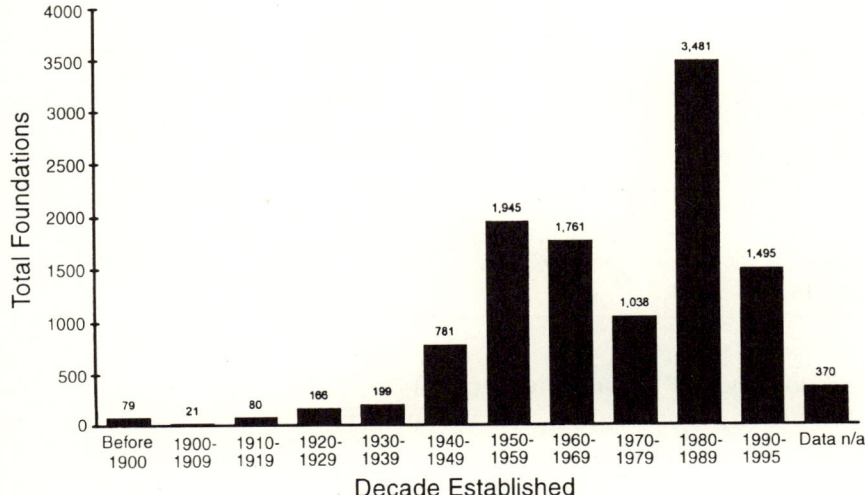

Figure 4.2. Period of establishment for larger foundations in the United States.

pre-1918 cohort and 76.3 percent for the interwar cohort to under 40 percent for the foundations established after 1983. At the same time, research as a grantmaking areas increases from 6.2 percent for the pre-1918 cohort to 32.7 percent for the 1983–1991 cohort. Similarly, art and culture activities increased their share from 6.5 percent to 29.2 percent. Other grantmaking areas that are more prominent in newly established foundations than in older ones are international activities, and environmental issues and health, whereas interest in family support appears on the decline, along with social services. The fields of education and religion, however, while fluctuating somewhat, have more or less maintained their share of grantmaking activities. Together, these results provide an image of stability and change; stability because the field of social services remains the most frequent area, together with the continued prominence of educational funding; change because newer foundations have become more diverse in their grantmaking activities and have oriented their support to fields such as research, art and culture, and the environment.

The recent expansion of the foundation sector did not heighten regional differences in the number of foundations. To the contrary (see Table 4.10a), the greatest birthrates were between 1983 and 1991, outside the traditional foundation centers of Hamburg and Bavaria, which have among the slowest growth rates. As a result, foundations are now more evenly distributed across the country than before, and they serve a broader range of activities and purposes.

Table 4.11a. Founding Period and Endowment of German Foundations ($1000)

Founding period	Mean	SD	CV	Kurtosis	Maximum	Percentiles		
						25th	50th	75th
1070–1918	2,474	11,327	458	55.6	109,698	37	118	683
1919–1945	1,689	6,394	379	62.7	60,000	42	144	608
1946–1968	13,099	180,356	1,377	229.8	2,735,734	66	250	981
1969–1982	7,208	47,289	656	176.9	720,000	118	478	2,000
1983–1991	3,200	12,092	378	54	113,039	150	500	1,743

How does the German situation compare to that in the United States? For comparative purposes, we use the same periodization, which may fit the U.S. circumstances less well than Germany, but it does point to historical intervals of similar significance. Moreover, information on the year of establishment is limited to a subset of foundations: those with assets over $1 million or $100,000 in grants made, and those established after 1987. Thus, we underreport on smaller foundations created prior to 1987, which implies that the results presented in Table 4.10b, 4.11b, and 4.12 are biased in favor of larger and "younger" foundations.

Foundations in the United States are, on average, younger than in Germany. While this may not seem surprising, it is the extent to which the U.S. foundation sector is a product of the post–WW II period that seems remarkable. Nine out of ten foundations were established after 1945, and only about one in one hundred predate the end of World War I. In Germany, one in five was established prior to 1918. The first U.S. foundations date back to the late eighteenth century, and their creation remained sporadic until about the 1880s. Only eleven foundations in our data have birth dates before 1914. It was only after World War I that the U.S. foundation sector gathered critical mass. Yet irrespective of historical roots and duration, as Tables 4.9a and 4.9b

Table 4.11b. Founding Period and Endowment of U.S. Foundations ($1000)

Founding period	Mean	SD	CV	Kurtosis	Maximum	Percentiles		
						25th	50th	75th
1070–1918	41,202	193,602	168	89.9	2,171,548	1,247	2,916	9,765
1919–1945	61,953	364,278	588	181.1	6,253,007	1,645	4,425	18,520
1946–1968	11,414	51,943	455	185.6	1,088,045	816	2,013	6,342
1969–1982	8,076	74,652	924	1,894.1	3,393,493	457	1,435	4,228
1983–1991	1,782	19,052	1,069	4,538.7	1,477,011	46	199	845

Table 4.12. Grant Making Domains for German and U.S. Foundations, by Founding Period in Percentages

Domain	Germany					United States				
	–1918	1919–1945	1946–1968	1969–1982	1983–1992	–1918	1919–1945	1946–1968	1969–1982	1983–1992
Social	73.7	76.3	51.7	50.1	39.6	24.3	17.8	17.1	19.0	19.2
Politics	0	0.3	0.6	1.4	1.3	4.9	4.7	3.8	4.1	3.4
Economy	0.5	1.3	0.6	1.4	1.4	1.4	1.3	0.7	0.7	0.5
Education	40.0	30.0	49.8	40.5	38.1	14.2	16.8	18.6	17.5	18.0
Religion	7.3	2.5	4.3	4.8	6.0	3.6	7.8	9.6	9.9	11.3
Family	19.5	8.2	3.2	3.1	2.9	4.9	2.5	1.7	1.9	1.9
Research	6.2	10.4	24.7	30.0	32.7	15.4	11.0	9.5	9.1	8.4
Health	4.8	3.8	8.2	12.3	12.7	14.7	16.5	17.3	16.8	16.2
Environment	1.1	0.9	2.6	8.1	9.9	3.4	3.7	3.2	2.9	2.8
International	0.3	2.5	3.5	4.6	6.7	1.7	1.9	1.3	1.4	1.5
Arts and culture	6.5	7.9	11.7	23.5	29.2	8.1	13.7	15.1	14.5	13.9
Other	6.1	3.8	9.5	12.9	15.3	2.9	1.7	1.7	1.7	2.3

show, the foundation sectors in both countries are by and large the products of the last decade. They differ in the sense that the U.S. foundation sector is even more a product of the last ten years than the German sector. One out of every two foundations (50 percent) in our data was established between 1983 and 1992, although we have to take into account that the bias in the data available to us favors post-1987 foundations. If we look at the subset of foundations with assets greater than $1 million and grants made in excess of $100,000 for 1990–1991, we find that 2,693, or 30 percent, of the nearly 9,000 foundations were established between 1980 and 1989 (Renz & Lawrence, 1993, p. 21).

Figures 4.1a and 4.1b display the number of foundations created per year since 1945 in Germany and the United States. In both countries, the late 1940s and 1950s were periods of steady growth in surviving foundations, with a slight slump between 1954 and 1955. Similarly, the 1960s saw a relative decline at first, and an absolute decline later in the rate of survivors. In both countries, we can assume that this decline is largely the result of two recessions (1965–1966 and 1973–1974), combined with changes in tax laws that seem to have discouraged the establishment and preservation of foundations. As Figures 4.1a and 4.1b show, the mid-1980s were a boon for the foundation sectors in both countries, with survival rates that dwarf previous epochs. This finding, while based on data possibly biased in favor of more recently established foundations, holds when we consider the larger U.S. foundations only, as displayed in Figure 4.3.

While we expect that temporal attenuation will produce a comparatively large number of recently born foundations in our cross-sectional data, the sheer magnitude of foundation startups in both countries in the mid-1980s suggests that other social forces were at work. In particular, the policies of the Reagan Administration in the United States and, to a lesser extent, the Christian–Liberal coalition government in Germany attempted to shift the responsibility of social welfare from the public to the private sector. In doing so, both governments created somewhat more favorable tax and legal environments for the establishment of grantmaking foundations than had been the case in the 1970s. Such policies are clearly reflected in the magnitude of surviving foundations born in the mid-1980s.

As Table 4.10b shows, the Pacific and Mountain regions of the United States have, on average, more surviving foundations established in the 1980s than other parts of the country. Here, all thirteen states have higher survival rates than the U.S. average, reflecting a shift in the foundation world away from the preeminence of the Midatlantic region. Renz and Lawrence (1993, p. 16) demonstrate that the share of the three Middle Atlantic states (New York, New Jersey, Pennsylvania) in total foundations assets held, declined from 43 percent in 1975 to 34 percent in 1991, whereas the Pacific region doubled its share from 7 percent to 14 percent. As Table 4.11b reveals, however, the

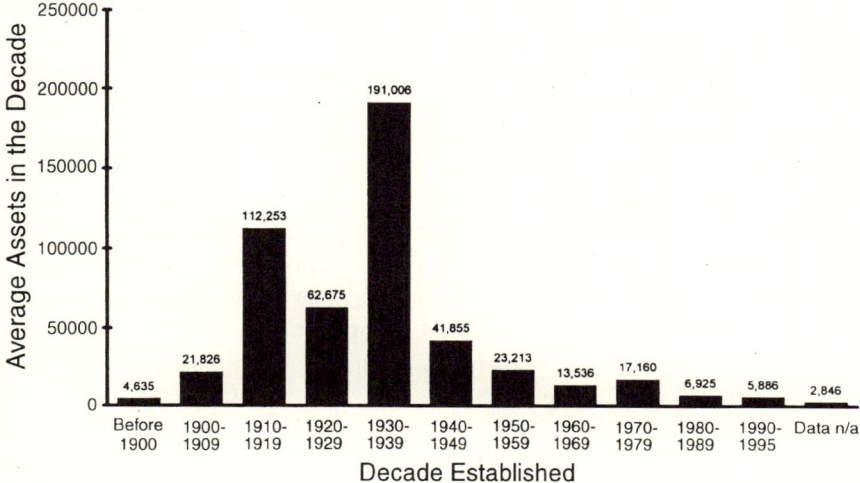

Figure 4.3. Average size of assets ($ million) of larger U.S. foundations, by founding period.

growth in the foundation sector, particularly in the 1980s, is more complex than suggested by a general shift westward. Substantial growth occurred in the northern New England states, Florida, as well as the east South-Central and United States and the Northwest. What differentiates these states and regions is their more pronounced growth in the 1980s, and not the absence of growth in other regions.

In terms of the relationship between assets birth date, the U.S. data show tendencies similar to those observed for German foundations. Tables 4.11a and 4.11b reveal that the most recent cohort of foundations (i.e., those established between 1983 and 1991), have, on average, smaller endowments than any preceding cohort. This tendency, whereby foundations become more numerous and smaller over time, is more pronounced in the United States than in Germany, perhaps a result of better data coverage of smaller foundations for post-1987 establishments. At the same time, and in contrast to German foundations, the coefficient of variability has substantially increased with time, as has the kurtosis, indicating that post-1968 cohorts are foundations characterized by very few very big foundations and many small foundations, with a relative decrease in the number and weight of medium-sized to large foundations. Thus, the U.S. situation, in terms of foundation assets for recent cohorts, is a more extreme version of what we concluded about the German case: New foundations, while more numerous, have much smaller endowments than older ones (Figure 4.1c). Given possible biases in the U.S. data, however, we should treat these tentative conclusions with caution.

How has the scope of U.S. foundations changed over time? As in the German case, we use the founding epoch as a way to analyze shifts in funding domains. A comparison with the German data in Table 4.12 shows three major results. First, in contrast to Germany, the United States reveals a higher degree of stability in funding domains over time, meaning that the grantmaking interests of U.S. foundations established in the early part of this century are closer to those of U.S. foundations created in the last two or three decades. For example, social services experienced only a slight decline, from 24.3 percent of the grantmaking activities among the oldest foundations (i.e., the pre-1918 cohort) to 19.2 percent of grantmaking activities in the youngest foundations (i.e., the 1983–1992 cohort). In Germany, however, the relative proportion of social services is reduced by almost half, from 73.7 percent to 39.6 percent for the same two age groups. For other funding domains in the United States, we also find relative stability over age cohorts: This includes such domains as politics, education, health, environment, and international interests. The stability of the health domain seems to indicate the persistent centrality of this type of grantmaking focus for U.S. foundations. The U.S. foundation sector does not show any of the major shifts found in the German foundation sector, where research, health, art and culture, and more recently, international and environmental domains, emerged as funding foci for the younger cohorts.

Second, and in marked contrast to Germany, we find that, in the United States, younger foundations are three times as likely to pursue the religious domain than older foundations. About 3.7 percent of the grantmaking activity among older foundations (pre-1918 cohort) is devoted to religious interest. Among the young foundations (1983–1992 cohort), religious activities capture as much as 11.3 percent of this group's grants. In Germany, religious grantmaking declines with the age of the foundation from a share of 7.3 percent for the oldest cohort to a share of 2.5 percent for the interwar cohort, and between 4 percent and 6 percent for the three youngest cohorts. These findings support the earlier conclusion about the structure of funding domains: The U.S. foundation sector appears to be more religious the less secular than the German sector, and it has become less secular over time.

CONCLUDING REMARKS

In *The Big Foundations*, Waldemar Nielsen writes that "foundations, like giraffes, could not possibly exist, but they do" (1972, p. 3). As quasiaristocratic institutions, they flourish on the privileges of a formally egalitarian society, they represent the fruits of capitalistic economic activity, and they organized for the pursuit of public objectives, which is seemingly contrary to the notion of selfish economic interest. Seen from this point, foundations are not only rare, they are also unlikely institutions: "strange creatures in the great jungle of American democracy," to paraphrase Nielsen. In this chapter, however, we have presented evidence, as have other before us (Renz & Lawrence, 1993; Neuhoff, 1992), that foundations are becoming increasingly frequent and more common. It seems as if the "golden age" of foundations neither began nor ended when the "big foundations" were established by Rockefeller and Ford, or Fugger and Bosch. More accurate would be a description that links the "golden age," if indeed one must use such expressions, to the present. Within little more than two decades, foundations in both the United States and Germany have passed from a period of relative decline through a phase of unprecedented growth.

In this chapter, we presented an initial comparison of foundations in Germany and the United States. While we were confronted with many limitations in the data available to us, it was nonetheless possible to analyze key aspects of the phenomenon by comparing the size, scope, and regional as well as age-cohort differences of foundations in the two countries. In summary, we found the following patterns:

- In terms of *legal forms,* we observe slight increases in commercial forms (corporate foundations and limited liability companies) and relative declines of public legal forms in Germany. Nonetheless, in both countries, we find relative stability in basic types.
- In terms of *size,* we found that the United States has a higher propensity to create foundations. Foundations in Germany are less frequent and smaller compared to foundations in the United States. Moreover, while both foundation sectors are highly concentrated and dominated in size by a relatively small number of large organizations, the German foundation sector, while smaller in size, appears as even more concentrated.
- In terms of *grants* paid, we find that differences reflect legally defined "default settings" in the tax regime under which German and U.S. foundations operate—one demanding minimum performance, the other a general disbursement of revenues combined with asset preservation. German foundations appear to have developed, on average, somewhat higher payout rates.
- In terms of *employment,* we find that the great majority of foundations in both countries employ neither full-time nor part-time staff. The U.S. foundation sector, however, appears more professional or formal, at least in terms of staffing, while German foundations rely more on voluntary inputs.
- In terms of *scope,* we find that both German and U.S. foundations show pronounced social service, educational, and arts and culture orientations. In the United States, health represents a major domain of interest for foundations, and religion emerges as one of the most significant differences between both countries. In the United States, religious philanthropy is linked to specific

funding domains in a much more pronounced way than in Germany. The U.S. foundation sector appears as the less secular one, not only in terms of the frequency of the religious motive, but also in the terms of domain structures. Moreover, and in marked contrast to Germany, cohort comparisons suggest that it has become less secular in recent decades.

• In terms of *regional variations,* we find that foundations in Germany, while less concentrated in one or two locations, are at the same time more unevenly distributed across states and regions than are U.S. foundations. The United States shows a consistently higher average propensity, with relatively lower degrees of regional variations, while Germany has a lower average propensity and greater regional differences. Regional variations have become less pronounced as a result of the foundation boom of the 1980s.

• In terms of *age,* we find convincing evidence, despite restrictions in the available data, that foundations in each country are relatively young, whereby a disproportionate number of surviving foundations were established in the last decade.

Thus, the German and the U.S. foundation sectors are similar in the sense that they both represent essentially a late twentieth-century phenomenon, and that they have expanded significantly in the recent decade. In both countries, foundations have become more numerous and, on average, smaller in terms of assets. To some extent, the reduced average endowment size of more recent foundation cohorts relative to that of older cohorts could be a function of the greater longevity of larger foundations. In this sense, the average asset size of older foundations increases over time as smaller foundations dissipate their resources and dissolve.

There is, however, a much more compelling explanation of the positive relationship between size of assets (or endowments) and age, which points to what may be one of the most essential feature of foundations in the capitalistic economies of the modern industrialized world: dead hand control. Like the Pharaohs of ancient Egypt, who tried to maintain control of their vast wealth after death by entombing it with themselves in the mighty stone pyramids, the modern industrial and financial Pharaohs of contemporary capitalistic economies may also attempt to control their grand fortunes by entombing them in the legal pyramid of the foundation. In this way, they can effect the disbursement of their wealth from the grave. But it is often the case that the foundation as a legal entity is first constituted prior to the death of the founding agent with a minimal endowment, only to be more fully invested after the founder dies. It is quite possible that many of the foundations established during the last two decades have live founding agents and therefore are not yet fully endowed. This would explain the observation that younger foundations have smaller endowments than older foundations. But all this must remain speculative, for our data do not contain the kind of observations necessary to adequately test hypotheses about the factors producing the observed relationship between assets and age in both countries.

Returning to our summary of findings, we have shown that the United States and Germany differ in a number of ways, including the legal forms available to foundations, the propensity to establish foundations, in terms of regional variations, and in the scope of grantmaking activities. Moreover, whereas the German foundation sector appears largely secular—despite the presence of church foundations—the religious motive plays a significant role in the U.S. foundation sector. For German foundations, we found a significant shift in funding domains, which seems to indicate more fundamental changes in that society toward an increased role of the state in social affairs since the 1950s. With the state taking on a comprehensive role in the financing of social services, this would suggest that foundations would shift to other areas such as arts and culture or research, which seem relatively underfinanced when compared to the social service field. Just as the funding shift in Germany's foundation sector seems indicative of some underlying political and social change, the remarkable stability of the funding domains of U.S. foundations seems to point to the equally fundamental continuity in the way social responsibilities are assigned to public and private sectors in the United States. The domain stability in the United States is suggested by the country's continuity in its basic social and economic setup.

In a recent paper on U.S. foundations, Margo (1992, p. 232) writes that "the size of the foundation sector appears to have been fueled by long-run economic growth and tempered by short-run business cycle fluctuations and variations in federal tax policy." While there is certainly much truth in Margo's conclusion, we suggest that a fuller comparative analysis would lead us to modify this statement: The long-term development of the foundation sector seems to be largely based on political stability combined with economic prosperity, as exemplified by the stability and prosperity of the post–World War II period in both countries. Within this general trajectory, growth rates are influenced by business cycles and tax policies, suggested by the relative decline in the overall importance of foundations in the 1970s in the two countries.

In summary, this is the conclusion we can draw from the German and U.S. foundation sectors. Our findings, then, invite us to address what emerges as a central question of comparative research in this area: Does the foundation boom of the last decade signal a fundamental shift in the general developmental trajectory of the foundation sectors, or was it largely a function of a relatively long upward trend in business cycles? Perhaps we will soon have to recognize that the key to understanding the present state of the foundation world lies—not in the distant—but in the very recent past.

NOTES

1. We would like to thank Rupert Graf Strachwitz and Elizabeth Brummer for their kind cooperation and invaluable assistance in making a computer-readable version of the 1992 German Foundation Directory available to us. We also thank the Bundesverband Deutscher Stiftungen in Bonn for to use the data for research purposes. In the United States, we are indebted to Loren Renz and her staff at the Foundation Center for providing a computer tape on U.S. grantmaking foundations and their great advice on how to handle the data.

2. As we demonstrate later in the chapter, some of the foundations for which data are missing are currently small, not fully operational entities of recent vintage. Indeed, they appear as no more than legal entities that are not fully funded or staffed to operate, and will not be so until some time in the future when founders die. Thus, the foundations that are fully represented in our data make up a good sample of operational foundations in the two societies under study.

3. As we further indicate in the section on variations, we do not have actual longitudinal data on all the foundations established during a given year or period. The foundation directory includes only currently existing foundations and does not provide information on foundations that may have dissolved, merged, or terminated. Reference to the variable "Year of Establishment" is therefore used as a proxy measure.

4. For convenience, we transformed all currency information into US dollars, using and exchange rate of DM 1.6 to $1.

5. The German data on assets are based on self-reported information requested in the survey form. Given the difficulty to assess the true value of foundation assets, in particular nonliquid and nonmonetary ones, the survey asked for two estimates: asset value at the time of establishment, and fair value of assets at current market prices. Since most foundations reported on current market value, we rely on data about the value at establishment only when information for the former is missing.

6. This estimation involves several steps. For the upper-bound limit, we assume that assets in the total population of foundations are distributed as they are in the "sample" of the 1,425 foundations that provided asset information, and multiply the "sample sum" by the ratio of "sample size" to "universe." For the lower-bound limit, we assume that the next 1,425 foundations would account for only 50 percent of the asset sum of the first 1,425 foundations in the "universe," and the third only 50 percent of the second, and so on. The lower-bound estimate is based on the assumption that larger foundations supplied asset information more frequently than smaller foundations, and that we have better coverage of larger foundations than of smaller ones. The figure of $2.5 billion in total assets is the average between the upper-bound ($28.5 billion) and the lower-bound estimate ($14.5 billion). The same procedure is used to estimate total employment and grant disbursements.

7. An analysis of grant disbursements and payout rates is complicated by the limited comparability between the reporting categories used in the German Foundation Survey and those used by the Foundation Center. The German Survey, while asking about maximum and minimum awards for different types of grants, did not collect data on actual grant disbursements. As a proxy measure, we assumed that reported total expenditure minus administrative costs and set-asides (additions to asset base) would equal the sum of grants made.

8. The U.S. data are based on the 1992 Foundation Center survey of foundations with at least $1 million in assets or $100,000 in grants made (Renz & Lawrence, 1993, p. 15). This implies that actual staff figures may be somewhat higher.

9. The Foundation Center provides a detailed coding of purpose and mission of U.S. foundations, using close to 200 descriptors such as "agriculture," "animal welfare," or "recreation" to the scope of grant activities. By contrast, the German Foundation Survey used a more limited array of grant areas. For comparative purposes, we mapped the U.S. activity classification into

the German one, which yields twelve larger categories: social services, political economy, education, religion, family, research, health, environment, international, arts and culture, and a residual category "other." While far from being a perfect classification system of grant areas and activities, it is allows at least for some initial comparisons between the scope of grantmaking in Germany and the United States.

10. Within the sequence of events in U.S. history, 2 percent of German foundations still in existence predate the year 1492, 6.6 percent the year 1776, and about 12 percent the end of the Civil War.

REFERENCES

Anheier, H. K. (1998). Das Stiftungswesen in Zahlen. Eine sozial-ökonomische Struktur-beschreibung deutscher Stiftungen. In Bertelsmann Stiftung (Ed.), *Handbuch Stiftungswesen.* Wiesbaden, Germany: Gabler.

Arias Foundation for Peace and Human Progress. (1992). *The State of Philanthropy in Central America.* San Jose, Costa Rica: Fundacion Arias. (mimeo)

Australian Association of Philanthropy. (1993). *The Australian Directory of Philanthropy,* 7th ed. Port Melbourne, Australia: Thorpe.

Berkel, U., & Neuhoff K., et al. 1989. *Stiftungshandbuch,* 3rd ed. Baden-Baden Germany: Nomos.

Biermann, B., Cannon, L., & Klainberg, D. (1992). *A Survey of Endowed Grantmaking Development Foundations in Africa, Asia, Eastern Europe, Latin America, and the Caribbean.* New York: The Synergos Institute. (mimeo)

Boris, E. (1987). Creation and Growth: A Survey of Private Foundations. In T. Odendahl (Ed.), *America's Wealthy and the Future of Foundations* (pp. 65–126). New York: Foundation Center.

Brummer, E. (Ed.). (1996). *Statistiken zum Deutschen Stiftungswesen 1996.* Munich, Germany: Maecenata.

Bundesverband Deutscher Siftungen. (1991). *Verzeichnis der Deutschen Stiftungen.* Darmstadt, Germany: Hoppenstedt.

Bundesverband Deutscher Siftungen. (1992). *Nachtrag zum Verzeichnis der Deutschen Stiftungen.* Ausgabe 1991. Darmstadt, Germany: Hoppenstedt.

Canadian Center for Philanthropy. (1991). *Canadian Directory to Foundations,* 9th ed. Toronto: Canadian Centre for Philanthropy.

Foundation Center. (1993). *The Foundation Directory,* 15th ed. New York: Foundation Center.

Fundacao Oriente. (1992). *Guia das Fundacoes Portuguesas.* Lisbon, Portugal: Romos Afonso & Moita.

Karl, B. D., & Katz, S. N. (1987). Foundations and Ruling Class Elites. *Daedalus, 116*(1), 1–40.

Leat, D. (1992). *Trusts in Transition: The Policy and Practice of Grant-making Trusts.* York, UK: Joseph Rowntree Foundation.

Margo, R. (1992). Foundations. In C. T. Clotfelter (Ed.), *Who Benefits from the Nonprofit Sector?* (pp. 207–234). Chicago: University of Chicago Press.

Neuhoff, K. (1978). Sonderdruck aus SOERGEL—*Kommentar zum Bürgerlichen Gesetzbuch* (11. Auflage), Band 1: Allgemeiner Teil. Stuttgart: Kohlhammer (also as: Materialien aus dem Stiftungszentrum, Heft 10).

Neuhoff, K. (1992). "Stiftung" and "Stiftungsrecht" in R. Bauer (Ed.), *Lexikon des Sozial- und Gesundheitswesens* (pp. 1967–1974). Munich and Vienna: Oldenbourg.

Nielsen, W. A. (1972). *The Big Foundations.* New York: Columbia University Press.

Odendahl, T. (1987). Independent Foundations and the Wealthy Donors: An Overview. In

T. Odendahl (Ed.), *America's Wealthy and the Future of Foundations* (pp. 1–26). New York: Foundation Center.

Renz, L., & Lawrence, S. (1993). *Foundation Giving: Yearbook of Facts and Figures on Private, Corporate and Community Foundations.* New York: Foundation Center.

Rudney, G. (1987). Creation of Foundations and their Wealth. In T. Odendahl, (Ed.), *America's Wealthy and the Future of Foundations* (pp. 179–202). New York: Foundation Center.

Salamon, L. (1992). Foundations as investment managers: Part I. The process. *Nonprofit Management and Leadership,* 3(2), 117–137.

Schiller, T. (1967). *Stiftungen im gesellschaftlichen Prozeß.* Baden-Baden, Germany: Nomos.

Ylvesaker, P. N. (1987). Foundations and nonprofit organizations. In W. W. Powell (Ed.), *The Nonprofit Sector: A Research Handbook.* (pp. 360–379). New Haven, CT: Yale University Press.

Part III

Management and Organization

While we still know little about the comparative quantitative dimensions of foundations in different cultures in terms of their size and scope of activities, we know even less about their management and organizational behavior. Even in the United States, where research on these institutions is more frequent, the question of how foundations work has not yet been thoroughly investigated. Indeed, foundations represent a largely uncharted territory in organizational research.

In view of the many new responsibilities and challenges that currently confront foundations, however, this void is no longer tenable. In an age of government devolution and privatization, a realistic assessment of the actual capabilities and limitations of foundations must be informed by an understanding of how they operate and behave as organizations.

The first three chapters of this part explore central aspects of the organization, management, and behavior of organizations. Diana Leat investigates British grantmaking trusts and develops a typology of three "grantmaking cultures." Her chapter also brings to light dilemmas and constraints typical of foundation management. William Diaz discusses the programs of a number of large U.S. grantmaking foundations in the light of three distinct models of organizational behavior.

Reminiscent of Leat's contribution, Heinrich Beyer calls for a new entrepreneurial approach to foundation management in his chapter, also mapping the prerequisites of such an approach in terms of foundation goals, strategy, and program operations. While grantmaking foundations clearly dominate the foundation communities in Anglo-American countries, they by no means constitute the only form of foundation. In this respect, Stefan Toepler examines the role and behavior of operating foundations with a special emphasis on the U.S. situation.

Chapter 5

British Foundations

The Organization and Management
of Grantmaking

Diana Leat

INTRODUCTION

A recent study of British charities estimated that 75 percent of the largest charities had a grantmaking function (Osborne & Hems, 1994). This chapter focuses on the narrower group of charitable organizations (foundations) whose sole or primary purpose is to give grants to other organizations and individuals for charitable purposes. These are organizations that do not produce any direct outputs; their immediate tangible outputs are checks written and grants given. There are two very broad types of grantmaking foundations in Britain: those deriving all, or a majority, of their income from endowment, and those solely, or primarily, dependent on fund-raising. In reality, some British foundations straddle these two types. However, for all foundations, British charity law requires that governance of, and benefit from, charitable organizations are kept very separate.

It is estimated that there are at least 2,500 foundations in Britain distributing an unknown total sum in grants. Kendall and Knapp (1995) suggest that in 1990, grantmakers had an income of £1.169 billion, if public funding of

Diana Leat • Visiting Senior Fellow, VOLPROF, City University Business School, London EC2Y 8HB United Kingdom.

Private Funds, Public Purpose: Philanthropic Foundations in an International Perspective, edited by Helmut K. Anheier and Stefan Toepler. New York, Plenum Press, 1999.

quangos is included, and £862.6 million if this is excluded. In 1994, the income of the top 500 grantmakers was estimated to be £864.7 million (assets: £12.5 billion), of which £705.1 million was given in grants, £54 million spent on administration, and the remainder added to the endowment. (Leat & Charities Aid Foundation Information Unit, 1996).

In Britain, as in the United States, the assets and income of grantmaking foundations are very unevenly distributed among the total population of foundations. Even within the top 500 foundations, the vast majority of assets, income, and grantmaking is concentrated within the top fifty foundations. For example, in 1991–1992, the top fifty foundations (10 percent) owned around 60 percent of the total assets of the 500, had around 60 percent of total income, and distributed around 75 percent of the total value of grants (Saxon-Harrold & Kendall, 1995).

Until very recently, data on foundations have not included fund-raising grantmakers, and data on these may still be incomplete. Fund-raising grant-makers include broadcast appeals on radio and television, of which there is no comprehensive systematic record—not least because their number varies from year to year, often in response to local, national, and international crises (Leat, 1989, 1990). A conservative estimate of the annual amounts given in grants from broadcast appeals might be £30–40 million. The category of fund-raising grantmakers also includes the National Foundation for Sport and the Arts, funded from weekly subscriptions by football pool promoters, giving over £60 million in grants in 1993, as well as an unknown number of other such organizations. Since 1995, the total amount given in grants by nonendowed charitable organizations has been increased by the recently introduced National Lottery. In the thirteen months to the end of December 1995, £991 million had been distributed by the five National Lottery Boards, of which the National Lottery Charities Board (NLCB) is one. In 1995, NLCB gave £159 million in grants, but voluntary organizations are also eligible to receive grants from the other four Boards (arts, sports, heritage, and millennium). The projected total of grants to "good causes" (i.e., from all five Boards) over the seven-year license is £8.96 billion (Fitzherbert, Guissani, & Hunt, 1996). The effects of this level of grantmaking on grant recipients and on the level of demand for continuing funding (falling on foundations) will not become apparent for some years.

There is another group of other grantmaking organizations that do not fit neatly into either the endowed or fund-raising category. This "mixed" category includes, for example, the growing number of Community Foundations, fund-raising in order to build an endowment and giving grants along the way. It also covers the small but growing number of charitable organizations set up as a channel for the distribution of government funds (discussion to follow).

TRADITIONAL ROLES AND PRACTICES
OF GRANTMAKING FOUNDATIONS

Whatever the total income available for grantmaking in Britain, it certainly constitutes only a small proportion of total voluntary-sector income estimated by different studies to be between £8 billion and over £20 billion in 1990–1991 (Posnett, 1993; Clare & Scott, 1993; Kendall & Knapp, 1995). But there are those who would argue that such calculations miss the essential contribution of charitable foundations. Grantmaking foundations may make only a small contribution to voluntary-sector income, but that contribution is particularly significant because it is the source of innovation, especially in areas of the sector that lack popular or political support.

The funds of foundations may also be viewed as significant, irrespective of size, because they are relatively secure and their distribution is free from market and political constraints. The security of trust funds is, however, open to question. Endowed foundation funds may be rather more secure than those of fund-raising foundations but even the former may be less secure in uncertain financial markets. However, the immunity of trust fund distribution from political and market constraints may heighten their significance insofar as foundations are able "to concentrate millions of dollars on selected projects, give these an aura of importance, and do this with a minimum of political accountability" (O'Neill, 1989, p. 137).

The contribution of foundations is also of particular significance as British voluntary organizations increasingly work under contract to the state. Grants from foundations will become one of the only sources of funding unhampered by contracts, political constraints, and popular priorities and prejudices. Indeed, a recent controversial report on the future of voluntary action in Britain has suggested that charitable foundations should be the major funders of voluntary organizations not providing services on contract to the state and thus forming the "true" voluntary sector (Knight, 1994).

Arguments emphasizing the significance of foundation giving tend to revolve around foundations' freedom in grantmaking or, to put it another way, their lack of public accountability. In recent years the "public subsidy without accountability" argument has been given a new twist as government has used charitable foundations as a conduit for its own spending in certain areas (e.g., in relation to disabled people and people suffering from HIV/AIDS). As an ex-Permanent Secretary at the Department of Health recently remarked: "The advantage for government is that people can't ask questions in the House. They [the government] can simply say, if necessary, 'Well that's done by the Family Fund.'" (Lattimer, 1990, p. 10). In this respect, foundations may be seen as channels in the development of third-party government and/or as politically retrogressive in substituting charity for rights.

Whatever the merits of these arguments, the reality is that remarkably little is known about the number, resources, policies and pratices, and record of grantmaking of foundations in Britain. We have very broad estimates of total income and assets, and we are reasonably certain that, as in the United States, foundation income is unevenly distributed among foundations, among beneficiary groups, and among different geographical regions (Leat, 1990). Lack of clarity in financial data is more than matched by lack of knowledge of how foundations operate. As the secretary to the Carnegie UK Trust has said: "The strength of the trust sector is its individualism; the weakness its secrecy" (Lord, 1989). In recent years, the "individualism" of foundations has been somewhat reduced by the establishment of an Association of Charitable Foundations, which, among other functions, meets to discuss issues of common interest.

Traditionally, British grantmaking foundations have emphasized five key principles in their work (Leat, 1992):

• *Doing what the state doesn't do.* Defining their role in this way was not only legally encouraged, it also sidestepped political controversy. In addition, it served to distance trusts from the arena of public policy while buttressing their claims to independence, difference, and avoidance of public scrutiny. "Doing what the state doesn't do" also had the advantage of allowing trusts considerable choice and flexibility in expending their limited resources on the wide range of groups, organizations, and activities not wholly supported by the state.

• *Pump priming.* In some cases, pump priming means starting something new that will then, it is assumed, be funded by local government. In other cases, it is better described as leverage—giving a small sum of money that will act as a lever on others to contribute further funding. In both cases, the underlying assumption is that there is money around to feed the primed pump.

• *Innovation.* Emphasis on innovation is closely related to that on pump priming. Like the voluntary sector in general, foundations have cultivated the notion that they are pioneers in provision even though there is little systematic evidence to support or refute this claim (Kendall & Knapp, 1995).

• *Unpopular causes.* One foundation described this as a "counter Stock Exchange approach—trying to spot the losers." But the definition of unpopular causes is not clear. It may mean funding groups that have little public appeal, or types of work or items for which it is difficult to raise funds, or simply groups or projects that do not currently have adequate or secure income.

• *Emergency funding.* In addition to one or more of the aforementioned, some foundations have seen providing "emergency" funding as one of their key roles. These foundations argue that one of their distinctive strengths is that they can work quickly without bureaucracy. Emergency funding may also be related to limited resources, which, it is argued, rules out larger, longer-term funding.

These perceptions of their role have gone hand in hand with traditional practices that stress being responsive rather than proactive, making smaller short-term grants; giving grants for specific projects rather than for core funds, and often for capital rather than revenue purposes. Foundations have also emphasized the value of making quick decisions, which in turn is linked to emphasis on the practice of risk taking. Risk taking has been related to innovation and to funding unpopular causes. Finally, as in the United States, traditional foundation practice has been marked by a lack of accountability (Nielsen, 1972; Odendahl, Boris, & Daniels, 1985). Little has been expected from grant recipients and little has been given by foundations to the public, even by those foundations that depend on fund-raising from the general public. Foundations have jealously guarded their privacy, a privilege that they extend to beneficiaries. Lack of accountability may also be related to a belief in giving without glory, to a positive belief in giving without strings, and to a desire to keep administrative costs low.

In an important sense, the role and practice of British charitable grant making foundations have been created in the "space" left by the state. As the role of the welfare state expanded into new provisions, the role of grant making foundations altered accordingly. In recent years, as successive Conservative administrations attempted to rein back the expansion of the state, foundations have begun to question traditional roles and practices. As the state withdrew from areas of provision, "doing what the state doesn't do" became an increasingly "leaky" barrier to limit demands on foundations' overstretched funds. Pump priming was a nice idea if there was a nearby well with water, but in a terrain in which statutory funding had largely dried up, it was increasingly seen as an ineffective use of resources.

Against this background, the first exploratory British study of the policy and practice of grantmaking foundations was undertaken. In-depth interviews were conducted with thirty British chartiable foundations regarded by their peers as "leaders" in the field. Foundations were selected to include a range in terms of income (from £150,000 to over £10 million), age (from three years to over 100 years), area of interest, and geographical location. Both fund-raising and endowed foundations were included; foundations covered included those with living donors/family active on the board and those whose original donors were long dead. All of the foundations studied were involved primarily in giving grants in the broad field of social welfare. Foundations solely involved in giving grants for research were excluded (for further details of the study, see Leat, 1995).

THE ORGANIZATION AND MANAGEMENT
OF GRANTMAKING

Despite the growing body of research into the organizational structures and processes of British voluntary nonprofit organizations, little research attention has been devoted to grant-giving foundations. Purely grant-giving foundations are particularly interesting and challenging to the organizational theorist for a number of reasons. These are organizations that have no profit and no direct product; and their immediate consumers are not typically their intended beneficiaries. Furthermore, endowed grant-giving foundations are not resource-dependent in any conventional sense; in this respect, they are quite unlike most other types of organization.

In theory charitable grantmaking is about meeting needs as specified by the trust deed. However, as in other organizations, the grantmaking foundation must pursue its mission in the light of organizational resources and environment. In achieving the best "fit" between pursuit of the foundation's mission and its internal and external resources and constraints, foundations face a number of dilemmas. Some of these dilemmas stem from the peculiar business of grantgiving, others from the structure of British charitable foundations and their relationships with others. Thus, some constraints and associated organizational and management dilemmas are common to all purely grant-giving foundations, whereas others vary between different types of foundation.

Among British charitable foundations, the notion that grantmaking is influenced by anything other than the organization's mission and financial resources is rarely discussed. Existing typologies of foundations indirectly acknowledge constraints on operation, but in distinguishing between independent and other types of foundation, both underplay the complexity of constraints on foundation operation and imply that such constraints are unfortunate aberrations from the ideal of independence (see, e.g., Ylvisaker, 1987).

GRANTMAKING CULTURES

The immediate, day-to-day task of purely grantmaking foundations is to spend money. Clearly, the broad activity of spending money takes a wide variety of forms—purchasing, investing, paying taxes, giving pocket money, and so on. How did the foundations interviewed perceive grantmaking? On the basis of interview data, three ideal-typical cultures of grantmaking were constructed. These three cultures represent the norms, values, beliefs, and assumptions that inform the ways foundations approach the task of making grants. As will become apparent later, these three ideal-typical cultures of grantmaking have very different implications for the resources required by foundations and for organizational processes and procedures. Depending on the structure of the foundation, its freedom of choice over human resources, and the nature and source of its financial resources, the foundation will be more or less constrained in changing its culture of grantmaking.

Gift-Givers

Foundations that adopt the gift-giving culture do not usually have any very clear priorities; they wait and see what people ask for. Gift-givers generally prefer not to give all their money to a few; they like to give as many presents as possible. The presents may be big or small—usually fairly small—and they may or may not be exactly what the recipient ideally wanted or asked for. Often the gift is 'a little something towards...' but within the gift-giving culture that does not matter. A gift is a gift and whatever its size it is better than nothing and is bound to be of some help and have some beneficial effect. Anyway, the gift-giver argues, you should not necessarily give applicants everything they ask for because it is good for them to have to make some effort. Grants given by gift-givers are usually one-off and the recipient should not rely on another next year.

Because the gift-giver is giving gifts and not expecting any specific return there is little need to do extensive investigation before choosing recipients. But, of course, gift-giver foundations want to know that the recipient is reliable and will spend their gift on some worthy cause. Some gifts are given without any strings but many are given to buy something specific rather than as a contribution to running expenses. Many gift-giving foundations want to see what their gift bought but, having given the gift, there is little follow-up or evaluation. Evaluation is not a major issue for gift-givers because success and failure are not dominant words in their vocabulary—gifts are gifts and success and failure do not really come into it. Some gift-givers may go and see what their gift bought and most would like a thank-you letter and report on how useful the gift was; if they do not get one the recipient is likely to be crossed off next year's present list.

Investors

Unlike gift-givers, foundations subscribing to the investor culture usually spend considerable time deciding into which specific areas they want to put their money. Like more conventional investors they may choose safe, solid options likely to produce steady, if unexciting, results or they may go in for riskier venture because this is where the future lies, or because if the investment pays off, the beneficial effect will be great.

Investor grant-makers do considerable research before investing money. Foundations look very carefully at the areas of activity, at the abilities and structures of the organizations, at the plans and projected costs. Investor grantmakers want to be reasonably sure that there is going to be a return and relate the size of the grant to what is needed to achieve the maximum effect. Within this culture, grantmakers may choose to have a portfolio of investments (grants)—not least as a way of spreading risk—or they may choose to invest more heavily in just one or two ventures. Investors may make one-time investments or may continue to invest over a period of years: it all depends on what is needed. If investments seem to be going less well than anticipated, investors may give another grant or they may cut their losses and run. Unlike the gift-giver, the investor talks in terms of success and failure. Investors always prefer success but are not afraid of failure; they know that investments are, by their very nature, risky and that there is something to be learned from failure.

It follows, then, that investors monitor their investments (grants) and are prepared to put time and money into this. They do not, however, typically become very involved in the management of the organizations to which they make grants. Like shareholders, they may have some token involvement and may require reports but, in general, they adopt a hands-off approach, letting grant recipients get on with their job in the way they see fit. Investors invest in ventures created and run by others and do not typically seek to be an initiators or partners.

Collaborative Entrepreneurs

This culture of grantmaking has much in common with the investment culture but differs in some important respects. Whereas gift-givers and investors are limited in how they spend their money by what the market—the voluntary sector—presents, collaborative entrepreneurs do not accept such limitations. This type of foundation knows what it wants and if what it wants does not exist, it goes out and finds a voluntary organization to work with to create what it wants. The foundation specifies the broad outlines of what is to be done and in negotiation with a supplier agrees on a price and a plan of action. The plan of action may be quite detailed, specifying clear objectives, performance targets, quality controls, and so on.

The foundation's financial commitment will almost certainly be over a period of years, and its size will be related to what is needed to make the project work. The relationship between foundation and grant recipient is one of partnership rather than straight investment. They work together to achieve mutually agreed objectives, and the foundation may be fairly heavily involved in the management of the project. Monitoring and evaluation are key elements in this approach and are likely to be built into the very design of the work rather than being an "end-of-term" activity.

It is important to stress that these are ideal-types. It is also important to note that any one foundation may adopt all three cultures of grantmaking in different parts of its work, although, in fact, this was rare. As one director remarked after the study had been published: "I see now that we have been gift-giving in some parts of our program and trying to be investors in other parts—this has created all sorts of problems because the standards for selection and follow-up are quite different."

By far the most common culture of grantmaking among the foundations studied was that of the gift-giver. Less systematic data on a wider range of foundations in Britain suggest that gift-giving is the generally dominant style of grantmaking. In many respects, the dominance of this culture is not surprising. Gifts and giving are central to the British charitable vocabulary. Some foundations, influenced by the changing political and economic environment, and disenchanted with the results of gift giving, were moving toward the investor and collaborative entrepreneur approaches. But there were often difficulties in achieving this cultural change. In order to understand approaches to grantmaking and, in particular, the dominance of gift giving, it is necessary to look more closely at the peculiar business of grantmaking and the organizational pressures and constraints on British foundations.

THE BUSINESS OF GRANTMAKING

Some of the organizational and management problems of British grantmaking foundations are inherent to the business of grantmaking. In part, these problems stem from the fact that the vast majority of British foundation deeds today express the purpose of the trust in broad, not to say, vague terms. "For the benefit of", "and other charitable purposes such as the trustees may think fit" are typical phrases. Thus, most grant-giving foundations have a broad purpose but not an entirely free choice. They must work within the trust deed that expresses the donor's intentions and that can only be changed in exceptional circumstances by application of a cy près scheme (Chesterman 1979).

Broadness of Purposes

The effect of broad purposes is to leave trustees with a blank sheet—they know where the edges are but there is nothing on the paper. The broad purposes with which trustees are expected to work may provide an exhilarating freedom or be like asking a business to operate successfully with no objective other than pleasing, say, middle-aged customers. At best, the trust deed is akin to a mission statement that needs considerable further work before specific policies and practices may be formulated.

Among the foundations interviewed, some tried to work with little more than the trust deed; for these foundations, legitimate demand for grants must always exceed supply of money. Without clear foundation priorities, applicants cannot deselect themselves, nor can administrative staff easily reduce the volume of applications to be considered by trustees. Without clear priorities and criteria, the range of applications is wide and every one requires individual consideration. Other foundations believed that it was impossible to work without some boundaries and began to fill in the blank sheet with more specific policies and priorities. But because of the peculiar business of grant giving, outlined here, management had few of the conventional means of formulating priorities and subsequently assessing the relevance of those priorities.

In British law, charitable foundations hold money on trust for the benefit of their ultimate beneficiaries as specified by the deed incorporating the donor's intentions. But this exacerbates rather than solves foundations' management problems. Beneficiaries recognized within charitable purposes in British law are usually (although not always) large in number, not easily or immediately identifiable, dispersed, and have neither the skill nor the means to articulate their claims.

Because of the characteristics of most beneficiaries many, but not all, grant-giving foundations work through suppliers. They attempt to benefit their designated beneficiaries not by giving money directly to them but by giving it to charitable organizations, and others, who will supply the appropriate benefits.

As the study revealed, a number of profound management difficulties arise from the practice of working through suppliers. One important consequence is that because they have not direct communication with their beneficiaries, foundations may come to identify the needs and priorities of suppliers with the needs and preferences of beneficiaries. They may come to see what the voluntary sector requests as a perfect reflection of need. Gift-giver foundations, in particular, argued that their job is to respond to what suppliers tell them they need. Collaborative entrepreneurs were less happy with this approach and identified their own priorities, which might be based, in part, on perception of unmet or future needs of beneficiaries not adequately reflected by suppliers' demands/applications.

But whichever approach is adopted, in an important sense, grantmaking foundations can only be as good as their suppliers. Thus, foundations have to ask themselves not only whether what they are spending money on is relevant to the needs of their beneficiaries but also whether their suppliers are capable of carrying out the work. But, as I shall suggest, the capacity of foundations to assess suppliers may be hampered by a range of other characteristics of foundation structure and management.

The fact that many grantmaking foundations do not produce anything except via suppliers has other consequences. Perhaps the most fundamental of these consequences is that purely grant-giving foundations have no immediate way of assessing success and failure in achieving their missions. The immediate product of grant giving is an empty checkbook and a list of grants, so it is not surprising that some British foundations publicly measure their success in terms of their expenditure in grants.

Because they have no substantive product, foundations may only judge their success and failure in meeting beneficiaries' needs or fulfilling their missions by assessing the success and failure of their suppliers. But this in turn presents problems. First, as several foundations emphasized, there is the problem of what counts as success and failure in a project and how to measure it. Concentrating on the problems of evaluation misses the second, more fundamental, difficulty, arising from the fact that foundations work through suppliers. A project may be successful in achieving its objectives but this does not necessarily mean that it was successful in terms of the foundation's goal of providing maximum benefit to beneficiaries. As some foundations noted, the success or failure of a particular project does not tell the foundation whether its priorities were "right" or not. The third problem in judging success and failure via the success and failure of suppliers is that, as one foundation director has pointed out, "Trusts can take only indirect responsibility for the success of their protégés and, worse still, can disclaim all responsibility for their failures" (Burkeman, 1991, p. 3).

As one respondent noted, foundations face a very peculiar difficulty in judging their success and failure and the "rightness" of their policies and priorities. They have no product but lots of customers. But these customers come to beg, not to buy, and whatever the foundation decided to "sell," whatever its priorities were, its customers would tailor their "needs" to what the foundation offered. So, unlike the business, a foundation cannot say: "We can measure our success, the relevance of our priorities, by customer demand." And it cannot do so because customers would keep on coming whatever its priorities and because its customers do not necessarily perfectly reflect the needs of its ultimate beneficiaries.

Trustee Constraints

The second source of organizational and management dilemmas in purely grant-giving foundations is their formal and informal structures. These structures create operational constraints and management dilemmas that are all the more important in the light of the peculiar business of grant-giving outlined earlier.

In British law, charitable foundations are governed by trustees and all decisions made by the foundation are the legal responsibility of those trustees. Under British charity law, trustees may receive no remuneration. Thus, the choice of trustees is limited to those who can afford to give time to the task of being a trustee. This in turn imposes constraints on the types of people, their knowledge, experience, and skills, who may be recruited as trustees.

Some grantmaking foundations in Britain face a further formal constraint on the choice of trustees. In some foundations, the trust deed specifies that trustees must be selected from the donor's family or be of a particular religious faith. These restrictions, combined with the fact that trustees cannot be remunerated, means that grantmaking foundations are hampered in their ability to start with a definition of what is needed for the task and then recruit trustees to fulfill those needs. The more common pattern, at least among British foundations, seemed to be grantmaking that is tailored to the interest, knowledge, and experience of trustees rather than vice versa.

These restrictions on the selection of trustees created a further organizational problem: restricted time due to volunteer trustees' need for financial support, and their other commitments. Again, the time available for grantmaking is likely to be dictated not by the needs of the task but by the time trustees are able or willing to give.

An increasing number of grantmaking foundations (although in Britain still only a small minority) attempt to resolve these management dilemmas by stretching the knowledge, experience, interests, and time of trustees with paid staff and paid or volunteer advisers. However, as the study revealed, the involvement of paid staff and volunteer or paid advisers may create new management problems. Trustees may see the role of paid staff as purely administrative—an extra pair of hands to deal with practical rather than policy matters. Staff, especially if they are well qualified and well paid, may see their role as something more than simply pushing paper (Odendahl, Boris, & Daniels, 1985). In the study of British foundations on which this chapter is based, the relationship between trustees and paid staff emerged as one of the central and most sensitive issues in foundation management. One staff member suggested that some trustees saw him as "an overpaid postman." The problem of relationships between trustees and paid staff exists in service-providing nonprofits, because in those organizations paid staff may generally claim some recognized professional expertise in the organization's key task/client group (see, e.g., Harris, 1992, DiMaggio, 1988). In grant-giving foundations, staff may regard themselves as professionals but some questioned whether professional expertise in grantmaking is more widely acknowledged. As one director put it: "Is there a profession of spending?"

Some of the foundations studied recruited paid or unpaid advisers instead of, or in addition to, paid staff to supplement the time and knowledge of trustees. However, as some foundation members remarked, recognition of professional expertise brings its own problems. If advisers are recruited because "they know better" than trustees, what implications does this have for the autonomy and responsibility of trustees in decision making?

Donor Constraints

The management of foundations must address not only the organizational constraints and dilemmas created by government by trustees but also those stemming from the involvement of donors. British charity law places very special emphasis on the intentions and rights of donors. Donor's intentions are built into the formation of foundations and even when the cy près doctrine is employed for purposes of rescue and modernization, the donor's intentions play a key role (Chesterman, 1979).

In practice in some British foundations, or at some periods, trustees and donors may be one and the same, but because there is this dual emphasis built into the organization, all charitable foundations in theory, and many in practice, have to negotiate a balance between control by donors and government by trustees. The problem of accommodating donors' intentions took different forms in different types of foundation.

At a superficial level, it might be thought that endowed foundations are likely to be more independent or freer from donor control than sponsored or fund-raising foundations dependent for future income on continuing donor goodwill (see, e.g., Ylvisaker, 1987). But source of income does not, of itself, predict degree of donor control. There are endowed foundations that have lost all links with the original donor. Conversely, there are endowed foundations that are still very clearly controlled by the donors and/or their immediate family. Similarly, there are foundations relying in whole or in part on fund-raising that allow for direct donor control over the destination of gifts. Other fund-raising trusts receive nonspecific donations from thousands of unknown donors; in these cases, donors are quite unlikely to exert any direct control. The foundation may nevertheless feel a strong pressure, via thoughts of future fund-raising, to accommodate donors' intentions in its management of giving. Thus, if source of income per se does not predict the management problems created by the need to accommodate donors' intentions, what factors are likely to influence such problems?

This study suggests that four factors influence donor constraints: whether donors are alive or dead; the number of donors; social and geographical dispersal and available channels of communication; and public visibility (for further discussion of donor constraints, see Leat, 1995). When donor's intentions or preferences are perceived as an organizational constraint, this may affect not only the type of work or group aided but also any number of other factors. For example, the principle adopted by the British commercial television Telethon that money raised locally must be spent locally was acknowledged to do little to redistribute wealth between richer and poorer regions but was justified managerially in terms of its assumed effects on fund-raising (Leat, 1989).

Resource Constraints: Time and Money

Foundations, like all other organizations, have to work within certain resource constraints. The most obvious, and only widely publicly acknowledged resource constraint for grantmaking foundations is the size of the foundation's total annual income. But concentration on total annual income should not be allowed to obscure the other resource constraints within which foundations may have to operate.

Apart from size of income, security of income may also constitute a constraint. Fund-raising foundations are most likely to need to manage within the constraint of uncertain future income; but the annual income of endowed foundations is not, of course, 100 percent certain.

In attempting to maximize their total income and reduce its uncertainty, foundations are likely to encounter organizational dilemmas. In some cases, income may be maximized, but only at the expense of straying from the ethical investment policies that an increasing number of British foundations have adopted. Fund-raising foundations may encounter similar ethical dilemmas in choice of fund-raising strategies and techniques. But quite apart from ethical considerations, fund-raising foundations have to balance increasing income against the direct and indirect costs of fund-raising. Furthermore, some respondents suggested, there is always a danger that the fund-raising tail begins to wag the dog of grantmaking. As one grantmaker pointed out: "At one level this may be logical—you can't spend it unless you've got it—but it is also true that £10 million spent badly will be less effective than £1 million spent well."

Uncertainty over future income may affect grantmaking in various ways, the most obvious of which may be the size and duration of grants and the amount of innovative work requiring sustained financial support in which the foundation feels able to engage.

In addition to the constraint of size and security of overall annual income, the foundations studied also emphasized that grantmaking must be managed within constraints on "reasonable" expenditure on administration. Regardless of any legal limits on administrative costs, the prevailing ideology of British foundation management still stresses the virtue of spending as little as possible on both fund-raising and grantmaking. Only a tiny minority of British foundations publicly assert the need to spend money in order to spend well. Again, this constraint may be particularly important in the management of fund-raising foundations dependent for resources on continuing credibility with the general public.

Time is a further constraint. As noted earlier, the time available from trustees is likely to be limited and further management dilemmas arise when attempts are made to stretch trustees' time with paid staff and volunteer or paid advisers. Data from the study suggested that fund-raising foundations in particular may face other constraints on management of time. The fund-raising schedule itself may influence both the timetable and the type and scope of grantmaking. One British fund-raising foundation studied felt obliged to spend all of its substantial income within a matter of weeks because that was what the fund-raising message (stressing urgent need) was seen to require. A less extreme constraint is felt by some fund-raising foundations afraid of the effects on fund-raising of being caught with money in the bank. For these foundations, speed in grant-making becomes a virtue and a necessity. With little time to spend obtaining information and considering applications, such foundations may respond to inadequate knowledge by spreading the risk around large numbers of small grants.

One of the most important effects of these various financial and time constraints on foundation management may be to reduce the amount of knowledge available for informed grantmaking—knowledge that may be already restricted by the composition of the governing body of trustees. The pressure for speed and for low administrative costs may reduce the likelihood of obtaining adequate information on suppliers, both before and after grantmaking.

Managing without Feedback

The management of foundations may be further hampered by lack of feedback on the effects of grantmaking. Grant-giving foundations in Britain are talking about monitoring and evaluation but few are, as yet, doing anything systematic. Without feedback on the effects of foundation's grantmaking, it is difficult to learn from mistakes and build upon successes.

Apart from technical difficulties, there are other organizational constraints on evaluation of grants. First, evaluation costs money in addition to the grant itself. Spending money on evaluating the work of grantees conflicts with the pressure, noted earlier, to keep administrative costs to a minimum. But some foundation staff expressed the view that the cost of lack of evaluation is the cost of ineffectual grants and the loss of the opportunity to learn positive and negative lessons from experience.

In part, this lack of commitment to the practice of evaluation as, at the least, an essential management tool may be related to British foundations' traditional emphasis on gift-giving and on small, short-term pump-priming grants (Leat, 1992). When each grant was relatively small, spending money on evaluation was simply not cost-effective, but, perhaps more significantly, the ideology of pump-priming in effect emphasized the foundation's lack of responsibility for results—the ongoing effectiveness of the grant was up to others. Having primed the pump, the foundation had fulfilled its role and had no further interest. The emphasis on risk taking in traditional foundation ideology may have also devalued the importance of evaluation: The foundation's role was to take risks and thus, in a strange way, success and failure—outcomes—were irrelevant. A strategy—risk taking—became an end in itself.

Lack of commitment to evaluation may also be related to the notion, still accepted in many British foundations, that spending money is easy, and that spending money on "good causes" must, by definition, achieve good effects. The idea that this might not always be so, or that it is possible to learn from experience how to do better, has yet to gain widespread acceptance even among the leading foundations studied.

One of the peculiarities of the business of charitable grant giving is that, in an important sense, purely grant-giving endowed foundations do not need to be successful in order to survive. The endowed grant-giving foundation already has money and does what it does in order to spend that money. For the endowed foundation, grant outcomes are irrelevant to survival—what matters is its investment policy, not its spending policy and practice. In that sense, the endowed foundation does not need evaluation because it does not need to know; spending money on "good causes" rather than achieving good outcomes is what matters.

The foundation dependent upon fund-raising is, in theory, in a rather different position. The fund-raising foundation does not already have money; it must raise it afresh every year, and in order to do this, it must satisfy its donors. In practice, however, there is little pressure in Britain for fund-raising foundations to produce results, little pressure for evaluation, but strong pressures to keep administrative costs low. Some British fund-raising foundations do not even produce an annual report and those that do tend to contain generalized accounts of how the money was spent and not what it achieved.

CONCLUSION

Some British foundations are changing. The growing practice of making larger, longer-term grants, largely in response to the current lack of adequate continuation funding within the voluntary sector, is creating pressure for a train of other changes in foundation management and practice. The need for larger, longer-term grants has led the management of some foundations to become more proactive, to identify clearer priorities, to select applicants more carefully, and to evaluate the effectiveness of these larger injections of money. In some foundations, what began as small changes in practice has led to radical questioning of the deeply embedded culture of grantmaking and of every aspect of foundation management and practice (Leat, 1992).

Purely grantmaking foundations are different in certain important respects from some other types of nonprofit organization. As yet, however, we are very far from being clear about the nature and range of those differences. This chapter has attempted to highlight some of the organizational constraints and dilemmas exhibited by British grantmaking foundations. This attempt is only a first tentative step in the process of identifying and understanding similarities and differences between purely grantmaking foundations and other nonprofit organizations.

The descriptive data mentioned here have also suggested differences within the category of grantmaking foundations. Grantmaking foundations in Britain differ in their culture of grantmaking, in structure, and in nature and source of income. Further work is needed both on cultures of giving and on the way in which structures, financial and other resources, are related to grantmaking cultures. For example, fund-raising foundations, those with uncertain income (for whatever reason) and those constrained in choice of trustees may find it especially difficult to adopt the collaborative entrepreneur grantmaking culture requiring extensive knowledge, high expenditure on administration before and after grant decisions, and a willingness to take risks. More generally, further work is needed on differences between grantmaking foundations. For example, in what ways, if at all, does the part-operating foundation differ in culture, structure, and practice from the purely grantmaking foundation?

There are also questions concerning the implicit theories of social change and development with which foundations operate and the ways in which these influence the practice of grantmaking (Biggs & Neame, 1995).

Finally, further empirical and theoretical work is needed on the similarities and differences between grantmaking charitable foundations and different types of organization in the for-profit sector. What similarities and differences exist between grantmaking foundations and for-profit organizations that work through suppliers, with little or not contact with the end-user/consumer? What similarities and differences exist between grantmaking foundations and for-profit service providers, perhaps especially those supplying financial services? In what ways, if any, do some foundations work in ways similar to banks making loans in response to applications from customers? Or is grant giving more akin to business purchasing and marketing? What role do perceptions of risk and trust play in grantmaking, as compared with, for example, bank lending and business purchasing? How are risk and trust defined and recognized in these different activities? These questions are important not only in understanding the business of grantmaking but also at a practical level in recruitment and training of staff. As in other areas of research, the location of organizations within the voluntary nonprofit sector should not be allowed to obscure the exploration of similarities and differences between organizations across sectors (Leat, 1993).

REFERENCES

Batsleer, J., Cornforth, C. & Paton, R. (Eds.). (1992). *Issues in Voluntary and Non-Profit Management.* London: Open University/Addison-Wesley.

Biggs, S. & Neame, A. (1995). Negotiating room for manoeuvre: Reflections concerning NGO autonomy and accountability within the new policy agenda. In M. Edwards & D. Hulme (Eds.), *Non-Governmental Organizations: Performance and Accountability* (pp. 31–40). London: Earthscan Publications.

Burkeman, S. (1991). *Reflections In The Joseph Rowntree Charitable Trust Report for the Years 1988–90.* York; UK: Joseph Rowntree Foundation.

Chesterman, M. (1979). *Charities, Trusts and Social Welfare.* London: Weidenfeld & Nicholson.

Clare, R., & Scott, M. (1993). Charities' contribution to gross domenstic product: The results of the CSO Survey of Charities 1990 and 1991. *Economic Trends, 482,* 134–141.

DiMaggio, P. (1988). Nonprofit managers in different fields of service: Managerial tasks and management training. In M. O'Neill & D. R. Young (Eds.), *Educating Managers of Nonprofit Organizations* (pp. 51–69). New York: Praeger.

Fitzherbert, L. & Eastwood, M. (Eds.). (1989). *A Guide to the Major Trusts.* London: Directory of Social Change.

Fitzherbert, L., Giussani, C. & Hunt, H. (Eds.). (1996). *The National Lottery Yearbook.* London: Directory of Social Change.

Harris, M. (1992). The role of voluntary management committees. In J. Batsleer, C. Conforth, & R. Paton (Eds.), *Issues in Voluntary and Nonprofit Management* (pp. 134–148). London: Open University/Addison-Wesley.

Kendall, J. & Knapp, M. (1995). *Voluntary Means, Social Ends: Policy Issues for the UK Voluntary Sector in the 1990's, Personal Social Services Research Unit.* Canterbury, UK: University of Kent.

Knight, B. (1994). *Voluntary Action.* London: Home Office.

Lattimer, M. (1990, February). Whitehall wisdom. *Trust Monitor,* pp. 10–11.

Leat, D. (1989). *Fund-raising and Grantmaking: A Case Study of ITV Telethon '88.* Tonbridge, UK: Charities Aid Foundation.

Leat, D. (1990). *Broadcast Charitable Appeals.* London: Directory of Social Change.

Leat, D. (1992). *Trusts in Transition, the Policy and Practice of Grant-Giving Trusts.* York, UK: Joseph Rowntree Foundation.

Leat, D. (1993). *Managing across Sectors, Similarities and Differences between for-Profit and Voluntary Non-Profit Organizations.* London: VOLPROF, City University Business School.

Leat, D. (1995). British foundations: The organization and management of grantmaking. *Voluntas,* 6,(3), 317–329.

Leat, D. & Charities Aid Foundation Information Unit. (1996). CAF's Top 500 grantmaking trusts. In *Dimensions of the Voluntary Sector 1996* (pp. 53–56). Tonbridge, UK: Author.

Lord, G. (1989). Grantmaking trusts in a changing society. In L. Fitzherbert & M. Eastwood (Eds.), *A Guide to the Major Trusts* (pp. 243–244). London: Directory of Social Change.

Nielsen, W. A. (1972). *The Big Foundations*. New York: Columbia University Press.

Odendahl, T., Boris, E. & Daniels, A. (1985). *Working in Foundations*. New York: Foundation Center.

O'Neill, M. (1989). *The Third America: The Emergence of the Nonprofit Sector in the United States*. San Francisco: Jossey-Bass.

O'Neill, M. & Young, D. R. (Eds.). (1988). *Educating Managers of Nonprofit Organizations*. New York: Praeger.

Osborne, S., & Hems, L. (1994). *Survey of the Income and Expenditure of Charitable Organizations in the UK: Summary of Findings*. Public Sector Management Research Centre, Aston Business School, Birmingham, UK.

Posnett, J. (1993). The resources of registered charities in England and Wales—1990–1991. In S. Saxon-Harrold & J. Kendall (Eds.), *Researching the Voluntary Sector* (1st. ed., pp. 1–9). Tonbridge, UK: Charities Aid Foundation.

Powell, W. W. (Ed.). (1987). *The Nonprofit Sector: A Research Handbook*. New Haven & London: Yale University Press.

Saxon-Harrold, S. & Kendall, J. (1995). *Dimensions of the Voluntary Sector*. Tonbridge, UK: Charities Aid Foundation.

Ylvisaker, P. (1987). Foundations and Nonprofit Organizations. In W. W. Powell (Ed.), *The Nonprofit Sectors: A Research Handbook* (pp. 360–379). New Haven & London: Yale University Press.

Chapter 6

The Behavior of Grantmaking Foundations

Toward a New Theoretical Frame

WILLIAM A. DIAZ

INTRODUCTION

Any examination of issues confronting grantmaking foundations is diminished in value without a theoretical framework that gives these issues a larger meaning within the study of philanthropy and provides both scholars and practitioners a means to analyze them in some systematic way. Until recently, however, students of organizational behavior have neglected grantmaking foundations as objects of scholarly study, leaving a major theoretical lacuna for understanding and predicting the behavior of these important social institutions. The lacuna is especially evident in understanding those *internal* forces that shape grantmaking programs and decisions. Such a lacuna stands in stark contrast to the rich organizational theories developed to explain the behavior of for-profit firms and public agencies. As a consequence, foundations remain "black boxes," little known and even less understood, "shrouded in mystery, inspiring in some the highest hopes and expectations and in others dark fears and resentments" (Nielsen, 1985, p. 4). This chapter's purpose is to suggest

WILLIAM A. DIAZ • Senior Fellow, Hubert Humphrey Institute of Public Affairs, University of Minnesota, Minneapolis, Minnesota 55455.

Private Funds, Public Purpose: Philanthropic Foundations in an International Perspective, edited by Helmut K. Anheier and Stefan Toepler. New York, Plenum Press, 1999.

three broad models of organizational behavior with which to begin building a theory of foundation behavior. Each model provides hypotheses that can be tested through field research and, particularly, the systematic collection of case studies. The three models are the Rational Actor Model, the Bureaucratic Politics Model, and the Organizational Process Model.

THE THREE MODELS DESCRIBED

The three models or "theoretical frames" described below draw heavily upon Graham Allison's (1971) *Essence of Decision: Explaining the Cuban Missile Crisis* and Lee Bolman and Terence Deal's (1991) *Reframing Organizations: Artistry, Choice and Leadership* for their formulation. For illustrative purposes, they have purposely been formulated in as broad a way as possible.

Rational Actor Model

The Rational Actor Model is theoretically rooted in the sociology of Max Weber and his efforts to develop rational norms for the creation of new organizational forms improving on older, arbitrary, "patrimonial" organizations (Weber, 1947). Weber's work was extended and further developed after World War II by Blau and Scott (1962), Perrow (1986), and Hall (1963), who have examined various elements of structure and their impact on morale, productivity, and effectiveness. This model assumes that organizations operate as unified actors, usually through a hierarchical decision-making process. To make decisions, they act as gatherers of information and circumstances from their perceived environments to which they *react* in order to achieve their stated goals. One implication of understanding organizations as unified to this extent is that their decision-making analysis is understood as only perceiving one set of goals, options, and estimates of consequences. Accordingly, "action is conceived as a steady-state choice among alternative outcomes (rather than, for example, a large number of partial choices in a dynamic stream)" (Allison, 1971, p. 33).

Resting on the above assumptions, the second dominant explanatory characteristic of this model is that organizations' behavior and actions result directly, and solely, from rational decision making. None (or very few) of an organization's actions are random or inexplicable. An organization's goals are based on the perceived probability that preferred consequences will occur if certain specific actions are taken. A course of action is pursued based solely on the perceived benefit of the consequences of the action; that is, organizations calculate an implicit (sometimes explicit) cost–benefit analysis; and then actions are undertaken on the basis of this calculation.

From the Rational Actor Model's perspective, therefore, foundations are goal directed and hierarchical in their decision-making structures and processes. Their trustees set their overall policies and grantmaking agendas after a careful consideration of their options. Staff, directed by a chief executive, then pursue these policies and strategies by stimulating grant proposals that would implement these grantmaking programs in the "real world." Foundations, through this conceptual lens, behave as "unified" actors, with complete internal coherence concerning program choices and priorities.

The Bureaucratic Politics Model

In contrast to the Rational Actor Model, in the Bureaucratic Politics Model, organizational decisions about final action do not result from orderly consideration at a macrolevel and are not dominated by static organizational systems, structures, or standard operating procedures; instead, actions reflect an amalgamation of choices, games, compromises, internal politics, prior resultants, and actions that were executed by chance, not as a result of an explicit decision. "The goals structure and policies of an organization emerge from an ongoing process of bargaining and negotiating among the major interest groups" within an organization, often in the competition among staff for scarce resources (Bolman & Deal, 1991, p. 203). It focuses on the power of individual personalities or actors, groups, and coalitions within organizations in determining an organization's actions (Bolman & Deal, 1991). Organizational goals are set through internal negotiations among coalitions (Cyert & March, 1963). Much of this theory finds its basis in political science and in studies of the presidency, especially Neustadt's (1960) *Presidential Power,* which described the president's power not in terms of his power to *command* but his power to *persuade.* Neustadt and others made much of our constitutional government as one not of separated powers but of separated institutions sharing powers (Neustadt, 1960). Because power is fractionated, those who share it must come together to get things done. It is but a short leap from understanding government this way to understanding all large organizations in a similar fashion. In this model, therefore, organizations are conceived of as political arenas and organizational behavior is understood as a "resultant": "a mixture of conflicting preferences and unequal power of various individuals, and internal coalitions—distinct from what any person or group intended" (Allison, 1971, p. 145).

From this model's perspective, foundations are internally divided into individuals, groups, and coalitions that differ over programming priorities. These differences can reflect ideological differences between programs, or differences in position. The grantmaking budget is often the arena in which foundation staff dedicated to different functions or areas compete to promote their interests. Richard Magat has written of "the competition among divisions [at the Ford Foundation] for the overall budget and for both new work and the continuation of current programs" (1979, p. 35). Foundation grantmaking programs, therefore, emerge from an ongoing, dynamic process of bargaining and negotiation among staff and trustees.

From the Bureaucratic Politics Model's perspective, foundation decision making is not hierarchal, but often horizontal, staff to staff, and "bottom-up" from staff to trustees. In this model, staff may have more influence over the foundation's grantmaking program than its chief executive or trustees because of their "gatekeeper function." They are the first to see proposals and to decide which shall be considered for a grant. In addition, they initiate and shape grantmaking options for trustees' consideration.

The Organizational Process Model

This third and final model draws as its source the relatively new field of organizational theory and a group of books written between 1937 and 1947, such as Chester Barnard's *The Function of the Executive* (1938) and Herbert Simon's *Administrative Behavior* (1947) (March, 1965). A rich brand of this theory takes as its focus decision-making processes within organizations, and Simon is the seminal figure in this branch. Simon's (1947) interest has been to understand organizational structure and function as they derive from the characteristics of human problem solving and rational choice. He focuses on the limits of human capacity in comparison with the complexities of the problems that individuals in organizations must face, leading him to the concept of "bounded rationality" that forces the extraction of the main features of a problem without capturing all its complexity.

In the Organizational Process Model, therefore, large organizations are understood as generally bureaucratic. Because bureaucracies, to function, must divide knowledge, resources, and decision-making authority among various departments, there is not one decision maker that can coordinate and control all of the actions taken by the organization. Instead, "behavior . . . [is] understood . . . less as deliberate choices and more as *outputs* of these large organizations functioning according to standard operating procedures" (Allison, 1971, p. 67). This is particularly evident in large organizations, where their size prevents any single, central authority from making all important decisions or directing all important activities. Although bureaucratization permits more specialized attention to particular facets of problems than would be possible with one central decision maker, there is less "control" over the overall mission, or goals, of the organization. "Things make leaders happen instead of the other way around" (Edelman, 1977, p. 73).

In place of any "rational" analysis to determine decisions, the Organizational Process Model assumes that established "programs," standard operating procedures, and routines drive organizational activity. These are the gears that move the organization on particular paths. Examples of these procedures include preparing budgets (with the previous year's budget as the baseline), attending regular meetings, writing reports, and attending to other "inputs." Although people who work in organizations spend much of their time engaged in such processes, the processes themselves can obscure and interfere with their intended outcomes. Nevertheless, over time, these procedures and routines become reinforced through repetition. Consequently, an organization's behavior in the present can best be understood by its behavior in the past.

Because "both learning and change are influenced by existing organizational capabilities and procedures," the organization does not choose actions that are radically different from that which its systems have been directing (Allison, 1971, p. 79). Thus, the role of any one leader is marginal in terms of affecting organizational outputs, partially because procedures and routines limit the range of options available to leaders. In addition to an organization's history, there are other constraints that direct its behavior. These include resources, demands from the outside environment, and bargaining and compromises among components of the organization.

This model suggests that foundations' grantmaking programs are highly constrained by their standard operating procedures and routines, which have become reinforced through repetition. This model would suggest that the best predictor of a foundation's behavior in the future would be its behavior in the past (i.e., to understand what a foundation will do next year, one should read this year's annual report).

The Implicit Rational Actor Bias

Students of foundations have offered a variety of motives and theories to explain their behavior, especially in responding to social issues, and their level of engagement in public policy. These explanations include the payout requirements and other restrictions of the 1969 Tax Act that alternately encourage and discourage public affairs engagement; a rise in society's needs tied to a growing independence among foundation staff professionals, leading to greater altruism and public spiritedness; and a range of social control theories wherein foundation support is considered "reactive" and designed to dampen social dissidence (see, e.g., Colwell, 1993; Jenkins, 1987).

These explanations and theories are limited by their tendency to treat foundations as "rational actors," that is, with an implicit bias toward the Rational Actor Model. Foundations' actions are generally treated as goal-directed and as if the outcomes of their behavior (grants) follow from rational choices about specific programmatic or broad societal goals. For example,

Colwell (1993) argues that foundations' trustees and leaders use foundations to help the nation's economic elite exercise major influence over the public policy process. Nielsen (1972; 1985), on the other hand, focuses on the intentions and actions of the chief executive officers of the largest foundations to explain their foundations' behavior. These analyses, as others, accept the "Rational Actor" model, albeit differently, without testing or exploring other models of organizational behavior to explain the role of foundations in responding to social issues, or their behavior more generally.

As a result, none of these explanations adequately captures the reality that foundations, especially large ones, like all human organizations, are complex, surprising, and ambiguous institutions (there are now twenty-five foundations with assets of over $1 billion, and giving programs of $45 million or more annually; Foundation Centre, 1998).

THE MODELS ILLUSTRATED

A brief examination of how three of the largest U.S. foundations, the Rockefeller Foundation, the Ford Foundation and the Carnegie Corporation, began addressing the enormous growth in population and need of U.S. Hispanics in the 1970s and 1980s (a population growth of 61 percent between 1970 and 1980) illustrates how these models could help to illuminate and explain the grantmaking behavior of foundations.

Carnegie Corporation

Carnegie's entry into Hispanic grantmaking is, perhaps, the most straightforward of the three foundations. Both John Gardner, its president between 1955 and 1965, and his successor, Alan Pifer (1965–1982) expressed strong individual concerns for issues of social justice and equity (Nielsen, 1972, p. 31). These views quickly were expressed to staff for action by the Corporation. In 1964, Gardner noted to his senior staff that a decade after the Supreme Court's decision desegregating America's public schools, *Brown vs. Board of Education,* the Corporation had done little in the area of race. This led to a $1 million request to the trustees to improve opportunities in higher education for African Americans. The resulting grants went predominantly to African American institutions or elite white institutions, such as Princeton or MIT, willing to create special workshops or programs for African Americans (Finberg, Personal Communication, November 7, 1996).

When Alan Pifer succeeded Gardner, who had left to become Lyndon Johnson's Secretary of Health, Education, and Welfare, he wanted to place greater emphasis on social justice and created a staff task force to explore and recommend what to do. The task force recommendations included helping minority organizations to seek social justice within the Corporation's general field of interest of education. While, up to then, the Corporation's interest in minorities had been restricted to African Americans, because the staff task force's leader was a Coloradan familiar with the needs of Native Americans and Hispanics, these groups were included within the new social justice initiative (Finberg, Personal Communication, November 7, 1996).

This brief history shows the applicability of the Rational Actor Model, with its emphasis on top-down, problem-focuesed hierarchical decision mark-ing, as illustrated by the strong impact of Gardner and Pifer in opening Car-negie to greater social justice concerns. However, it also shows the power of the bureaucratic politics framework to illuminate the role of staff and internal coalitions in shaping organizational decisions. In this case, Hispanic and Na-tive American organizations were included in the foundation's new initiative because of the staff task force leader's personal experience and interest.

Rockefeller Foundation

The Rockefeller Foundation began in 1909 with a broad charter: "To promote the well-being and to advance the civilization of the peoples of the United States and its territories and possessions and of foreign lands in the acquisition and dissemination of knowledge, in the prevention and relief of suffering, and in the promotion of any and all of the elements of human progress" (Nielsen, 1972, p. 50).

John D. Rockefeller, however, was "convinced that good health was of first importance to human well-being, and this soon became the foundation's main interest" (Nielsen, 1972, p. 53). For example, early on, it focused on the eradication of hookworm in the South and then in other countries. Over the years, this commitment to "hard" science and medicine led to successes that further reinforced this single-minded view and strengthened the hand of the scientists and doctors on the foundation's staff preventing the foundation from attempting or achieving comparable successes in other fields—the social sci-ences, the arts and humanities—in which it had also professed interest. As described by Nielsen by the late 1940s, "Rockefeller had become so set in its habits—emphasis on pure research, advanced training, institutional develop-ment, and working through universities—that the introduction of any ba-sically new program was made only with great difficulty. To some degree the foundation had become the prisoner of its own successes" (Nielsen, 1972, p. 63).

In 1962, however, a program review identified five priority areas for future action; among them was "equal opportunity for all American citizens" (Nielsen, 1972, p. 67). However, broad policy statements proved to be one thing and the actual implementation of programs another. For the next nine years, the foundation's president, George Harrar, implemented some priorities with great vigor while neglecting others, including "equal opportunity."

It was only with great difficulty, and with great and persistent exertion by the Rockefeller trustees and a new president, John Knowles, that the foundation was able to break out of its "prison," leading to a 1981 special trustee appropriation of $1.5 million for an "equal opportunities" program for minorities. Knowles, in addition, had in 1978 hired Dr. Bernard Anderson, an African American economist, to develop a major program on inner-city black youth employment. Anderson, familiar with employment data on various ethnic groups, realized that Hispanics, too, suffered high rates of youth unemployment. Therefore, in the foundation's earliest work in this area, Hispanics were included as a target group and a Latina Ph.D. was hired as a research associate to help direct the work (Bernard Anderson, Personal Communication, January 21, 1997).

This history illustrates that despite numerous opportunities and demands from the external environment for Rockefeller to address domestic policy and minority concerns, and the efforts of some staff and trustees prior to John Knowles to respond to those opportunities and demands, the foundation's long-established "programs" and "standard operating procedures" successfully resisted change, as the Organizational Process Model would predict. Nevertheless, Knowles and several trustees were finally able to crack through this inertia, suggesting that Rational Model, with its emphasis on top-down hierarchal decision making and leadership, adds further insight to the story.

Ford Foundation

In 1984, the Ford Foundation announced a new major program initiative addressing the needs of the nation's growing Hispanic population. The new initiative consisted of the following:

1. Research and policy analysis on the Hispanic population.
2. Efforts to promote Hispanics' participation in public affairs, including a new Hispanic Leadership Development program.
3. Public education about Hispanics to non-Hispanics in light of "the potential for increased intergroup tension."

Finally, the new initiative would include a special effort to create a new community foundation in Puerto Rico. From one perspective (the Rational Actor), the decision to create the Hispanic program, and its shape and contents, can be viewed as a rational response by Ford's Trustees to the emergence, through immigration and other population factors (high fertility rates, etc.), of a "new American minority," facing serious problems of poverty and unemployment, as well as language barriers and discrimination. From the perspective of the Bureaucratic Politics Model, however, the creation of the Hispanic program can be viewed less as an initiative of the Trustees in response to a "sea change" in American society than the result of what a former Foundation Trustee has called a "gathering restiveness on the part of staff" to address the Hispanic population's needs (Wyman, Personal Communication, October 6, 1995).

In October 1979, five years before the new initiative was launched and just as a change in Foundation leadership was about to occur (from the retirement of its president, McGeorge Bundy), the Foundation had created an internal Delegated Authority Program (DAP) for various Latino programs and organizations (Ford Foundation, 1979). The DAP, in essence, allowed program staff to make small discretionary grants under a broad delegation of authority from the Foundation's president. The DAP provided funding in the amount of $100,000 over one year and was renewed again in 1980 for $150,000. The DAP's creation was in large part the result of internal lobbying by Foundation staff from the National Affairs Division that had long been involved in Hispanic grantmaking. There had been a sense on the part of this staff and other sympathetic to their view that the Foundation, in addressing minority concerns, had focused its attention disproportionately on the needs of the nation's African Americans, in spite of the growing diversity of the U.S. population and Hispanics' growth as a population in need (Oppenheimer-Nicolau, Personal Communication, August 8, 1995; Forman, Personal Communication, July 21, 1995). The staff grant recommendation for the DAP notes that "when the nation began to recognize social inequality in the 40s and 50s, it focused on the Blacks. The Mexican Americans did not attract the attention of Eastern liberals who made an important contribution in the early days of the civil rights movement" (Ford, 1979, p. 3). In this Bureaucratic Politics Model version of events, this group of staff eventually succeeded in persuading the Foundation's new president, Franklin Thomas, and its Trustees to call for a paper on Hispanics at their October 1980 Trustees meeting to be delivered at their meeting in October 1981. (It should be noted that Thomas, himself an African American, was prepared to be receptive to this initiative, having served as a trustee of the John Hay Whitney Foundation, which had been among the earliest foundations to fund work on Hispanic issues.) In the Bureaucratic Politics Model version, the process was competitive; "horizontal," (staff to staff), and "bottom-up," (staff to Trustees), rather than vertical, top-down, and "unitary," as the Rational Model would suggest.

EVALUATING THE MODELS

As these brief "cases" suggest, it is likely that the Rational Actor Model is probably quite weak in its ability, standing alone, to illuminate "what really happens in foundations." To draw an analogy to the world of the for-profit corporation, to know that all are somehow "rational" in their pursuit of profit tells us little about why Apple chooses to pursue a different strategy than IBM. Rather, it would seem that we need the Bureaucratic Politics and Organizational Process models to help explain their behavior. The Bureaucratic Politics Model appears particularly powerful on issues of internal resource allocations and budget. It helps to illuminate conflict and cooperation among staff and trustees regarding genuine differences over grantmaking priorities. The Organizational Process Model illuminates how organizational histories and cultures, prior decisions, and standard operating procedures influence and constrain available options and choices in the present. Their greatest power may lie in their combination as each brings illumination to different facets of a foundation's decision making "system."

THE EXTERNAL ENVIRONMENT

Although these models focus on internal organizational forces and processes that shape foundations' decision making, it is important to note two important external factors that also help shape their programs. First, is the "ecology" of people, ideas, organizations, and issues that shape their grantmaking opportunities. Put somewhat differently, foundations exist within a social, political, and economic reality that gives definition to the grantmaking avenues they have available to pursue. The second factor is the various financial markets in which a foundation's assets are invested. The performance of these markets dictates the level of grantmaking the foundation can pursue. These external factors are noted here as a reminder that, ultimately, any theory of foundation behavior will have to account for the interplay between foundations' internal and external environments.

CONCLUSION

Because of our habits of mind, it is easy to fall into the trap of believing that foundations, especially large ones, are run by their trustees, that they are goal directed, operate on a rational analytical basis, and are unitary in the way they define and address societal and other problems. Perhaps this trap is so difficult to avoid because it represents the way we like to think of ourselves: as rationally directed individuals, free from internal conflict, and possessing options unlimited by our own earlier, perhaps bad, choices.

This chapter has attempted to suggest that this Rational Model or perspective, while satisfying to our habits of mind, is highly limited in its ability to explain the behavior of foundations and, most importantly, their "outputs," the grant programs, and grants they pursue. A full understanding of foundations and their grantmaking "outputs" must take into account the internal dynamics, especially around resource allocation, represented in the Bureaucratic Politics Model, and the organizational habits and processes that constrain current options and decisions captured in the Organizational Process Model. Therefore, consistent with the "new institutionalism" in organizational theory and sociology, as scholars move toward developing a better understanding of American foundations, they need to move way from an exclusive reliance on the Rational Model (Powell & DiMaggio, 1991). Their understanding will have to capture the complex internal life of these institutions that other models, such as the Bureaucratic Politics Model and Organization Process, help to explain. This is particularly important to any understanding of foundations' roles in American society. Generally speaking, scholars appear to be prone to view them as monolithic instruments of an economic "elite" operating through their boards of trustees, when in reality, they may be driven as much by staff, organizational habit and, yes, on occasion, plain confusion. Foundation grants and grantmaking programs, in other words, may be less than the results of an objective and "rational" process than the "resultants" of internal staff competition and bargaining, and the outputs of organizational routines and procedures. Perhaps, they are best viewed as a mix of the intended and unintended, the rational and irrational.

If this is the case, we may find that the grantmaking behavior of endowed foundations is best explained by a "garbage can" model of organizations developed by James C. March (1965) and his associates. The model suggests that for people within the organization,

> problems are convenient receptacles into which they can toss solutions that happen to interest them, or for interests that are not being met at the time. The can with its problems, become an opportunity or resource. Depending on the number of cans around, the mixes of problems in them, and the amount of time people have, they stay with the particular can or leave it for another. The problem, then, gets detached from those that originally posed it, may develop, or get transformed into quite another problem. Solutions no one originally intended or even expected may be generated or no solutions at all. (Perrow, 1986, p. 135)

Foundations, especially large ones, may particularly fit this model for two reasons. First, at any one time, there is a broad range of problems in their environments that they can be addressing. Therefore, the opportunity for the creation of new "garbage cans" by staff and/or trustees seems endless. Second, the creation of "garbage cans" is encouraged when there is organizational "slack"—an excess of resources (money, time, personnel, equipment, ideas). Foundations are created from excess resources and generally manage their endowments to generate excess resources either for new grantmaking and/or to maintain and grow the original endowment. In short, they generally operate with a good deal of "slack."

These thoughts are intended to be suggestive only of one direction a theory of foundation behavior might take. At this time, however, we remain far from such a theory. In order to construct one, analysts will need to examine many more cases of foundation process and test explanatory models far more rigorously than was the intent of this chapter. This might proceed by "testing" hypotheses suggested by these three models with foundations of various sizes and types such as independent, community, corporate, and family foundations, which can be expected to have very different internal dynamics (e.g., one might test the hypotheses that corporate foundation behavior is best explained by the Rational Actor Model because of a clearer focus of these foundations on their parent corporation's interest). As this process proceeds, these models would be refined, discarded, or replaced. It is important to ¯ recognize, too, that the models described are, admittedly, ethnocentric; they are based entirely on American organizational theories and experience. A comprehensive international theory of foundations would require the incorporation of foreign theories and the testing of hypotheses on an international basis.

One possible obstacle to such further research and hypotheses testing may be the unwillingness of foundations to cooperate with research that might conclude they operate "irrationally." It would seem that, in the long run, foundation managers would have an interest in the building of a strong theory of foundation behavior to help inform practice. Clearly, managers armed with a better understanding of the bewildering shifts, turns, and unexpected outcomes in daily organizational life will be better prepared to achieve their goals. This would seem particularly true at a time when government cutbacks will place new demands on foundations to respond to needs in the area of public affairs. Relatedly, a second incentive to building a body of research on foundation process is to create greater transparency around these processes that would perhaps help to reduce public, press, and governmental mistrust of foundations, their intentions and their methods of operations: to remove, in Waldemar Nielsen's words, the shroud of mystery that surrounds them in the hopes of dispelling the "fears and resentments" they inspire in some. But foundation managers would have to be willing to admit that their institutions are not perfect, but subject to the same foibles and forces affecting other (large) organizations.

The opportunity, in summary, exists for analysts and foundation practitioners to come together to build a rich body of literature no the organizational behavior of foundations that would help inform both theory and practice. I hope this chapter provides some initial encouragement for this to occur.

REFERENCES

Allison, G. T. (1971). *Essence of Decision: Explaining the Cuban Missile Crisis.* Boston: Little, Brown.

Barnard, C. I. (1938). *The Functions of the Executive.* Cambridge, MA: Harvard University Press.

Bolman, L. G., & Deal, T. E. (1991). *Reframing Organizations: Artistry, Choice and Leadership.* San Francisco: Jossey-Bass.

Blau, P. M., & Scott, W. R. (1962). *Formal Organizations: A Comparative Approach.* San Francisco: Chandler.

100 Largest Foundations by Assets (1996). *The Chronical of Philanthropy, 3*(11), 18.

Colwell, M. A. C. (1993). *Private Foundations and Public Policy: The Political Role of Philanthropy.* New York & London: Garland.

Cyert, R. M., & March, J. G. (1963). *A Behavioral Theory of the Firm,* Englewood Cliffs, NJ: Prentice-Hall.

Edelman, M. J. (1977). *The Symbolic Uses of Politics.* Madison: University of Wisconsin Press.

Ford Foundation. (1979). *Recommendation for Grant/DAP Action,* No. 799–0708. Ford Foundation Archives.

The Foundation Center. (1998). *Foundation Giving.* New York: Author.

Hall, R. H. (1963). The concept of bureaucracy: An empirical assessment. *American Journal of Sociology, 49,* 32–40.

Jenkins, J. C. (1987). Nonprofit organizations and public advocacy. In W. W. Powell (Ed.), *The Nonprofit Sector: A Research Handbook* (pp. 296–318), New Haven, CT: Yale University Press.

Magat, R. (1979). *The Ford Foundation at Work.* New York & London: Plenum Press.

March, J. G. (1965). *Handbook of Organizations.* Chicago: Rand McNally Chicago University Press.

Neustadt, R. (1960). *Presidential Power, The Politics of Leadership.* New York: Wiley.

Nielsen, W. A. (1972). *The Big Foundations.* New York & London: Columbia University Press.

Nielsen, W. A. (1985). *The Golden Donors.* New York: Truman Talley Books Dutton.

Perrow, C. (1986). *Complex Organizations: A Critical Essay* (3rd ed.). New York: Random House.

Powell, W. W., & DiMaggio, P. J. (1991). *The New Institutionalism in Organizational Analysis.* Chicago: University of Chicago Press.

Simon, H. (1947). *Administrative Behavior.* New York: Macmillan.

Simon, H. (1957). *Models of Man: Social and Rational; Mathematical Essays on Rational Human Behavior in a Social Setting.* New York: Wiley.

Weber, M. (1947). *The Theory of Social and Economic Organization* (T. Parsons, Trans.) New York: Free Press.

Chapter 7

Toward an Entrepreneurial Approach to Foundation Management

HEINRICH BEYER

BACKGROUND

Following the tradition of Ronald Coase (1937), who first worked out the fundamental differences between market coordination and internal coordination within enterprises, we can assume that management is a phenomenon of collective action in all organizations—for-profit corporations, government agencies, and foundations alike. In contrast to the "invisible hand" of the market, where changes in relative prices initiate individual adaptation processes (e.g., a decrease or increase in demand for a specific product), the coordination of economic activities within organizations is realized by the "visible hand of management" (Chandler, 1977). The differences between markets and organizations regarding the regulation of individual behavior are emphasized by Coase (1937, p. 388): "If a workman moves from department y to department x, he does not go because of a change in relative prices, but because he is ordered to do so."

In contrast to the market model, where individuals act autonomously, organizations are charactgerized by regulating and controlling individual activities to achieve organizational goals (Beyer, 1993). The output of business

HEINRICH BEYER • Economics Program, Bertelsmann Foundation 33311, Gutersloh, Germany.

Private Funds, Public Purpose: Philanthropic Foundations in an International Perspective, edited by Helmut K. Anheier and Stefan Toepler. New York, Plenum Press, 1999.

enterprises, nonprofit organizations, and foundations is not produced by entrepreneurs or donors alone, but is the result of what Alchian (1984) called a team-production process. Team production implies that "a group of people can by 'joint' action achieve more than the sum of their separate results, where the total is not the sum of separate amounts of each member. The action does not entail an exchange of identifiable products of one person to another person. The reward to each is a portion of the team's salable output value" (Alchian, 1984, p. 35).

This "joint action" does need to be managed. When we talk about foundation management, we must see that foundations are indeed established by donors and that foundation activities are guided by a set of objectives and specified purposes. However, it is also apparent that foundations, like enterprises, are institutions of team production, where objectives must be formulated and realized, where individual activities must be coordinated, and where employees must be motivated to participate actively in realizing organizational goals. Apart from their nonprofit character, foundations may thus face similar organizational problems as other organizations. From this perspective, there are no fundamental differences between several types of institutions. Management is a general attribute of all organizations with a strategic, an operative, and a motivational dimension:

1. Team production is characterized by the common activities of individual members in achieving organizational goals. To do so, these organizational goals—for example, the social intentions and philanthropic interests of a donor—must be defined and transformed into operational objectives and practical activities.

2. Team members' activities must be coordinated: Coordination can be described as creating and controlling rules for individual behavior. The existence of rules, regulated decision processes, and some kind of work organization is a general characteristic of all institutions (Vanberg, 1982).

3. Finally, an organization must give monetary and non-monetary incentives to its members to ensure their active participation, to reduce governance costs and to establish efficient performance. Therefore foundation management has to fulfill leadership functions exactly like other organizations.

Besides these similarities, there are, of course, some fundamental differences between firms on the one hand and nonprofit organizations and foundations on the other. The most important features are as follows:

- There is no apparent market for what foundations offer, and competition is limited or nonexistent.
- Foundations do not make profits based on their grantmaking and operational activities.

- Foundations do not distribute profits to owners or their equivalents, such as board members.

At first, traditional management concepts do not seem to be applicable to foundations because they are not geared to the market and are not established to make profit (except for asset management). Rather, their explicit purpose is to achieve goals such as sponsoring cultural, social, political, scientific, and educational activities to serve the common welfare and other similar objectives specified by the donor. However, operating and grantmaking foundations do meet special demands by supporting other institutions and individuals. In doing so, foundation management must decide, for example,

- What projects should be granted
- How to use available assets
- How to control the performance of projects
- How to inform the general public about its activities.

As in the case of enterprise management, strategic and operational goals must be defined, plans must be worked out, decisions must be made, employees must be motivated, and a "foundation culture" and a "foundation identity" must be established. In short, foundation management has to meet performance criteria that may be just as demanding as those of enterprise management. Although foundations cannot be penalized for inefficiencies by the market, foundation management requires an efficient use of capital, labor, and other resources to realize the donor's purposes and to meet tax law stipulations. Such requirements entail a need for what could be called "entrepreneurial foundation management."

ENTREPRENEURIAL FOUNDATION MANAGEMENT

Of course, there are many differences among specific types of foundations (e.g., grantmaking foundations, operating foundations, family foundations, corporate foundations, and community foundations), but they are all concerned with issues surrounding the use of resources, solving managerial and organizational problems, and how to plan for the future. How foundation management copes with these demands depends on the attitude of donors and managers toward methods of operation and the general functions of a foundation. We can distinguish between two different (ideal) approaches to foundation management.

1. The "administrative" approach in reference to Max Weber's (1968) model of bureaucracy: This type of foundation management has a prevailing passive character. Grants are made in response to applications from external

institutions and clients, the management function is reduced to the bureaucratic execution and control of projects, and the internal organization is structured along hierarchical principles. Among European foundations at least, this notion of foundations as "quasiadministrative institutions" is still the dominant one (Dümcke, 1993).

2. The "entrepreneurial" approach in reference to Schumpeter (1976) is the more actie type of foundation management. A foundation is understood as an active part of civil society, which uses its creative power to discover social needs and opportunities. The foundation is actively involved in the definition, execution, and presentation of projects and other activities, and practices organizational and personnel development to make better use of human capital (Weger, 1992).

In this view, there is no remarkable difference between the function of an entrepreneur and the function of foundation management. If we understand foundations in that way, then traditional management concepts are of great importance for these institutions, too (Weger, 1992; Zimmer, 1993).

DEFINING FOUNDATION GOALS

Donors have specific as well as very general motives when creating foundations; but to realize their implied purposes, such motives must be transformed into operational goals. Nielsen (1972, pp. 312–313) suggested that "although donors have often been remarkably far-seeing and creative in their businesses, they generally have been shortsighted and inept in launching their foundations." To avoid this and to reduce goal ambiguity, foundations need, like business enterprises, some kind of "market researach." Donors must have detailed information about specific needs in the area of interest, and they must know where their foundations will be most effective. A detailed definition of goals combined with a foundation philosophy and operational guidelines can help highlight specific foundation profiles and accentuate donors' purposes and attitudes. Because nonprofit organizations may have less well-defined objectives and traditional efficiency criteria as guidelines for evaluating activities may not apply, a detailed goal formulation of priorities and expected outcomes becomes a strategic management tool for greater efficiency.

STRATEGIC FOUNDATION MANAGEMENT

Strategic management of business enterprises has to make basic decisions on products, markets, competitive strategy, diversification, and future policy directions in general. Donors and foundation managers have to decide on their fields of activity. They have to set priorities as to which activities to support and concentrate their investments on these projects and programs. To reduce problems arising from limited information, lack of knowledge, and uncertainty about possible outcomes ("bounded rationality"), foundation management may frequently be dependent on management methods and instruments similar to ones used in for-profit organizations (Porter, 1980). Their usual forms of organizational rationality, which can be described as efforts to make efficient use of scarce resources to realize conflicting objectives, can in fact support the achievement of business as well as philanthropic goals.

OPERATIVE MANAGEMENT AND PROJECT MANAGEMENT

Strategies once defined must be realized. Particularly big foundations with extensive staff need an organization with prescribed responsibilities, job descriptions, governance, and incentive structures. In addition, an important task of foundations is to establish professional project management, which values all activities in the context of foundation goals and ensures that criteria of social utility on the one hand and economic efficiency on the other are achieved. The planning, budgeting, realizing, and evaluating of projects are also comparable to corresponding management task in business enterprises (Weger, 1992).

Marketing

The marketing approach ascribes the adjustment of all institutional activities to the wishes and needs of customers, clients, and other interest groups. It is not formulated exclusively for enterprises but is also applicable to nonprofit organizations (Kotler & Levy, 1983; Zimmer, 1993). An analysis of "demand structures" and of activities of other foundations is as useful as defining and controlling strategies in order to achieve a specific position in the "charity market." To give instances of charitable work and to influence public opinion, foundations should present some kind of annual report to inform the public about specific activities. In particular, foundations that offer grants for social, cultural, or scientific research projects should take care that the results of these projects are published appropriately. This should not (only) be done to promote its public image, but also, for example, to support the diffusion of knowledge. Additionally, an intensive cooperation and communication with other relevant institutions and authorities, the arranging of symposiums, public hearings, workshops, and press conferences or the publication of own editions are important marketing instruments for foundations.

Leadership

In contrast to business enterprises, labor–management relations in foundations or other nonprofit organizations are not characterized by a structural conflict between labor and capital. Yet both groups of institutions face similar problems regarding practical cooperation among employees, management, and the board. Conflicts arising from work organization and financial restrictions can affect the corporate culture and organizational efficiency in foundations no less than in enterprises. In particular, big foundations should accept their role as employers and their tasks in organizational and personnel development. To motivate employees to participate actively in realizing goals, it is not enough to refer to the philanthropic character of a foundation or its statutes. Instead, modem leadership accepts conflicts, supports employees' participation in decision making, and offers possibilities for promotion. In the absence of structural distribution conflicts, the conditions for implementing participatory labor–management relations in foundations should be quite favorable (Beyer & Nutzinger, 1993).

This short overview of some managerial aspects shows that running foundations in an entrepreneurial manner demands almost the same management methods as business enterprises. If foundations are understood as instruments for realizing private intentions aimed at furthering common welfare, and if donors and foundation management do not react only to "market demands" but do actively develop programs, projects, and fields of activities, then a professional management is needed that ensures an efficient use of scarce resources—in the interest of both the donor and the public.

Foundation Culture

Besides different goals and the absence of the profit motive, the creative power of foundations, not limited by market constraints, and their independence of initiative from political constraint are the most significant differences between foundations and private business enterprises and public agencies, respectively. Additionally, the philanthropic "mission" guiding foundations' orientation gives rise to a specific operational culture (Beyer & Nutzinger, 1993). As a result of their normative character, foundations have the chance to develop an internal organization that is characterized by a high degree of identification and motivation. To make extensive use of these key resources, grantmaking and operating foundations need professional management to regulate labor–management relations as well as to work out plans and strategies.

The characteristics of foundations imply advantages as well as risks. On the one hand, freedom to act is a precondition of entrepreneurial and private commitment to social and philanthropic affairs, enabling foundations to discover and satisfy social needs without being limited by market or political constraints. In addition, this comfortable situation helps foundations achieve a specific balance between philanthropy and organizational rationality. On the other hand, the problem of governance and efficiency is present throughout. To what extent managers and boards of trustees can guarantee the balance between philanthropy and operational efficiency remains an open question.

CONCLUSION

Philanthropy and organizational rationality need not be inconsistent. On the contrary, the development of specific efficiency criteria and entrepreneurial thinking can promote the usefulness of foundations and their activities. Frequently, foundations face organizational problems similar to business enterprises. To make efficient use of scarce resources and to organize the "philanthropic enterprises," a formal structure, a high degree of coordination, and professional management are increasingly required to ensure goal fulfillment. Managerial strength and expertise will not restrain philanthropy but will actually transform foundations into active, efficient instruments of philanthropy.

REFERENCES

Alchian, A. A. (1984). Specificity, specialization, and coalitions. *Journal of Institutional and Theoretical Economics 140,* 34–49.

Beyer, H. (1993). *Interne Koordination und Partizipatives Management—Eine mikroökonomische Analyse·neuer Management und Führungstechniken.* Marburg, Germany: Metropolis.

Beyer, H., & Nutzinger, H. G. (1993). Hierarchy or co-operation: Labour–management relations in church institutions. *Voluntas, 4*(1), 55–72.

Chandler, A. D. (1977). *The Visible Hand: The Managerial Revolution in American Business.* Cambridge & London: Belknap Press.

Coase, R. (1937). The nature of the firm. *Economica, 16*(4), 386–405.

Dümcke, C. (1993). Kulturförderung als Managementaufgabe—Zum Dilemma von Managementansätzen in der Kulturförderung. In R. Graf Strachwitz & S. Toepler (Eds.), *Kulturförderung—Mehr als Sponsoring* (pp. 385–393). Wiesbaden, Germany: Gabler.

Kotler, P. & Levy, S. (1983). Broadening the concept of marketing. In P. Kotler, O. C. Ferrel, & C. Lamb (Eds.), *Cases and Readings for Marketing Nonprofit Organizations* Prentice-Hall. Englewood Cliffs, NJ.

Nielsen, W. (1972). *The Big Foundations.* New York & London: Columbia University Press.

Porter, M. E. (1980). *Competitive Strategy: Techniques for Analysing Industries and Competitors.* New York: Free Press.

Schumpeter, J. A. (1976). *Capitalism, Socialism, and Democracy.* London: Allen & Unwin.

Seibel, W. (1992). *Funktionaler Dilettantismus—Erfolgreich scheitemde Organisationen im "Dritten Sektor" zwischen Markt und Staat.* Baden-Baden, Germany: Nomos.

Vanberg, V. (1982). *Markt und Organisation.* Tübingen, Germany: Mohr.

Weber, M. (1968). *Economy and Society*. New York: Bedminster Press.

Weger, H.-D. (1992). Wie man Stiftungen gestaltet statt verwaltet. In *Frankfurter Allgemeine Zeitung, Blick durch die Wirtschaft, May 26, 1992*.

Zimmer, A. (1993). *Management und Marketingprobleme kultureller Vereine. In R. Graf Strachwitz & S. Toepler (Eds.), Kulturförderung—Mehr als Sponsoring* (pp. 395–411). Wiesbaden, Germany: Gabler.

Chapter 8

Operating in a Grantmaking World

Reassessing the Role of Operating Foundations[1]

STEFAN TOEPLER

INTRODUCTION

Foundations appear in a wide variety of types, legal forms, and sizes, and pursue a broad range of objectives. This makes it hard to get a firm grasp of the institutional form as a whole. Nevertheless, there are some basic commonalities. Foundations can generally be defined as asset-holding entities, usually endowed by a single donor, that are dedicated to charitable or philanthropic causes and have organizational structures to fulfill their objectives. The ways in which goals are pursued allow for a general distinction between operating and grantmaking foundations, the former of which are more actively involved in carrying out the intended activities than the latter. Accordingly, foundations are either restricted to making grants to other agencies, or deliver services directly. The common understanding of foundations is mostly determined by this distinction.

However, this basic distinction is often overlaid with foundation typolog-

STEFAN TOEPLER • Research Associate and Lecturer, Institute for Policy Studies, Johns Hopkins University, Baltimore, Maryland 21218-2588.

Private Funds, Public Purpose: Philanthropic Foundations in an International Perspective, edited by Helmut K. Anheier and Stefan Toepler. New York, Plenum Press, 1999.

ies that focus on the origin of the endowment (e.g., types of founders, and a general emphasis on grantmaking), as the distinctive characteristic of foundations. While this is the case with the U.S. Foundation Center's definition, which was developed to specifically target grantmakers, similar approaches were chosen by the European Foundation Centre and the Asia Pacific Philanthropic Consortium (Strachwitz, 1998). Although operating foundations are historically the older form, the surge of grantmaking foundations in the twentieth century—and among them, towering institutions such as the Ford, Rockefeller and Carnegie foundations—has directed most attention and research toward the grantmaking aspect. Indeed, the relatively few largest grantmaking foundations began to symbolize in popular understanding the essence of foundations in the United States (cf. Margo, 1992, p. 208). As a result, seldom has an organizational form been more neglected than that of operating foundations, and recent research overlooks this type of foundation almost entirely. Based on the common assumption that foundations are primarily grantmaking institutions, research is largely guided by a paradigm, which treats foundations solely as funding intermediaries for the nonprofit sector and defines their role predominantly in relation to their grantees (see, e.g., Margo, 1992; Freeman, 1991; Nason, 1989; Odendahl, 1987; DiMaggio, 1986). The research focus has therefore been on the distributional impact of foundations on the nonprofit sector rather than on the way foundations operate. In most studies, operating foundations receive thus only a brief mention, such as "[their] work is performed mostly in-house (usually in the form of direct service and/or research) and only occasionally by subsidizing the activities of others" (Ylvisaker, 1987, p. 361). Interestingly, the situation in Europe is somewhat different. Medieval hospice foundations survived over the centuries[2], and transformed into modern hospitals or homes for the elderly, the disabled or the needy, they remain vital parts of the European foundation communities. Joined more recently by research institutes and cultural institutions in foundation form, operating foundations either dominate the foundation sectors in some countries, such as Italy and France (see Barbetta, Chapter 10, and Archambault, Boumendil, & Tysboula, Chapter 9; this volume), or account for a substantial part of the total foundation universe, as is the case in Germany with approximately one-third of all foundations (Toepler, 1996).

While operating foundations maintain a strong and visible presence in European foundation communities, the U.S. bias toward grantmaking might be due to incorrect perceptions of the actual size and scope of the operating part of the foundation sector. Indeed, it is a widespread belief—even within the operating foundation field—that there are only very few operating foundations in the United States. The 1991–1992 Report of the J. Paul Getty Trust, for instance, states: "As a private operating foundation, the Trust belongs to the relatively small group of philanthropic organizations that create and ad-

minister their own non-profit programs, in contrast to grantmaking foundations, which fund the programs of others" (p. 1). The apparent obscurity
certainly contributes to the lack of knowledge about and interest in operating
foundations. Especially with respect to their scope of activities and fields of
interest, deeper insight than the somewhat monolithic assumption that operating foundations either provide services or conduct research is not easy to
obtain. Anecdotal evidence, however, suggests that operating foundations engage in a broad variety of purposes and "virtually every endeavor humankind
has ever conceived" (Foote, 1985b, p. 14). Activities range from the distribution of cash assistance to indigent persons from Britain and the Common-
wealth, as is the purpose of the St. George's Society of New York[3] to the
operation of museums, as is the case with the Getty Trust, the largest of its
kind. This variety and scope itself justifies a more thorough analysis.

In part, the focus on the grantmaking activities of those operating foundations that have such programs contributes to an underestimation of the operating segment of the foundation field as well. Operating foundations with grants
programs constituted only 5.3 percent of the more than 33,300 U.S. grantmaking foundations in 1991 and accounted for only 1.6 percent of the total value
of all grants (Renz & Lawrence, 1993, p. 2). Although the number of corporate
foundations was roughly the same, they disbursed more than 16 percent of all
grants. Even community foundations, though five times smaller in number,
contributed three and a half times more in grant money to the nonprofit sector
(ibid.).

The common emphasis on grantmaking leads, however, to a mispercep-
tion of the U.S. foundation community as a whole. Of a total of about 35,700
U.S. foundations, as detailed in the Foundation Center's *Guide to U.S. Foundations, Their Trustees, Officers, and Donors* (Murphy & Seabourne, 1993), total
assets of those operating foundations with $1 million or more in assets ex-
ceeded $15.2 billion (see Table 8.2) and represented 9.3 percent of total
foundation assets. In terms of numbers and assets, operating foundations thus
constitute a far more important part of the foundation community than corporate and community foundations combined. Symptomatic of this "grantmaking bias" is the fact that only the J. Paul Getty Trust, which has an incidental
grant program, was listed among the fifty largest U.S. foundations in 1991
(Renz & Lawrence, 1993, Table 16), although in terms of assets, at least two
other operating foundations, the Casey Family Program and the Kimbell Art
Foundation, would have qualified for inclusion as well.

The purpose of this chapter is to shed some more light on this long-
neglected segment of the foundation sector in the United States. A brief discussion of the characteristics of operating foundations is followed by an empirical
overview of scope and structure and an exploration of the general tax and legal
regulation governing U.S. foundations in order to determine legal factors that

Table 8.1. The Ten Largest U.S. Operating Foundations by Asset Size
(in Thousand Dollars), 1991

	Grants	Assets	Gifts received	Expenditures
J. Paul Getty Trust	8,227	5,251,845	86	86,959
Casey Family Program	0	728,644	565,883	23,696
Kimbell Art Foundation	0	577,467	73	4,781
Norton Simon Art Foundation	0	403,431	0	615
Norton Simon Foundation	2	362,084	309	139
Longwood Gardens	72	244,227	1,469	21,458
Mather Foundation	844	145,790	3,246	8,535
Liliuokalani Trust	0	142,470	0	7,203
Lannan Foundation	1,795	141,375	0	4,350
Liberty Fund	197	140,673	0	5,449
TOTAL	11,137	8,138,006	571,066	163,185

SOURCE: Compiled from listing in Murphy and Seabourne (1993).

might give shape to the operating foundation universe. As we will see, the U.S. tax regulation of foundations provides a somewhat haphazard definition of operating foundations that does not appear to be appropriate for analytical purposes. In order to assess the potential distortions that might arise from following the tax law in matters of classification, I contrast the American legal definition with a more functional one, as common in Europe.

WHY OPERATING FOUNDATIONS?

While the structural differences between grantmaking foundations and other nonprofits are considerable, in the case of operating foundations, however, it might be argued that "[c]onceptually, they are closer in function to the typical nonprofit firm than the other types of foundations" (Margo, 1992, p. 210). In a way, operating foundations combine the economic independence, inherent to the endowed foundation form, with the service-delivery aspects of nonprofit service providers. The main difference to grantmaking foundations is that operating foundations do not rely on third parties (i.e., grantees) to pursue their purposes and thus allow for "more direct donor participation in specific charitable operations" (Rudney, 1987, p. 195). The key distinction to typical nonprofits relates to the financial independence from other stakeholders (e.g., funders). Operating foundations leave the donor a high degree of control (cf. Foote, 1985a, pp. 14–15). Such control and participation is less likely in other nonprofit service providers, where funding restraints may also lead to compromises in regard to the services offered and shared control between different groups of demand-side stakeholders (Gronbjerg, 1993).

Perhaps more importantly, operating foundations not only allow donor participation and control, but also the pursuit of very specific preferences or demands of the donor that might not otherwise be addressed by the nonprofit sector. As indicated earlier, data on operating foundations are scarce and do not allow for more than exemplary evidence. So far, the only sources for some descriptive background information on operating foundations are two articles in *Foundation News* (Foote, 1985a, 1985b). Some of the examples given there tend broadly to support the assumption. For instance, the James F. Lincoln Arc Welding Foundation—offering awards to innovative research on this process— was established when the further development of arc welding depended on more research (Foote, 1985b, pp. 20–21). In instances such as this, operating foundations indeed reflect very specific demand. This form may be the better choice, since the success of grantmaking foundations as financial intermediaries depends on the availability of suitable grantees for carrying out the intended purposes that perhaps may not yet exist. In some cases, such as Deutsches Altenheim in Massachusetts or Altenheim–Home for the Aged in West Virginia, there are indications that even ethnic heterogeneity results in the establishment of operating foundations. In other instances, operating foundations occupy niches that are not likely to be covered by more generally supported organizations. Museums for Western heritage, glass, dolls, toys and miniatures, and combat jets, for example, would fall into this category. Additionally, operating foundations will be the means of choice for the preservation of memorials or monuments if other support is not available, or for maintaining collections in a specific context. John Paul Getty's original stipulation to display his collection in his home[4]—as well as the quite famous case of the Barnes Collection, can serve as examples for the latter case. Considering the scarce information that is available, it seems safe to assume that operating foundations indeed are designed for very specific purposes, reflecting the donor's preferences; or as a foundation officer put it: "The donor says, 'The world needs an organization to do such and such, and nobody else is doing it, so I'll do it.' It has the notion of uniqueness, the notion of doing something in your own image in your lifetime" (quoted in Foote, 1985a, p. 19). But what is it that operating foundations do, and what means do they have at their disposal?

OPERATING FOUNDATIONS IN THE UNITED STATES: AN EMPIRICAL SKETCH

Scope

As commonly held, operating foundations either directly provide services or conduct research. Since they have not attracted much attention so far, it is almost impossible to gather correct data as to the kind of services provided. The listing in the Foundation Center's *Guide to U.S. Foundations, Their Trust-*

ees, Officers, and Donors (Murphy & Seabourne, 1993) does not include information on purpose and activities. A well-founded and comprehensive picture, therefore, is not yet achievable. For most of the 849 operating foundations with $1 million or more in assets in 1991,[5] however, a tentative classification is possible[6] (Table 8.2) if information on operating foundations included in the *Foundation Directory*, periodical articles, and available foundation reports are taken into account. In other cases, the foundation's name (museum, home for the aged, arboretum, etc.) gives a safe clue as to the type of the provided service. Nevertheless, this grouping is still quite vague, and a review necessitates some caution.

Of 849 operating foundations, 511, or 60 percent, have been classified. These represent roughly 73 percent of total assets, 72 percent of expenditures, 70 percent of grants paid, and 59 percent of gifts received.[7] In terms of numbers, almost 30 percent operate homes for the aged and disabled. One-fourth operate in culture and recreation, most of which run museums, galleries, and art collections. Almost 17 percent conduct research and other educational activities. Animal protection and environmental purposes—the latter including parks, gardens, arboreta, and nature preserves and conservancies—rank fourth, with slightly more than 11 percent, followed by social services, development and housing, health services, and other (Table 8.2).

Looking at the assets, the situation is quite different. Even without the Getty Trust, cultural and arts foundations (44 percent) held more than twice as many assets as research and educational organizations, which accounted for one-fifth. Homes held 15.5 percent, and environmental foundations 10 percent. Homes for the aged or disabled and research foundations together accounted for more than half of all expenditures, and museums and environmental organizations accounted for an additional twenty percent. With respect to gifts received, the fields of arts and culture received almost 38 percent, education and research almost 32 percent, homes roughly 13 percent, and environment 11.5 percent.

It becomes quite clear at this point that the activities of operating foundations concentrate in these four areas. Moreover, within these areas, a further concentration can be identified. Museums, galleries, and collections dominate culture and recreation; homes are the single most important type of institution; educational purposes are virtually unimportant compared to research; and environment—mostly arboreta, parks, and gardens—towers above animal protection. The data thus suggest that the operating form is especially suitable for a few specific purposes.

However, do these major fields of activity significantly differ from the main funding domains of grantmaking foundations or, more generally, those of the nonprofit sector as a whole? Table 8.3 compares the percent distribution of expenditures of operating foundations with the distributions of grant dollars of grantmaking foundations and operating expenditures of the nonprofit sector. As demonstrated in Table 8.3, significant differences emerge between the fields of activity of operating and the funding domains of grantmaking foundations. The field of arts and culture drew about one-fourth of operating foundation expenditures but only 14 percent of grant dollars. While one-fourth of all grant dollars went to education, operating foundations maintain hardly any presence in this field, with only 4 percent of their expenditures. By contrast, operating foundations are considerably more strongly engaged in research, with 26 percent versus 9 percent of grantmaker dollars. Health and human services take up about the same share of expenditures and grant volume, respectively, with slightly more then 30 percent. However, in the case of operating foundations, nursing and residential homes account for most of the expenditures. Operating foundations show twice the presence in the environmental field (11 percent vs. 5 percent), but are significantly less active in the international and public/society benefit (i.e., civic activities, community development, philanthropy, and public affairs) areas.

Perhaps more interesting are the differences that emerge in comparing the expenditures of operating foundations and the nonprofit sector. Given the assumption that operating foundations are conceptually closer to other nonprofit organizations, a lesser degree of variations should be expected. However, as Table 8.3 shows, this is not the case. Indeed, the fields of arts and culture, research, and environment are considerably more strongly represented in the operating foundation segment than in the nonprofit sector as a whole, exemplifying the prevalence of museums, research institutes, or arboreta and nature preserves among operating foundations.

On the other hand, operating foundations are significantly less present in key fields of nonprofit activity such as education and health and human services. Specifically, the share of operating foundation expenditures in the area of education is one-fifth of that of the nonprofit sector as a whole and about half in health and human services. This finding might be explained by the fact that certain types of institutions accounting for major parts of general nonprofit expenditures do not take the form of operating foundation. In particular, these are colleges and universities, which account for 65 percent of overall nonprofit operating expenditures in education, and hospitals, accounting for 71 percent of combined nonprofit operating expenditures in health and human services (computed from Salamon, Anheier, & Sokolowski, 1996, Table 9.1).

Finances

In principle, one would expect operating foundations—like their grantmaking counterparts—to enjoy a certain financial independence due to

Table 8.2. U.S. Operating Foundations, Classified by ICNPO Groups, 1991

Groups	Number	%	Assets	%	Expenditures	%	Gifts received	%
Arts and Culture	125	24.5	2,969,343	43.7	128,853	23.4	83,992	37.6
Museums, galleries, etc.[a]	55	10.8	1,829,657	27.0	68,875	11.1	61,638	27.6
Libraries	15	2.9	138,647	2.0	7,486	1.4	1,514	0.7
Historic preservation, etc.	22	4.3	186,119	2.7	16,662	3.0	7,765	3.5
Arts unclassidied	33	6.5	814,920	12.0	43,830	8.0	13,075	5.9
Recreation	3	0.6	22,874	0.3	2,440	0.4	94	0.0
Total culture and recreation	128	25.0	2,992,217	44.1	131,293	23.8	84,086	37.6
Education	12	2.3	206,476	3.0	20,263	3.7	7,593	3.4
Research	74	14.5	1,152,992	17.0	141,792	25.7	63,181	28.3
Total education and research	86	16.8	1,359,468	20.0	162,055	29.4	70,774	31.7
Health services	19	3.7	94,798	1.4	22,855	4.1	2,922	1.3
Homes	153	29.9	1,053,716	15.5	135,625	24.6	29,628	13.3
Social services[b]	20	3.9	114,319	1.7	11,359	2.1	3,083	1.4

Income support	12	2.3	154,747	2.3	7,326	1.3	1,982	0.9
Total social services	32	6.3	269,066	4.0	18,685	3.4	5,065	2.3
Environment	40	7.8	619,206	9.1	51,814	9.4	22,773	10.2
Animals	18	3.5	64,553	1.0	6,243	1.1	2,810	1.3
Total environment	58	11.4	683,759	10.1	58,057	10.5	25,583	11.5
Community development	6	1.2	52,720	0.8	4,116	0.7	2,412	1.1
Housing	12	2.3	32,974	0.5	5,474	1.0	744	0.3
Other	2	0.4	2,502	0.0	173	0.0	122	0.1
Total development and housing	20	3.9	88,196	1.3	9,763	1.8	3,278	1.5
Other	15	2.9	246,452	3.6	12,494	2.3	2,094	0.9
TOTAL	511	100.0	6,787,672	100.0	550,827	100.0	223,430	100.0
Total classified	511	60.2	6,787,672	44.6	550,827	62.5	223,430	23.7
Getty/Casey	2	0.2	5,980,489	39.3	110,655	12.6	565,969	60.0
Total unclassified	336	39.6	2,459,065	16.1	219,909	25.0	153,804	16.3
GRAND TOTAL	849	100	15,227,226	100	881,391	100	943,203	100

Note. Assets, grants, expenditures, and gifts in thousands: [a]excludes J. Paul Getty Trust; [b]excludes Casey Family Program.
SOURCE: Compiled form listing in Murphy and Seabourne (1993).

Table 8.3. Fields of Activity of Grantmaking and Operating Foundations
and the Nonprofit Sector, 1990–1991

	Operating foundations (% of expenditures)	Grantmaking foundations (% of grant dollars)	Nonprofit sector (% of operating expenditures)
Arts and culture	24	14	3
Education	4	25	20
Research/science	26	9	3
Health and human services	32	31	63
Environment	11	5	1
Public/society benefit	2	10	3
International	0	4	1
Other	1	2	6
TOTAL	100	100	100

SOURCE: Table 2; Renz & Lawrence (1993); Salamon, Anheier, & Sokolowski (1996).

endowment income. The median asset size, however, is around $4 million[8] (see Table 8.4). In this respect, for the majority of foundations, it is questionable whether endowment income suffices in order to operate an institution. A comparison between median and average endowment sizes highlights certain differences between the four main types of operating foundations. On average, arts foundations are considerably better endowed than any other type, indicating that some museums hold very large assets. Interestingly, the assets of homes for the aged or disabled range even below total average, and this foundation type also receives the least in gifts. Both facts may imply that there is an "optimal" asset size for different types of operation depending on the scope of operations and on the availability of other sources of income. The low ranking of homes in terms of assets and gifts received can probably be best explained by their ability to raise income in form of fees for services. Nursing homes, in general, receive 49 percent of their spending from private consumers (Salamon, 1992, p. 59), whereas earnings—including admission, store, and restaurant revenues—account for only 17.5 percent of all revenue sources in the case of art museums[9] (Rosett, 1991, p. 142). In contrast to grantmakers, which due to the very nature of their mode of operation do not necessarily need other financial sources even when they have few assets, it seems that the majority of operating foundations have to generate additional income. On the other hand, in the isolated case, even smaller endowments can provide enough income for the intended operations.

For example, the Tudor Place Foundation maintains a museum in a historic house and garden in Washington, DC, with assets only slightly higher than the median size for foundations operating museums. Its investment in-

Table 8.4. Median and Average Financial Structure in Selected Areas (in Thousands)

	Grants	Assets	Gifts	Expenditures
Museums, galleries, collections (n = 55)				
Median	0	4,410	97	373
Average	48	33,883	1,141	1,127
Homes (n = 153)				
Median	0	3.771	10	412
Average	9	6,886	194	888
Research (n = 74)				
Median	2	3,936	146	503
Average	140	15,581	854	1,916
Environment (n = 40)				
Median	0	4,299	122	404
Average	35	16,396	597	1,361
All (n = 847)				
Median	0	3,278	33	315
Average	68	10,917	446	910

come and dividends, however, account for close to 77 percent of revenues, and 79 percent of operating expenses in 1991. The remainder comprises primarily private contributions. Two grants from governmental agencies, such as the Institute of Museum Services, represent only a small fraction of that year's budget. The foundation's relative financial independence in this case is certainly made possible by an extensive and successful volunteer program (see Tudor Place Foundation, 1992). Another DC foundation, the Cato Institute, which conducts public policy research, relies heavily on sophisticated fundraising through a sponsors program. With an endowment of about $5 million, private contributions are actively sought. Accordingly, the foundation's self-description reads: "In order to maintain an independent posture, the Cato Institute accepts no government funding. Contributions are received from foundations, corporations, and individuals, and other revenue is generated from the sale of publications."

The size of assets, however, does not necessarily give the right clues as to the financial self-sufficiency of an operating foundation. Even some of the larger foundations seek other sources. The Charles F. Kettering Foundation, for instance, a project-oriented organization working in the policy field as well, ranks eleventh under the largest U.S. operating foundations. An informational folder, nevertheless, contends: "Kettering works primarily through partnerships with other organizations in the United States and around the world. . . . Its endowment of $140 million provides roughly a third of the resources for the programs. Therefore, the Foundation actively seeks joint ventures with organizations that share in similar interests." In conclusion, the degree to which endowment income covers the operating expenses of operating foundations varies widely. It seems more dependent on the type of activity than on the size of the endowment. Nevertheless, operating foundations appear to be largely self-funded and rely less on external private or government funding than other nonprofit organizations. One of the major reasons for this, however, lies in the legal definition, as operating foundations would be reclassified as public charities, if they were to receive substantial government or private funding. The following section discusses the legal regulation of operating foundations to explain some of the findings.

LEGAL DEFINITIONS AND REGULATION[10]

Earlier, I defined foundations as asset-holding institutions, usually endowed by a single donor, that are dedicated to charitable or philanthropic causes and have organizational structures to fulfill their objectives. This definition largely follows legal definitions as common in Europe, and, like the general legal regulation in the European tradition, it does not distinguish between grantmaking and operating foundations. Indeed, in countries other than the United States, the difference between operating and grantmaking foundations is seen as a functional one, depending mainly on donors' intentions or the way a foundation sees itself, but has no further legal bearing.

Whereas European legal systems usually adopt positive definitions of foundations, similar to the one used in this chapter, U.S. tax law differs considerably in this respect. According to section 501(c)(3) of the Internal Revenue Code, a private foundation is an organization that is organized and operated exclusively for charitable, religious, educational, scientific, literary, and so on, purposes. In the logic of the tax system, section 501(c)(3) is primarily designed for private foundations, although the majority of organizations qualifying under it are public charities: "Every organization that qualifies for tax exemption as an organization described in section 501(c)(3) is a private foundation unless it falls into one of the categories specifically excluded from the definition of that term" (Internal Revenue Service, 1992, p. 18). Accordingly, even if an organization falls into the excluded categories, it is presumed to be a private foundation until it gives timely notice that it is not. Private foundation, therefore, is a residual category, and the term *foundation* is negatively defined.

Four categories of exclusions are laid out in section 509(a). Section 509(a)(1) defines the main types of excluded organizations. Explicitly mentioned are churches, schools or colleges, and hospitals or medical research organizations; other publicly supported organizations also fall into this section as well as organizations operated for the benefit of certain state and municipal colleges and universities, and governmental units. All publicly supported organizations, except the specifically mentioned types, must pass a support test, which is satisfied when the organization normally receives at least one-third of its total support from governmental units and/or from contributions made by the general public. Section 509(a)(2) excludes publicly supported organizations that are not only governmentally or publicly supported, but also receive income on their own. In these cases, organizations must receive at least one-third of their support from grants, contributions, and related income, but no more than one-third from investment and unrelated business income.

So far, organizations are excluded from private foundation status under section 509(a) that either conduct specific, explicitly mentioned types of activities or that are broadly supported by the general public. Section 509(a)(3) furthermore excludes organizations that may be endowed by a single donor, family, or corporation. Entities classified here are supporting organizations that have close relationships with 509(a)(1) or (2) organizations, and are established exclusively for the benefit of, for performing the functions of, or for carrying out the purposes of the latter. 509(a)(3) organizations must be operated, supervised, or controlled either by or in connection with publicly supported organizations. They give up a significant degree of independence and cannot be controlled by disqualified persons, which include, among others, family members of the founder as well as all substantial contributors to the foundation. The fourth category excludes organizations for the purpose of testing products for public safety.

The residual (i.e., all 501(c)(3) organizations not exempted under section 509) are classified as private foundations that have in common the fact that they lack significant public support. For private operating foundations, an additional subcategory was introduced by the Tax Reform Act of 1969. According to the then-introduced definition, operating foundations "make qualifying distributions directly for the active conduct of their educational, charitable, and religious purposes, as distinct from merely making grants to other organizations for these purposes" (Internal Revenue Service, 1992, p. 31). Although most of the restrictions on private foundations in general also apply to operating foundations, they enjuoy some advantages. For instance, donors can deduct charitable contributions at the same percentages as for donations to public charities. Contributions to private grantmaking foundations, in contrast, have considerably lower deduction limits. Grantmaking foundations that contribute to operating foundations face lighter monitoring burdens, as they do for contributions to other grantmakers. Furthermore, operating foundations are not subject to the 5 percent payout requirement.

To qualify for the status of operating foundation, a private foundation must pass an income test and one other test that can be either an asset, a support, or an endowment test. The basic income test prescribes that qualifying distributions for the active conduct of activities must equal at least 85 percent of either the adjusted net income or the minimum investment return, whichever is less. Qualifying contributions include administrative expenses as well as assets acquired for the direct execution of the tax-exempt purposes. Each of the additional tests is basically designed to reflect the specific needs of certain types of purposes. The assets test is intended to apply to museums, libraries, and similar institutions; the support test to special-purpose foundations; and the endowment test to organizations such as research foundations (for details, see Internal Revenue Service, 1992, p. 31).

Another subcategory, exempt operating foundations, was created in 1984. Exempt operating foundations are—in contrast to other operating and non-operating foundations—not subject to the excise tax on net investment income. In order to qualify, an organization must already be an operating foundation and have received public support for at least ten years. In addition, at all times of the year, the governing body has to be broadly representative of the general public, and not more than one-fourth of its members can be disqualified individuals. Furthermore, disqualified individuals may not serve as foundation officers.

THE EXCLUSIONARY NATURE OF THE U.S. TAX CLASSIFICATION

This sophisticated system of exclusions and its resulting negative definition of foundations leads to a number of complications concerning the difference between operating foundations and public charities.

First, since churches, schools and colleges, hospitals, and medical research organizations are explicitly mentioned in section 509 of the Internal Revenue Code, these kinds of institutions receive public charity status automatically, even if they would not pass the public support test. Although many of these organizations could be regarded as operating foundations from a functional point of view, they are usually not counted as such by virtue of their tax classification. Therefore, the differences in composition between the operating foundation segment and the nonprofit sector as a whole in the education and health and human service fields appear to be due to the fact that colleges and hospitals cannot be operating foundations *per definitionem*. On the other hand, the artificial exclusion of such institutions from the operating foundation field might obscure the real size of this sector. The twenty-five best-endowed institutions of higher education would qualify for inclusion among the fifty largest foundations with respect to asset size (see Nicklin, 1993). Moreover, in addition to endowment funds, many universities have related foundations. Since these foundations often are technically part of the university systems (Foote, 1985a, p. 16), they are generally not included in foundation statistics.

Clearly, from a functional point of view, the boundaries between operating foundations and public charities are somewhat fuzzy and may be blurred even further by discretionary classification decisions at the tax administration level. The salient example is the Howard Hughes Medical Institute (HHMI), which, according to a settlement agreement with the Internal Revenue Service, is classified as medical research organization, although it is formed by an endowment and held assets of almost $7 billion in 1991 (Renz & Lawrence, 1993, p. 11). Had the outcome of the "settlement" been different, the HHMI would be the largest foundation in terms of assets—considerably larger than the Ford Foundation. By the same token, the HHMI clearly stands out among medical research organizations. The *Nonprofit Almanac* (Hodgkinson, Weitzman, Toppe, & Noga, 1993, p. 278) shows that more than 70 percent of total assets of medical research organizations are concentrated in Maryland, where the HHMI is located.

Second, the somewhat volatile and artificial distinctions that the tax code draws also explain the strong presence of U.S. operating foundations in the area of arts and culture. Since museums, for example, are not explicitly mentioned in section 509(a)(1), endowed institutions of this kind are normally operating foundations. The introduction of the hybrid exempt operating form was actually intended to ameliorate the disadvantaged position of endowed museums and similar institutions vis-à-vis hospitals and colleges. Beckwith and DeSirgh (1987, p. 282) note in this context that the creation of an exempt operating foundation category was "a significant development in that it signals the inability of Congress to develop or specify a generic definition for institutions such as museums and libraries—as it has done for such entities as churches, universities, and hospitals. Consequently, many of these institutions are classified as private foundations." Without doubt, had museums and libraries been specifically included under section 509(a)(1), the U.S. operating foundation sector would be considerably smaller than it is today.

Last, the residual character of the classification of foundations contributes to blurry boundaries between operating foundations and other nonprofits in just another way. Following the tax definition, foundations are organizations that neither directly engage in specific activities nor receive broad support from government or the general public. Thus failed public charities (i.e., organizations that did not or have not yet succeeded in attracting a sufficient amount of public support) are automatically included in the private foundation category. Since these organizations are normally neither able nor willing to make primarily grants to other organizations, they end up classified as operating foundations. Since having significant assets is not a constitutive characteristic for a purely technical classification as operating foundation,

Table 8.5. Number and Assets of Endowed Institutions (Assets in Millions)

Type	Number	%	Assets	%
Nonoperating foundation[a]	31,586	73.7	153,419	32.2
Operating foundations[b]	849	2.0	15,227	3.2
Institutions of higher education[c]	3,382	7.9	125,799	26.4
Hospitals[d]	6,356	14.8	172,811	36.3
Medical research organizations	695	1.6	9,128	1.9
TOTAL	42,868	100.0	476,384	100.0

Note. Foundations circa 1991; all others circa 1988: [a]independent, corporate, and community founda-
tions; [b]assets of $1 million or more; [c]includes graduate/professional; [d]includes convalescent facilities.
SOURCES: Renz and Lawrence (1993): Table 2; Murphy and Seabourne (1993); Hodgkinson et al. (1993):
Tables 6.B.3, 6.E.3, 6.H.3.

many U.S. operating foundations are indeed not operating foundations, but "nonpublic charities," as John Simon put it. Of 484 operating foundations in the state of New York, for example, roughly one-third have assets of less than $50,000, and more than 5 percent have assets of less than $1,000.

It becomes clear at this point that the choice between the legalistic American and a more functional approach to the classification of foundations has a severe impact on the size of the operating foundation sector. If a functional approach is chosen, the combined assets of grantmaking foundations have to be put in perspective by including public charities with significant endowments in the analysis of operating foundations. Although those "nonpublic charities" currently listed as operating foundations would have to be subtracted, the loss would be offset by adding other endowed institutions. Judging from this point of view, the U.S. operating sector would be considerably larger than it appears to be now. Table 8.5 shows the accumulated assets of grantmaking and operating foundations, as well as the assets of some types of public charities that are specifically excluded by law from the private (operating) foundation category. Although grantmaking foundations still account for close to three-fourths of all endowed institutions, their combined assets constitute merely one-third of the total.

CONCLUSION

The intention of this chapter was to explore a segment of the U.S. foundation community that has long been neglected as well as misrepresented by analysts. While operating foundations in Europe have long been acknowledged as an important, sometimes even predominant, part of the local foundation communities, the "grantmaking bias" in the United States has relegated these institutions to a "shadow existence." However, as shown, operating foundations account for a much larger share of the total foundation sector in the United States than commonly recognized. The data presented here also demonstrated significant differences in structure and composition between the operating foundation, grantmaking foundation, and total nonprofit sectors. To a large extent, these differences can be explained with the peculiarities of the tax regulation and definition of foundations. The analysis also suggested that the tax law approach to defining operating foundations might not be the most appropriate way to capture this organizational form fully because of somewhat artificial exclusions.

Indeed, for comparative purposes, the divergent approaches to the definition of foundations may easily carry the danger of comparing apples to oranges, as long as the cross-national differences in the treatment of operating foundations are not sufficiently accounted for. One way to circumvent the problem is to restrict comparative analysis to grantmaking foundations (as done by Anheier and Romo, Chapter 4, this volume), thereby adopting the American view of foundations as financial intermediaries. However, this would exclude large segments of the foundation sectors elsewhere. This approach would substantially reduce the scope of the German foundation sector and likely let the small, largely operating foundation communities in countries such as France and Italy disappear from view completely. Adversely, as demonstrated, including operating foundations, that is, endowed institutions, into the analysis also leads to a number of significant problems. In this case, the question arises where to draw the line between true foundations and other organizations that happen to have endowments. Clearly, definitions that emphasize the existence of a single founder–donor as an additional characteristic to differentiate between foundations and other organizations are not on the mark either. While this might help preclude organizations that raised endowments from a large number of smaller donations, that same might be true for organizations that had a founder–donor providing a small initial endowment that grew, however, over time by additions from multiple sources.

To the extent that an operating foundation "essentially acts like a well-endowed nonprofit organization" (Schearer, 1997, p. 307), it might arguably indeed be preferable to adopt the first approach of concentrating on grantmaking foundations, as they embody the more distinctive characteristics of the foundation form. Especially with regard to foundations that basically operate service-providing institutions, such as nursing homes, hospitals, or museums, it appears questionable whether there are indeed sufficient differences between these foundations and similar, endowed institutions in other legal forms to justify a separate analysis. However, while such organizations constitute the majority of operating foundations in the United States as elsewhere, there is another type of operating foundation that perhaps deserves closer attention.

These foundations operate their own projects and programs rather than institutions. The recent emergence of a number of such project-oriented operating foundations in countries such as Germany is viewed as an indication of a new pattern in the establishment of foundations, which, according to some observers, may alter the future composition of the foundation sector (Strachwitz, 1994). Moreover, project-oriented operating foundations are also frequently seen as important carriers of societal functions (Strickrodt, 1977, p. 565). Whether or not this will be the case, these projections are based on the assumption that project-oriented operating foundations provide a more suitable organizational form for an "active" pursuit of foundation policies as opposed to the administrative-reactive character of traditional grantmakers. In the light of recent criticism of the short-term, uninvolved funding practices of U.S. foundations (see Letts, Ryan, & Grosman, 1997), a reevaluation of operating foundations as an alternative philanthropic vehicle might prove useful.

NOTES

1. This chapter is based on a research report that was prepared for the International Fellows in Philanthropy Program at the Johns Hopkins Institute for Policy Studies.
2. The oldest still existing foundations of this type in Germany date back to the tenth century (Strachwitz, 1994; Toepler, 1996).
3. The St. George's Society—established in 1770—is perhaps among the oldest still existing foundations in the United States.
4. In December 1997, the Getty Museum moved to a new, $1 billion complex in Los Angeles that also houses several other programs and institutes operated by the Getty Trust.
5. The exclusion of the vast majority of operating foundations seems justifiable insofar as a good part of the smallest are operating foundations only in a very technical sense. Due to the specifics of definition for tax law purposes, it is reasonable to assume the many of these are not foundations but regular nonprofits that have not been able so far to attract enough public support in order to classify as public charity (to be discussed).
6. The classification system used here is the *International Classification of Nonprofit Organizations* (ICNPO, Salamon & Anheier, 1997, Chapter 4).
7. In order to minimize distortions, the J. Paul Getty Trust and the Casey Family Program are excluded. Otherwise, 513 operating foundations would represent 84 percent of combined assets, 75 percent of expenditures, 70 percent of grants paid, and 84 percent of gifts received.
8. Not including the bulk of operating foundations with assets of less than $1 million.
9. Excluding endowment income.
10. This section draws heavily on the Internal Revenue Service (1992). For brief descriptions of the legal regulations concerning operating foundations, see also Freeman, 1991, pp. 169–170; Beckwith & DeSirgh, 1987, pp. 280–282.

REFERENCES

Beckwith, E., & DeSirgh, J. (1987). Tax law and private foundations. In T. Odendahl (Ed.), *America's Wealthy and the Future of Foundations* (pp. 267–293). New York: Foundation Center.

Coing, H. (1981). Remarks on the history of foundations and their role in the promotion of learning. *Minerva, 19,* 271–281.

DiMaggio, P. J. (1986). Support for the arts from independent foundations. In P. J. DiMaggio (Ed.), *Nonprofit Enterprises in the Arts* (pp. 113–139). New York: Oxford University Press.

Foote, J. (1985a). Service unlimited. *Foundation News, 26*(4), 11–19.

Foote, J. (1985b). You name it, they do it. *Foundation News, 26*(5), 14–25.

Freeman, D. F., & Council on Foundations. (1991). *The Handbook on Private Foundations.* New York: Foundation Center.

Gronbjerg, U. (1993). *Understanding Nonprofit Funding.* San Francisco: Jossey-Bass.

Hodgkinson, V., Weitzman, M., Toppe, C., & Noga, S. (1993). *Nonprofit Almanac 1992–1993.* San Francisco: Jossey-Bass.

Internal Revenue Service. (1992). *Tax-Exempt Status for Your Organization.* Publication 557 (Rev. Jan. 92). Washington, DC: Department of the Treasury, Internal Revenue Service.

Letts, C., Ryan, W., & Grosman, A. (1997). Virtuous capital: What foundations can learn from venture capitalists. *Harvard Business Review, 2,* 36–44.

Margo, R. A. (1992). Foundations. In C. T. Clotfelter (Ed.), *Who Benefits from the Nonprofit Sector?* (pp. 207–234). Chicago & London: University of Chicago Press.

Murphy, C., & Seabourne, J. (Ed.). (1993). *Guide to U.S. Foundations, Their Trustees, Officers, and Donors.* New York: Foundation Center.

Nason, J. (1989). *Foundation Trusteeship: Service in the Public Interest.* New York: Foundation Center.

Nicklin, J. (1993, February 10). Colleges' earnings on endowment averaged 13.1% in fiscal 1992. *Chronicle of Higher Education.*

Odendahl, T. (1987). Foundations and the nonprofit sector. In T. Odendahl (Ed.), *America's Wealthy and the Future of Foundations* (pp. 27–42). New York: Foundation Center.

Renz, L., & Lawrence, S. (1993). *Foundation Giving–Yearbook of Facts and Figures on Private, Corporate and Community Foundations.* New York: Foundation Center.

Rosett, R. N. (1991). Art museums in the United States: A financial portrait. In M. Feldstein (Ed.), *The Economics of Art Museums* (pp. 129–173). Chicago: University of Chicago Press.

Rudney, G. (1987). Creation of foundations and their wealth. In T. Odendahl (Ed.), *America's Wealthy and the Future of Foundations* (pp. 179–202). New York: Foundation Center.

Salamon, L., & Anheier, H. (1997). *Defining the Nonprofit Sector: A Cross-National Analysis.* Manchester, UK: Manchester University Press.

Salamon, L., Anheier, H. & Sokolowski, S. (1996). *The Emerging Sector: A Statistical Supplement.* Baltimore: Johns Hopkins Institute for Policy Studies.

Schearer, S. B. (1997). Building indigenous foundations that support civil society. In L. M. Fox & S. B. Schearer (Eds.), *Sustaining Civil Society: Strategies for Resource Mobilization* (pp. 305–325). Washington, DC: Civicus.

Strachwitz, R. G. (1994). *Stiftungen—nutzen, führen und errichten: Ein Handbuch.* Frankfurt: Campus.

Strachwitz, R. (1998). Operative and fördernde Stiftungen: Anmerkungen zur Typologie. In Bertelsmann Stiftung (Ed.), *Handbuch des Stiftungsmanagements.* (pp. 675–698). Wiesbaden, Germany: Gabler.

Strickrodt, G. (1977). *Stiftungsrecht—Geltende Vorschriften und rechtspolitische Vorschläge.* Baden-Baden, Germany: Nomos.

Toepler, S. (1996). *Das gemeinnützige Stiftungswesen in der modernen demokratischen Gesellschaft.* Munich: Maecenata.

Tudor Place Foundation (1992). *Annual Report.* Washington, DC: Author.

Ylvisaker, P. N. (1987). Foundations and nonprofit organizations. In W. W. Powell (Ed.), *The Nonprofit Sector* (pp. 360–379). New Haven & London: Yale University Press.

Part IV

Country Studies

Perhaps one of the main reasons for the predominance of the U.S. foundation experience in our understanding of foundations at the international level lies in the fact that many other foundation traditions have been, and remain, hidden from view. While some research and discussion may have taken place within the context of specific countries, this knowledge has not been communicated across national borders and has yet to reach the international research community.

The preceding parts of this volume have already highlighted key aspects of foundation sectors in a number of countries, especially the United States, the United Kingdom, and Germany. Other European nations, including the Netherlands, Sweden, Switzerland, Denmark, Belgium, and Spain, appear to boast strong foundation communities as well.

The country studies covered in Part IV, however, largely concentrate on countries where the foundation tradition for various reasons had been disrupted or significantly curtailed and the development of foundations accordingly slowed. As such, the chapters of this part do not explore the success stories, but examine the historical and cultural barriers in the evolution of foundations. The part begins with Archambault, Boumendil, and Tsyboula's discussion (Chapter 9) of the French case, where the Jacobin tradition and the belief in the superiority of government suppressed foundations. Even recent changes in the state's attitude toward foundations have not (yet) resulted in a major revival of this organizational form. A rather similar picture emerges from Barbetta's Chapter 10 on Italy. Interestingly, issues involving the privatization of the Italian savings bank industry are bringing new life to the Italian foundation scene. Both chapters discuss the respective historical and legal framework and also offer an empirical analysis.

Strachwitz's contribution (Chapter 11) explores the East German situation. After 40 years of communism, the break of the foundation tradition there is more recent than in the French case but no less significant. Chapter 12 by Quigley and Popson concerns the role of foundations, and especially Western foundations, in the rebuilding of Central and Eastern European civil societies. Drawing on extensive workshops conducted in the region, they discuss both the successes and drawbacks of the approaches chosen by foundations to assist the transition.

Largely, space constraints have prohibited us from taking this exploration to the next level by extending the analysis to the equally unchartered foundation terrains of Asia, the Arab World, Africa, and Latin America. However, the chapters of this part underscore the value of examining foundations, their history, and legal and policy environments in specific national contexts. We hope that the country chapters presented here will encourage others to conduct similar types of inquiry in their own country, thereby adding to our empirical knowledge and cross-national understanding of philanthropic foundations.

Chapter 9

Foundations in France

EDITH ARCHAMBAULT, JUDITH BOUMENDIL,
AND SYLVIE TSYBOULA

In the Western world, the French foundation sector is perhaps among the least developed. Currently, the sector comprises less than 500 "state-approved" private foundations (*fondations reconnues d'utilité publique*), another thirty corporate foundations, and 400 endowments administered by the *Fondation de France,* the single most important foundation in France. Without doubt, the main explanation for the relative scarcity of foundations in France is the deeply rooted Jacobin tradition, which emphasized centralization and etatism and led to long-lasting conflicts between the central government and foundations and other intermediary bodies. In addition, more recent economic and financial crises as well as depreciation of initial assets have curtailed the means at the disposal of many existing foundations, further limiting the importance and impact of foundations in France (Courtois, 1995). Given the limited size of the foundation community, its role is not well understood by the French public. Indeed, public opinion often vaguely equates foundations with charitable associations, without further distinguishing between these two very different types of organizations.

Besides its small size, the French foundation sector is also characterized by the lack of a grantmaking tradition. The majority of the foundations are

EDITH ARCHAMBAULT • Professor of Economics and Director of the Laboratoire d'Economie sociale, University of Paris 1 Sorbonne 75013, Paris, France.   JUDITH BOUMENDIL • Research Assistant, Laboratoire d'Economie social University of Paris 1 Sorbonne 75013, Paris, France. SYLVIE TSYBOULA • President, Fondation de Jouques, and former Deputy Director, Fondation de France, c/o LES–2 University of Paris 1 Sorbonne 75013, Paris, France.

Private Funds, Public Purpose: Philanthropic Foundations in an International Perspective, edited by Helmut K. Anheier and Stefan Toepler. New York, Plenum Press, 1999.

operating foundations. For example, several important museums and art institutions, such as Vasarely, Arp, Maeght, and the *Institut du Monde Arabe,* are operating foundations, as are the *Fondation Darty, Hôpital Rothschild,* or the *Fondation Garches* in the field of health. Other operating foundations are active in research with the *Institut Pasteur, Fondation Nationale des Sciences Politiques, Maison des Sciences de l'Homme, Fondation Royaumont,* and the *Fondation Curie* as prominent examples, while others again deal with environmental issues, including the *Cousteau* and *Ushuaia* foundations. The few existing grantmaking foundations are often quite small, with the exception of the *Fondation pour la Recherche Médicale* (1964), which was the first foundation to launch mass-media-based fund-raising campaigns, and the *Fondation de France* (1969), the first and only general purpose foundation in France with discretion over the distribution of its grant allocations, which allows it to pursue the venture capital role that has long defined the functions of foundations, especially in the American context. In contrast to other French foundations, the *Fondation de France* is a hybrid institution, both fund-raising and grantmaking in charactrer. In addition, it also embodies parts of the community foundation concept by administering smaller foundations under its umbrella.

On a general level, the underdevelopment of the French foundation sector must be seen in a political–historical context that is marked by a deeply rooted Jacobin tradition of centralization and state organization that, over long stretches of French history, nurtured a conflictual relationship between the central government and any form of local power or intermediary interest groups in general and foundations in particular (Archambault, 1997). Practically outlawed for nearly two centuries, specific legislation governing foundations was only reintroduced into French law as recently as 1987. In a way, the 1980s can be interpreted as a reversal of long-standing governmental attitudes toward foundations, as the 1987 law and subsequent initiatives intended to publicly encourage a revival of "*mécénat*" (i.e., maecenatism or patronage), especially in the field of arts and culture. Nevertheless, these recent legislative activities still place relatively heavy financial and regulatory restrictions on donors and foundations.

While the tacit governmental encouragement did lead to a better overall understanding of foundations in France, the growth of the foundation sector thereafter remained slow and is currently almost stagnant. This contrasts sharply with the dynamic evolution of the association field with approximately 700,000 associations currently in existence and more than 65,000 created every year (Archambault, 1997).

Against this backdrop, the following chapter outlines the historical background of these organizations and analyzes their legal position as well as the differences between the three kinds of foundations: state-approved foundations (*fondations reconnues d'utilité publique*), corporate foundations (*fondations d'enterprise*), and nonautonomous foundations (*fondations abritées*). After describing the size, scope, structure, and evolution of the French foundation sector, we conclude by discussing the contradictory nature of government policy toward foundations, with its mix of encouragements and restrictions.

HISTORICAL DEVELOPMENT

Throughout the Middle Ages, foundations developed in France much as they did in other Continental European countries, mostly in the form of hospitals and asylums to provide care to the poor, the sick, or the elderly under the auspices of the Catholic Church. The Church and some monastic orders, such as the Benedictine and Franciscan orders, successfully acquired bequests and donations, both in kind and in money, for the creation of such foundations. Accordingly, under the *Ancien Régime,* many poorhouse foundations, foundations supporting poor students and ecclesiastics, and also magnificent abbeys, churches, and schools in foundation form existed in France.

However, the wealth that some foundations acquired through legacies and donations began to arouse the suspicion of the state early on, which questioned the accumulation of inalienable property and power beyond the direct control of the state. Soon suspected by the French monarchs as a means to evade royal taxes, Louis XIV and Louis XV began to restrict the rights of existing foundations and prohibited the creation of new ones (Pomey, 1980). Among the central arguments against the control of patrimonies by the "dead hand" was the denunciation of economic inefficiencies resulting from the withdrawal of foundation property from the general circulation of goods. The negative attitudes toward the creation of large patrimonies at that time are perhaps most clearly expressed in Turgot's entry in the Great Encyclopedia edited by Diderot:

> A founder is a man who wants to eternalize his will. . . . No man-made work is everlasting. As foundations, multiplied by vanity, would absorb in the long run all funding and individual property, it is necessary to destroy them. If all the men who ever lived would have had a tomb, it would be necessary to knock down these sterile monuments to find soil to cultivate and to move the ashes of the dead to feed the living. (Quoted in Pomey, 1980, p. 35; transl. by the authors)

The suppression of foundations that had already begun under the *Ancien Régime* continued with renewed vigor after the revolution of 1789 under the influence of the political philosophies developed in Rousseau's *Du Contrat Social* of 1762. Accordingly, the Le Chapelier Act of 1791, while proclaiming the State's monopoly on activities in the general interest, was primarily directed against foundations as well as corporations, guilds, and other forms of intermediate entities, by stipulating that "no one shall be allowed to arouse in any citizen any kind of intermediate interest and to separate him from the nation through the medium of a spirit of corporation."

The ensuing struggle between State and Church led to further substantial consequences for the foundation field, as the property of the clergy and Church-related foundations were seized, and in some cases sold as *biens nationaux* to the rising bourgeoisie, with proceeds resulting from these sales benefiting the state. In the wake of these developments, many schools and charitable institutions had to close. Hospitals were nationalized and subsequently taken over by local government administrations. Although some indemnification to the Church took place during the Restoration Period between 1815 and 1830, foundations had lost their legal status and virtually disappeared until the end of the nineteenth century.

The *Institut Pasteur* was among the first and most notable foundations to mark a limited reappearance of the foundation idea in the late nineteenth century. Louis Pasteur was a prominent member of the civil service. Being disenchanted with the inefficiency of public academic research teams, Pasteur rejected governmental research support after his discovery of rabies treatment in favor of a privately supported research institute. After a successful fund-raising campaign, the *Institut Pasteur* was established in 1887 and remained independent of public subsidies until very recently (Moulin, 1992).

Following Pasteur's lead, a select number of other operating foundations were created before World War I, including the still-existing *Fondation Thiers* (1893), the *Musée Social* (1894), and the *Institut Océanographique* (1906). Others, such as the *Fondations Curie* (1921), *Rothschild* (1921), *Deutsch de la Meurthe* (1922), followed in the interwar period. However, the endowments of many of the institutions that emerged in this first renewal of the foundation sector in France proved vulnerable to the prolonged inflationary trends during and after World War I. As a result, interest in this institutional form ceased again until the mid-1960s.

Today, a second foundation renewal seems to be under way. Indeed, over the last few years, some large corporations have created company-sponsored foundations in new fields such as the environment and education, but above all, in the area of arts and culture. The recent emphasis on the arts has in part been due to the activities of Jack Lang, Minister of Culture in the Socialist governments of the 1980s, who tried to extend available resources for arts through the promotion of *mécénat,* or private sponsorship. The new positive posture of government toward the use of foundations, especially in the field of culture, continued under the conservative government, as the 1995 proposal by the then-Minister of Culture to create a Heritage Foundation demonstrated.

THE LEGAL POSITION

A closer analysis of the legal environment is essential to understand the development and current state of the French foundation sector. It is important to keep in mind that legislation concerning this field is still in the first phases of implementation, since there was no body of law specifically governing foundations until 1987. Before 1987, only general regulations, applicable to a range of nonprofit organizations, were in place. Although foundations were eligible for recognition by the state as a matter of administrative practice, foundations did not exist as a specific legal form and did not enjoy legal status. In all, about 400 of these State-approved foundations, or *fondations reconnues d'utilité publique,* existed prior to 1987.

Currently, foundations are governed by two laws, the Law of July 23, 1987, and the Law of July 4, 1990. The Law of July 23, 1987, aiming at foundations established by individuals, provided for the first time a legal definition, according to which a foundation is "the legal act through which one or several individuals or legal entities decide the irrevocable allocation of estate, rights or resources for a nonprofit making activity of general interest." This definition emphasizes the fact that foundations are based on goods or estates earmarked for public benefit aims as opposed to associations, which are member-based. The subsequent Law of July 4, 1990, spells out the specific conditions under which corporations may create foundations.

In contrast to other countries, the term *foundation* is now legally protected in France and can only be used for organizations covered under either of the two laws: the *fondation reconnue d'utilité publique* (State-approved foundation) or the *fondation d'entreprise* (corporate foundation). However, nonautonomous foundations without legal personality distinct from the one of the organization that administers or "shelters" it also exists as a hybrid form. In the following, we briefly outline the legal regulation applicable to these three types of foundations.

The establishment of a *fondation reconnue d'utilité publique* (RUP), is a lengthy, complicated, and centralized process involving highest state authorities. More specifically, founders must first seek preliminary state authorization signed by the Prime Minister and the Home Office. After this acknowledgment, legal personality is granted through a decree issued by the *Conseil d'État,*[1] and published at the *Journal Officiel.* The *Conseil d'État* also has the power to impose bylaws and to determine whether the endowment suffices to pursue the aim of the foundation. In any case, a minimum endowment of FF 5 million, or approximately $1 million, is required. Since the process may last more than two years, an association supporting the forthcoming foundation is frequently created to fill the gap between the preliminary authorization and the final response by the *Conseil d'État.*

Initially, a *fondation RUP* could only be established *inter vivos*. Since 1990, however, it is also possible to create such a foundation by will. Until 1995, no more than 445 of such foundations were created and the complexity of the authorization process may to a large part explain why. In view of the involvement of highest state powers in the process, it can fairly be assumed that the French government still considers it necessary to closely control and supervise the foundation field. This is further emphasized by the government's right to designate up to one-third of any *fondation RUP*'s board members.

Generally, the legal treatment of state-approved foundations is much stricter and provides considerably more controls than the laws governing other types of nonprofit organizations, especially the 1901 Act on associations. Accordingly, neither private companies nor any form of nonprofit organization (*associations, mutuelles*) are still subjected to this kind of authorization. Associations, for example, may simply register in a *Préfecture* and are under no obligation to invite representatives of public authorities to join its board (Archambault, 1997; Castro, 1997).

While state-approved foundations face close supervision and control, they also enjoy a number of special privileges in exchange. The first set of privileges refers to the legal capacity of these foundations, which is much wider than that of associations. While associations cannot own buildings or real estate, except if directly used for their operations, foundations face no such restrictions. Foundations may also receive gifts and legacies, but certain transactions such as transfers of properties or rights, or loans and mortgages, are subject to state supervision.

The second set of privileges relates to the tax treatment. *Fondations RUP* are allowed to engage in commercial activities, although profits are subject to regular taxation, and activities directly linked with the foundation's aim are generally exempt of V.A.T. and corporation tax. Individuals making donations to *fondations RUP* and registered associations that hold intermediary accounts with such foundations are entitled to a tax credit of 50 percent of the contribution on the taxes owed by the taxpayer up to 6 percent of the taxable income (Law of June 24, 1996). Legacies are exempt from heritage tax. Private companies can deduct donations up to 0.325 percent of their annual business turnover.

Governed by the 1990 Act, *corporate foundations,* or *fondations d'entreprise,* can be founded for nonprofit activities of public interest by one, or several, private or public corporations, cooperatives or mutual societies. Until 1995, however, only thirty corporations did take advantage of this option—mostly large companies and especially public enterprises, which account for half of the total number of corporate foundations. While corporate foundations also need administrative authorization, the process is less demanding than in the case of *fondations RUP*. A corporate foundation receives legal personality either through explicit authorization by the administration or through tacit consent in case of administrative silence within a period of four months after preliminary application.

In contrast to private, state-approved foundations, however, corporate foundations are initially only authorized for a period of five years, although the authorization may be repeatedly renewed thereafter. Corporate foundations must be established with a minimum endowment of approximately one-fifth of projected five-year programmatic expenditures, which must amount to a five-year total endowment of at least FF 1 million (Art. 19-6, Law of July 23, 1987). The governing board must include at least two employees of the founding corporation. The legal capacity of corporate foundations is as limited as that of declared associations, meaning that they can only own real estate used to carry on their activities. According to the Law of June 24, 1996, the founding company can deduct endowment payments from corporate tax for up to 0.225 percent of the annual business turnover. Corporate foundations cannot receive donations and legacies.

Finally, *nonautonomous foundations* do not have their own separate legal status, but are "sheltered" or hosted by other institutions. About 1,000 of such foundations are administered by the *Institut de France*[2] as a result of specific bequests to this venerable institution. With very few exceptions, such as the Kodak and Fiat Foundations, the endowments of these foundations are negligible. The vast majority of such foundations that do have economically significant endowments are "sheltered" by the *Fondation de France*. This includes about 400 nonautonomous foundations. The advantage of nonautonomous foundations is that neither minimum endowments nor annual funding commitments are required by law. The drawback, however, is the dependence on a host institution. Nonautonomous foundations can be created either by individuals—*inter vivos* or by last will—or by corporations. Indeed, about fifty corporate foundations are administered by the *Fondation de France*.

FOUNDATIONS IN FRANCE: A PROFILE

As indicated earlier, due to the Jacobin tradition to favor the monopolization of the public interest by the State (Archambault, 1997), foundations have remained rare organizational forms in France. In September 1995, the SIRENE file[3] recorded only 628 foundations, including operating and grantmaking foundations, and establishments run by foundations. Foundations thus constitute indeed only a very small part of the French nonprofit sector. According to our own very tentative estimates, total operating expenditures of the French foundation sector in 1995 may not have amounted to more than FF 10 billion, which likely represents less than 4 percent of the operating expenditures of the

French nonprofit sector as a whole. Similarly, foundation employment is less than 3 percent of total employment of the whole association and foundation sector. As Table 9.1 shows, the 628 foundations had 34,322 employees, which compares to 1,160,073 employees of 225,600 associations, as recorded in the SIRENE file.

On average, foundations employ more staff than associations. The average foundation establishment has a staff of fifty-five, compared to an average of five employees for associations recorded in SIRENE file. A breakdown of total employment by main foundation activities shows that more than half of foundation employment is in the health sector (Table 9.1; Figure 9.1), mainly in hospitals created before 1950. These hospitals are generally large organizations, averaging 214 employees. Social services account for nearly one-fourth of the employment, with an average of thirty-three employees. Other sectors of some economic importance include research (9.3 percent of employment), education (5.8 percent), and tourism and housing (2.1 percent). The extremely small share of arts and culture, both in terms of numbers of foundations devoted to this field and their share on total foundation employment (0.3 percent), appears to be most remarkable, as arts and culture are among the growth fields in the foundation sectors of other European countries (see F. I. Strachwitz & Toepler, 1996). The implication here is that the strong dominance of the central government in the cultural area has so far stifled private foundation initiative and that recent legislative encouragements especially targeted at the cultural area have not taken root yet.

Not only is the French foundation sector relatively small, but it also shows no signs of accelerated growth. Data provided by the Ministry of the Interior allow an assessment of the recent evolution in terms of number of

Table 9.1. Number of Foundations and Foundation Employment in 1995

NAF* Code	Sector	Number of establishments	%	Employment	%
55–70	Tourism and housing	78	12.4	730	2.1
73	Research	32	5.1	3,185	9.3
80	Education	54	8.6	1,984	5.8
85	Health	86	13.7	18,388	53.6
85	Social services	242	38.5	8,021	23.4
92	Culture	25	4.0	92	0.3
	Other and n.e.c.	111	17.7	1,922	5.5
	TOTAL	628	100.0	34,322	100.0

*NAF is the acronym for *Nomenclature d'activités Françaises*, the classification consistent with the International Standard Industrial Classification, in use in France since 1993.
SOURCE: SIRENE File, September 1995.

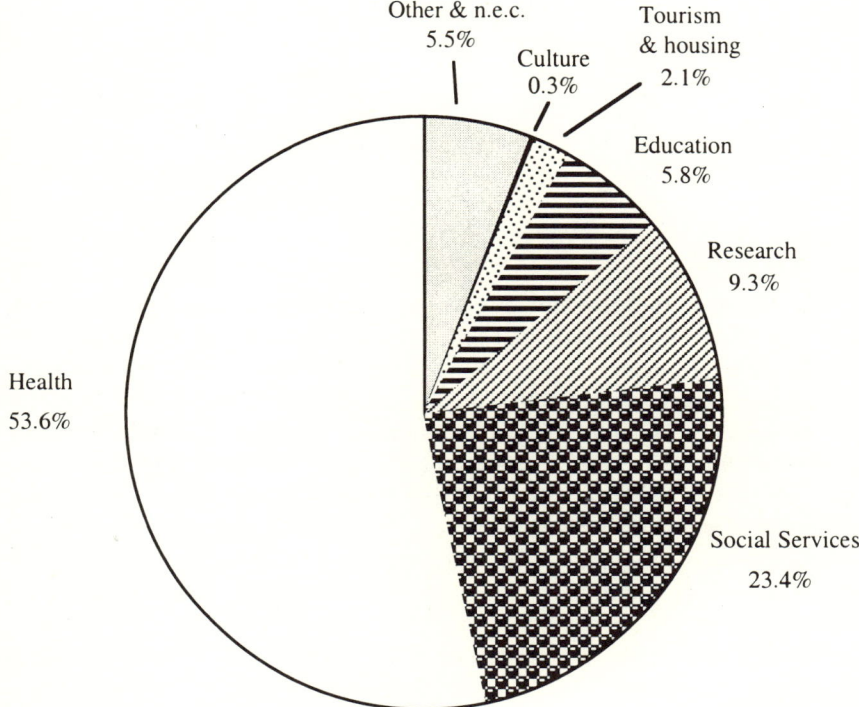

Figure 9.1. Foundation employment by sector of activity, in percentages, 1995. Source: SIRENE File, September 1995.

foundations and growth rates. As borne out in Table 9.2, no significant growth can be observed for state-approved foundations, despite the recent legislation. Over the last six years, the number of *fondations RUP* grew from 383 in 1989 to only 445 in 1995, or on average by approximately ten new foundations per year. This lack of significant growth is often attributed to the discouraging effects of the lengthy authorization and approval process and the high minimal endowment requirement.

Table 9.2. Number of *fondations reconnues d'utilité publique,* 1989–1995

1989	1990	1991	1992	1993	1994	1995
383	393	402	417	430	438	445

Source: Unpublished data provided by the Ministry of the Interior.

Table 9.3. Year and Number
of Foundations Sheltered
by Fondations de France

1990	1991	1992	1993	1994
326	351	358	364	395

SOURCE: Fondation de France, 1995.

In addition, the development of corporate foundations has been even more stagnant. Only thirty have been created since 1990, and some of those are not really new as they are reorganized associations or quasicorporate entities established prior to the 1987 law on foundations.

As indicated in Table 9.3, nonautonomous foundations administered by the *Fondation de France* grew at the slightly higher rate of 21.2 percent in the four-year period between 1990 and 1994. This translates into an average annual growth rate of 5 percent, or twice the growth rate of State-approved foundations over the same period, demonstrating that the high level of minimum endowments required for State-approved foundations might indeed have discouraging effects on potential founders.

Overall, the impact of the *Fondation de France* on the French foundation field is most significant. Its total assets amount to about FF 2 billion. Annual grant expenditures totaled more than FF 400 million. The *Fondation de France* raises more than FF 300 million in donations and legacies. As a multipurpose grantmaker, it distributes around 45 percent of its annual grants to social service field; around 22 percent to health and medical research, the same amount to culture and arts, and around 5 percent to international activities and the environment. Another noteworthy grantmaker is the *Fondation pour la recherche médicale,* which reported an annual revenue of more than FF 127 million in 1993 (Guide Annuaire des Fondations et des Associations; 1995).

RECENT TRENDS

As in many other European countries and despite their limited number, foundations are currently facing a renewed interest, although it is not yet clear what impact the new political environment and the deep economic recession will ultimately have on their development. The second foundation revival that is currently under way traces back to the encouragement of the central government for the creation of the *Fondation de France* in 1969. On the initiative of General de Gaulle and André Malraux, the *Fondation de France* received an initial endowment of FF 16 million from the *Caisse des Dépots et Consignations*, a public financial institution, and FF 17 million from other public and private banks. Independent from the government but with some civil servant trustees, it was set up to encourage philanthropy and foster private initiative by offering the option to shelter individual or corporate foundations.[4]

Perhaps even more significantly, the *Fondation de France* served as a role model by introducing the new and sophisticated concept of a multipurpose foundation to France. Its creation subsequently led to the establishment of a number of other foundations during the 1970s, which have been successful in their achievements but remained limited in size and assets. Most of these foundations are not fully supported by their endowments and have to solicit private donations and public subsidies to develop projects or to overcome financial difficulties.

During the 1980s, the foundation idea was further propelled by the unexpected attention that the new Socialist government paid to corporate involvement in public affairs, especially with regard to corporate patronage of the arts and culture guided by Anglo-American models of business sponsorships of the arts. Indeed, the intervention of the Ministry of Culture has been crucial, as it initiated the Law of 1990 with the intend of fostering and promoting the patronage of organizations or companies to diversify cultural financial resources. Of the thirty corporate foundations established since then, most are committed to arts and culture, but also to new issues such as the environment, education, and public health, as is the case with the foundations established by corporations like *Macif, France Telecom, Gan, Gaz de France, Crédit Coopératif, Total,* and *Air France.*

As much recognition as incentive, the 1990 Law on Corporate Foundations undoubtedly marks an important step in French attitudes toward business and corporate giving. The traditional view was that corporations should not be involved in public-interest activities as the endowment of corporate foundations and corporate giving in general was seen as an improper diversion of resources that could either be used to increase wages or shareholder dividends. While the Law of 1990 departed from this traditional approach and promoted a newer trend toward a socially responsible "citizen enterprise" culture in the French business sector, it has nevertheless raised some practical questions, as the law lacks flexibility, which serves as a constant source of criticism from the business community. Indeed, the option to create corporate foundations is often perceived as a mixed blessing, since business leaders view the required five-year financial commitment as too demanding in periods of economic recession. Moreover, the level of endowment has to be specified in the statutes of the foundation, necessitating costly modifications of the statutes for any changes.

At present, most corporate foundations as well as corporations that have
giving programs rather than separate foundations indicate the need to reduce
support levels in the coming years, showing how frail the corporate responsibility culture still is. But the economic and fiscal crisis may also give room to
new foundations, aimed at alleviating its consequences. A prominent example
is the foundation created by the Minister of Labor, Martine Aubry, gathering
public and private money to stimulate employment. A number of corporations
are also exploring ways to create foundations with the goal of motivating and
training former employees in early retirement to become active in voluntary
activities. Foam bubbles or deep waves, these initiatives clearly signal that a
lively corporate foundation culture may finally be taking root in France.

By contrast, the Law of 1987 concerning private, State-approved foundations raises more problems. Although state supervision is largely limited to
administrative matters and has little consequence for day-to-day operations, it
is still widely considered to be too restrictive by legal experts as well as
foundation executives and other observers (see Perrin, 1997). The French
administration continues to harbor suspicions vis-à-vis foundations, their
management, and sometimes their activities, and the administrative culture is
still deeply entrenched with an unabashed belief in the superiority of governmental provision for public needs and a distrust of independent privately
controlled institutions. Confronted with an administrative culture that has not
yet fully adapted to the complex reality of philanthropy, foundations—independent, but closely supervised—thus find themselves at a cross road between
two, often conflictuous, cultures.

But legal aspects and the administrative environment are not the only
cause for the scarcity of foundations in France. Though their visible achievements stand for them in many fields of public interest, foundations themselves
have yet to take a closer look at their identity and role in French society at
large. What seems to be missing to engage discussions on the larger meaning
of foundations in contemporary society is a "council of foundations," as institutional infrastructure similar to the French *Conseil National de la Vie Associative* (National Council of Associative Life).

Nevertheless, French foundations are a dynamic reality in motion. While
still not significant economically, and with a diffuse understanding of their
larger societal role, foundations currently have a unique opportunity to define
their place in the development of responses to the large and complex social,
cultural, and economic challenges that France is facing. Fundamentally,
though, foundations have still to overcome the deep-rooted French cultural
tradition, which identifies the State as uniquely responsible for the public
interest. The challenge that lies ahead for foundations in France is thus not
only political and legal in nature, but rather one of cultural legitimacy as well.

NOTES

1. The *Conseil d'État* is the highest court in France, ruling on the interpretation of legislation.
2. The *Institut de France* is not a foundation itself, but a state-approved public institution created in 1795 that houses the five academies (the French academy; science, letters, arts, and moral and political science).
3. SIRENE is the main register of economic activity in France: every enterprise, upon creation, receives an identification number that is referred to at every administrative operation; in this way, the register is automatically kept up to date. SIRENE data cover name and address, legal status, economic activity category, and number of employees. For nonprofit organizations, SIRENE records only those that have employees, pay VAT, or are subsidized by the central government.
4. In addition, the *Fondation de France* performs another "umbrella" type of activity. More specifically, declared associations that do not have *RUP* status can open an account at the *Fondation de France*. Donors to such associations (*associations titulaires d'un compte à la Fondation de France*) may claim the higher tax benefits—otherwise reserved for State-approved associations and foundations, parochial associations, relief and charitable organizations and religious communities—if their donation is made out to the association's *Fondation de France* account. In 1994, there were 388 of such declared associations with accounts at the *Fondation de France* (Fondation de France, 1994).

REFERENCES

Alfandari, E., & Nazdone, A. (1994). *Les associations et les fondations en Europe: Régime juridique et fiscal,* 2nd ed. Brussels: Librairie Européenne-Juris-Service.

Archambault, E. (1997). *The nonprofit sector in France.* Manchester, UK: Manchester University Press.

Bidet, E. (1993). Les différents types de fondations au regard de la loi Française *Revue des Etudes Cooperatives, Mutualistes et Associatives, 2,* 25–38.

Castro, S. (1997). France. In L. M. Salamon (Ed.), *The International Guide to Nonprofit Law* (pp. 100–117). New York: Wiley.

Courtois, G., & de Montalembert, A. (1989). *Droit et fiscalité des associations et des fondations.* Paris: Les nouvelles fiscales.

Courtois, G. (1995). Les fondations en France. *Guide annuaire des fondations et des associations.* Paris: SA2.

Debbasch, C. (Ed.). (1987). *Les fondations: Un mécène pour notre temps?* Paris: Economica.

Debbasch, C., & Langeron, P. (1992). *Les fondations.* Paris: PUF-collection Que-sais-je.

Delsol, X. (1991). *Mécénat et parrainage: Guide juridique et fiscal.* Lyon: SA2-Juris-Service.

Dupuy, R.-J. (1985). Le droit des fondations en France et à l'étranger. *Notes et études documentaires* n °4879. La Documentation Française.

Fondation de France. (1990–1995). *Rapports d'activité.*

Fondation de France. (1992). *Repères à travers le monde des fondations.*

Fondation de France. (1992). *Fondations, Donations et legs.*

Fondation de France (1994). Droit ete pratiques des fondations au service de l'intérêt général. *Les rencontres de la Fondation de France.* Paris: Avril.

GAFA. (1995). *Guide Annuaire des Fondations et des Asasociations.* Paris, SA2.

Leat, D. (1995). "British foundations: The organization and management of grant-making," *Voluntas, 6*(3), 317–329.

Moulin, A. M. (1992). *The Pasteur Institute and the logic of nonprofit.* Paper presented at the 3rd Conference on Research on Volunteering and Nonprofit Organizations, Indianapolis, IN.

Perrin, A. (1997). Cultural sponsorship—150 years in the service of creation. *Alliance—Critical Journal of Corporate Citizenship Worldwide, 2,* 10–15.

Pomey, M. (1980). *Traité des fondations d'utilité publique.* Paris: P.U.F.

Strachwitz, R., & Toepler, S. (1996). Traditional methods of funding: Foundations and endowments. In L. Doyle (Ed.), *Funding Europe's Solidarity* (pp. 100–108). Brussels, Belgium: Association for Innovative Cooperation in Europe.

Tsyboula, S. Foundations in Europe: The view from France. Presentation at the Voluntas and L.E.S. symposium, *Foundations: An International Research Symposium* Paris.

Van der Ploeg, T. J. (1995). "Supervisory powers relating to foundations: A comparative analysis of foundation law." *Voluntas, 6*(3), 317–329.

Chapter 10

Foundations in Italy

GIAN PAOLO BARBETTA

INTRODUCTION

From an American perspective, charitable foundations are a very rare type of institution in the Italian landscape. While foundations in the United States, such as the Ford Foundation, the Rockefeller Foundation, or the Carnegie Corporation, usually distribute grants to nonprofit organizations, only a few grantmaking foundations operate in Italy; their endowments and grants are generally very small, especially compared to their American counterparts, while their activities (generally disbursement of fellowships or subsidies) are very traditional.

Many factors explain the different attitudes of the two countries toward grantmaking institutions: religious and social beliefs; the role of the State and the Church in the provision of social services; the political and legal mistrust of any body that intermediates between the individual and the State—a legacy of the Enlightenment period; public concern about unproductive use of wealth; a fiscal system that makes it easy to get around inheritance laws and tax laws that allow only limited tax incentives for donations.

The lack of grantmaking institutions does not mean that foundations do not exist at all in Italy. Indeed, the legal form of the foundation is growing more common and gaining wider acceptance in Italy after many years of distrust by government and the public. Nearly all Italian foundations provide

Gian Paolo Barbetta • Research Scientist, Department of Economics and Finance, Università Cattolica del Sacro Cuore and Istituto per la Ricerca Sociale 20135, Milan, Italy.

Private Funds, Public Purpose: Philanthropic Foundations in an International Perspective, edited by Helmut K. Anheier and Stefan Toepler. New York, Plenum Press, 1999.

goods or services directly to the public, making them operating rather than grantmaking foundations.

One could therefore say that, in Italy, many foundations do not differ very much from other nonprofit organizations as far as activities and funding are concerned. In fact, a foundation is just one of the possible legal forms that can be adopted by Italian nonprofit organizations, in addition to associations (recognized or unrecognized), voluntary organizations, and social cooperatives.[1] With a few exceptions, Italian foundations (both operating and grantmaking) are small and their endowments are modest. Most foundations rely upon yearly contributions from the private or public sector for funding. In summary, the Italian nonprofit sector has not yet produced a larger set of specialized grantmaking organizations.

This situation is changing as a result of Law 218 of 1990, known as the Amato Law after the Treasury Minister who promoted it. This law and subsequent decrees started the transformation of Italian banks, part of the semi-public sector, into stock companies. So far, most of these banks had been registered under the unusual legal status of association or foundation. The process of transformation, now almost complete, created two different sets of organizations: about ninety banks with the new legal status of joint-stock companies, and some ninety well-endowed foundations that should act much like their American counterparts. Consequently, the law paved the way for the creation of a new sector of grantmaking foundations.

The creation of a sector of grantmaking institutions that is currently taking place in Italy will thus presumably be the result of government intervention and not of private benevolence. This remarkable characteristic differentiates Italian philanthropic foundations from those of the United States and many other countries. This is no surprise in a country that shaped its legal system after the French Napoleonic code, and then created a universal, though highly debated, welfare state.

FOUNDATIONS IN ITALY: LEGAL DEFINITION AND FISCAL TREATMENT

Legal Definition

According to Articles 12 to 35 of the Italian Civil Code of 1942, a foundation is a private nonprofit organization with an endowment that must be used to pursue the aims stated in its charter. The endowment is the defining characteristic of a foundation and differentiates it from other nonprofit organizations, such as associations or social cooperatives. While an association is a group of people pursuing common interests, a foundation is an "endowment dedicated to a goal" (Ristuccia, 1996, p. 35).

The Italian Civil Code does not specify any minimum endowment for the creation of a foundation. All that is required is that the endowment be "adequate" to pursue the aims stated in the foundation's charter. The law assigns the assessment of the adequacy of an endowment to administrative authorities, as described later in this chapter. The Civil Code does not prescribe any specific aims, although it is generally intended that a foundation should pursue the "public interest" and not the benefit of private individuals (Sanfilippo & Maniaci, 1990, p. 59; Guzzi, 1996, p. 49).[2]

In addition to the general definition provided by the Civil Code, many different laws[3] regulate particular types of foundations with specific aims (Ciriec, 1979, p. 35; Guzzi, 1996, p. 52; Sanfilippo & Maniaci, 1990, p. 54), such as the following:

- *Family foundations,* regulated by Royal Decree 99/1891, whose aim is to provide social and educational services to the members or offspring of one or more families.
- *Educational foundations,* regulated by Royal Decree 1297/1928 and by Presidential Decree 3/1972, whose aim is to provide economic support to deserving students in financial difficulty.
- *University foundations,* regulated by Royal Decrees 1592/1933 and 1269/1938, whose aim is to increase attendance of universities and to support deserving students with loans and subsidies.
- *Military foundations,* whose aim is to support members of the army and their families in case of economic hardship.
- *Religious foundations,* regulated by the Concordat of 1929 and the laws—approved in 1985—amending the Concordat, including many different type of organizations with religious or social welfare aims.
- *Banking foundations,* created in 1990, which will be discussed in greater detail later.

Legal Treatment

To acquire legal or juridical standing (so-called *personalità giuridica*) and commence activity, a foundation must apply for incorporation. Incorporation protects the founders from losses or damages by providing the foundation with limited liability. Incorporation is obtained by public decree enacted by the President of the Italian Republic, when a foundation acts nationwide, or by the President of the Region when activities are limited to local level.[4] The process of incorporation at the national level is quite difficult and can take several years. There is a wide degree of latitude and discretion on part of the the administration in terms of assessing the adequacy of a foundation's endowments and the merits of its aims. Incorporation at regional level is generally faster.

Incorporation, however, is not the only time when public authorities influence the life of a foundation. Indeed, local representatives of the government (known as prefects) maintain significant control over foundations. According to Article 25 of the Civil Code, they can control the board of a foundation; appoint or substitute board members if those proposed were not nominated in accordance with its charter; dissolve the board if its actions and decisions do not pursue the aims of the foundation or do not follow the will of the founders; force one or more foundations to coordinate their activities and to merge their boards and administrations to avoid any waste of resources (Art. 26); change the aims of a foundation (complying as much as possible with the founder's will) when they (1) become impossible to pursue, (2) are not beneficial to the community, or (3) when depreciation makes it impossible to pursue the original goals with the current endowment.

Due to these powers granted by law, the government maintains a very high degree of control over the activities of Italian foundations. This control is quite often more hypothetical than concrete, however, as the government has insufficient resources and usually does not place a high priority on actively participating in the policies of individual foundations. Nevertheless, this power is a clear sign of the legal suspicion and distrust of foundations, nonprofit organizations, and any body or institution located between the State and its citizens.

This body of laws and regulations was highly influenced by the French legal, economic, and philosophical traditions of the Enlightenment that developed in the seventeenth and eighteenth centuries. At that time, a new economic and political elite was emerging within a society still dominated by the aristocracy and the clergy. To affirm its primacy, the emerging bourgeoisie had to fight established powers and the ancient order. Foundations were considered part of this order, as most were Catholic and run by religious personnel. They often had large endowments, a legacy of the medieval period, but little income. To a certain extent, they were used by the Church as an instrument to affirm its power and pursue its mission (Ristuccia, 1996).

Early critics of foundations concentrated on a few aspects they interpreted as crucial shortcomings of the foundation form. From an economic point of view, French political philosophy held that welfare increases when savings directly finance investments, implying that foundations were "unproductive" accumulations of capital. Moreover, private benevolence toward the needy was seen to encourage laziness and dependency and could not solve the poverty problem. Furthermore, it was widely held that many foundations dissipated their resources and wasted their income in useless expenses. From a political perspective, this philosophy tried to affirm the primacy of the new democratic and lay State over the church, the aristocracy, and medieval corporations and guilds. As a result, any organization between the State and its citizens, including foundations and associations, were strongly opposed.

This tradition has strongly shaped the Italian legal system and its influence is still apparent, although the Republican Constitution, approved in 1948, guarantees freedom of association to individuals and freedom to pursue any goals (if not against the law) to organizations. Nevertheless, many legal provisions testify to a very recent past characterized by a deep aversion toward collective organizations and State control over their goals and activities (Onida, 1992, p. 24).

Fiscal Treatment

Nonprofit organizations as such are not tax-exempt in Italy and foundations are no exception to this general rule. Cartabia and Rigano (1997, p. 63) note that "the absence of the profit motive has never been a reason for tax exemption and thus we might say that nonprofit organizations do not enjoy a privileged position as far as liability to taxation is concerned." More generally, Italian fiscal law does not distinguish between nonprofit and for-profit organizations, but rather between commercial and noncommercial bodies and commercial and noncommercial activities.

Commercial bodies include organizations regulated by the fifth book of the Civil Code, such as public stock companies, limited liability companies and cooperatives, whose purpose is to carry out business, and organizations regulated by the first book of the Civil Code, such as associations and foundations that pursue business objectives on a permanent basis. Noncommercial bodies include both public and private sector organizations whose objects do not include pursuing a commercial activity.

According to the Civil Code, the following activities should be considered "commercial": (1) industrial activities aimed at the production of goods or services; (2) brokering for the circulation of goods; (3) land, sea, and air transport; (4) banking and insurance; and (5) activities that are auxiliary to the former. Activities other than those listed are considered noncommercial. While income generated from commercial activities is subject to corporate income tax (IRPEG), income produced from noncommercial activitity is not taxed when two conditions are met: the activity is directly related to the aim of the organization, and services are supplied "at cost" and without a dedicated organizational structure.

The law assumes that commercial bodies carry out commercial activities and therefore taxes their whole income, whatever its origin. Noncommercial bodies can carry out either commercial or noncommercial activities. Income generated by noncommercial activities is not liable to be taxed, under the conditions described earlier, although income derived from commercial activities is subject to taxation, even if noncommercial bodies carry out the activities.[5] In addition, there are five special provisions within fiscal law that particularly concern foundations:

1. While nonprofit organizations have to pay taxes on all commercial income, foundations enjoy several special fiscal advantages in this respect. According to Article 6 of Presidential Decree 601/1973 (amended by Art. 66 of Decree 331/1993) some organizations (including foundations) that carry out activities in the areas of social services, hospitals, education, research, and culture enjoy a 50 percent reduction in their tax on commercial income (IRPEG). Moreover, income generated from parks and gardens open to the public free of charge, as well as income generated by buildings used as museums, libraries, art galleries or archives, are tax exempt. As a further incentive, foundations can deduct costs incurred for "maintenance and restoration of the artistic and cultural heritage" from their income.

2. The fiscal regulation of the most important indirect tax (value added tax—VAT) does not differ significantly from that of direct taxation, although there are no special exceptions for foundations. Commercial activities generate revenue subject to VAT, while noncommercial activities do not. Likewise, nonprofit organizations pay VAT when they engage in commercial operations.

3. Incentives for foundations and nonprofit organizations are found in the fiscal laws of INVIM, a tax on property appreciation. Organizations, business, and, to some degree, individuals are subject to this tax when they sell real estate or after each ten-year period of ownership. Although abolished in 1993, this tax is still applicable to capital gains before 1993 that are still taxable when estates are sold or inherited. Donations of buildings to foundations and nonprofit organizations are exempt from INVIM when the buildings are used for social, educational, study, or research purposes. Foundations enjoy the advantage of being exempt from INVIM on buildings for institutional use that are owned by foundations recognized as noncommercial bodies. Moreover, regardless of the nature of the activities performed by foundations, all buildings used for social, health, educational, cultural, recreational, and sporting purposes are tax exempt. Noncommercial bodies also receive a 50 percent discount on INVIM on buildings not used for institutional purposes.

4. Donations and bequests to foundations with welfare, research, education, or other public interest purposes are exempt from taxes on inheritance and donations.

5. Some fiscal incentives are also available to individuals and companies donating money to foundations and nonprofit organizations. Tax concessions are available for donations to:

a. Legally recognized associations operating on a non-for-profit basis that are involved in study and research to promote cultural or artistic endeavors.
b. Nonprofit organizations that specialize in the promotion of cultural activities, such as theaters.
c. Programs aimed at improving conditions in underdeveloped areas as well as to recognized nongovernmental organizations working on projects in developing countries.
d. All three of the above deductions can be set against income tax (for both individuals and businesses) to a maximum of 2 percent of net income.

Business firms can also deduct donations to:

a. Registered organizations with educational, recreational, research, or religious aims, or those providing social or health services.
b. Organizations running programs in underdeveloped areas.
c. Registered organizations based in Southern Italy pursuing research.
d. Private foundations, associations, or cooperatives running community radio stations.

A total of two percent of declared income may be set against the tax, except for the last case where the limit is one percent (Cartabia & Rigano, 1997, pp. 67–68).

ITALIAN FOUNDATIONS: THE NONSPECIALIZED WORLD

The description of the legal environment by itself, however, does not provide a full picture of Italian foundations and their activities. Although the law emphasizes the differences between foundations and other nonprofit organizations, these organizations are very similar when their activities, size, and sources of income are considered. Some characteristics of Italian foundations, as well as features common to foundations and other nonprofit organizations, suggest that the Italian nonprofit sector has not yet produced organizations with specialized capabilities.

As already mentioned, philanthropic grantmaking foundations are rare in Italy. Analyzing 536 foundations of a total foundation universe that might comprise as many as 1,500 foundations, Demarie (1997) found that only 5 percent of these organizations are exclusively grantmaking foundations, while 39 percent are exclusively operating foundations. Of the 42 percent of foundations that are mixed in nature, most consider themselves as "mostly operating institutions" in which grantmaking plays a minor role (Table 10.1). With the

Table 10.1. Italian Foundation by Type
of Activity ($n = 529$)

Type of activity	Percentage
Fellowship/scholarship foundation	10.0
Other grantmaking foundations	5.3
Operating foundations	38.8
Mixed foundations	43.1
Mostly operating	33.3
Mostly grantmaking	9.8
Unspecified	2.8
TOTAL	100.0

SOURCE: Demarie (1997, p. 55).

disbursement of fellowships or scholarship grants, another 10 percent of Italian foundations perform only one, fairly narrow kind of activity. Strictly speaking, they shoud be classified as grantmaking organizations, but of a special type. They are generally small organizations[6] specializing in just one routine activity, unlike larger, more complex, multipurpose grantmaking foundations, common in the United States and other European countries.

This lack of grantmaking institutions indicates the nonspecialized nature of the Italian nonprofit sector. Most organizations—regardless of their legal form—provide services to the public, while only a few organizations provide (financial) services to other nonprofits. The wide range of activities performed by Italian foundations is indicative of this national characteristic. Italian foundations, most of which do not make grants, act in almost every field of the nonprofit sector. Some foundations are research institutions, such as the *Fondazione Giovanni Agnelli* in Turin, the *Fondazione Censis* or the much smaller *Fondazione Adriano Olivetti* in Rome, and constitute Italian versions of the American-style think tanks. A few foundations run hospitals, such as the large *Ospedale San Raffaele* in Milan, owned by the *Fondazione San Romanello del Monte Tabor,* or the many hospitals owned and run by Catholic organizations with endowments. Other foundations are active in the area of culture, such as the *Fondazione Cini* in Venice or the *Fondazione Poldi Pezzoli* in Milan, which runs a museum. Others are large and internationally well-known medical research institutions, such as the *Istituto Mario Negri* in Milan, or combine medical research and social service provision for particular categories of individuals, such as the *Fondazione Don Carlo Gnocchi* in Milan, which serves the disabled. According to Demarie (1997), most foundations are active in the field of "research" (with a slight prevalence of humanities over biomedical and artistic research), "education and training," and

Table 10.2. Field of Activity of Italian
Foundations ($n = 514$)

Field of activity	Percentage
Preservation of the cultural heritage	9.1
Education and training	28.8
Artistic, scientific, and medical research	32.1
Social services and health	25.1
Environment	1.2
International cooperation	0.8
Religion	2.9
TOTAL	100.0

SOURCE: Adapted from Demarie (1997, p. 33).

"social services and health." More than 85 percent of the foundations analyzed in this study operate in these areas (Table 10.2).

A third characteristic of Italian foundations concerns their size. Apart from a few, probably internationally known examples, foundations are relatively small in Italy, both in the size of endowment and number of employees. As Table 10.3 shows, 60 percent of Italian foundations rely on endowments of one billion lire or less (about $600,000 at 1997 exchange rates), and another 30 percent on endowments in the one to ten billion lire range ($600,000 to six million dollars). Less than 3 percent of Italian foundations have endowments of more than 50 billion lire ($30 million), or large enough to enable an operating foundation to act on a significant scale (Demarie, 1997). This feature is particularly remarkable since it is the endowment that should distinguish a foundation from other nonprofit organizations and serves as further evidence of the great similarities between foundations and other nonprofit organizations in Italy.

Because of their size, many foundations cannot rely exclusively on their endowments and must raise operating funds each year to balance their budgets

Table 10.3. Endowment Size of Italian
Foundations ($n = 515$)

Foundation endowment	Percentage
Less than 1 billion lire	58.5
1 to 10 billion lire	30.1
10 to 50 billion lire	8.5
More than 50 billion lire	2.9

SOURCE: Adapted from Demarie (1997, p. 27).

Table 10.4. Italian Foundations
by Employment Categories ($n = 536$)

Foundation with	Percentage
No employees	51.5
1 to 5 employees	30.6
6 to 20 employees	12.3
21 to 100 employees	3.1
More than 100 employees	2.4

SOURCE: Adapted from Demarie (1997, p. 51).

and run their activities. It appears that foundations are not very successful fund-raisers, given that most are quite small in financial terms: 74.3 percent of foundations spend less than 500 million lire ($300,000) per year, and almost 45 percent spend less than 100 million lire ($60,000) per year.

The 536 foundations studied by Demarie (1997) have a total of about 10,000 employees, with eighteen employees on average. However, this figure is somewhat deceiving since more than 50 percent of those foundations have no employees at all, 82 percent have less than five employees and about 94 percent have less than twenty employees (Table 10.4). Large foundations with more than twenty-five employees (representing less than 5 percent of this sample) account for almost 90 percent of total employment.

Such small staff is particularly surprising given the nature of Italian foundations. While grantmaking requires few employees, the provision of services should imply larger numbers of staff. This suggests that most Italian foundations act on a very limited scale and provide services to only a few beneficiaries. In this respect, they are no different from the large majority of other nonprofit organizations. Thus, in Italy, as opposed to other countries, a foundation is not necessarily a grantmaking organization but one of the many legal arrangements available to any persons wishing to undertake a "not-for-profit" activity. Consequently, Italian foundations provide services directly, raise funds to augment the annual income generated by endowments, and enter into contractual relationships with government bodies for the provision of services to the public, just as many associations or social cooperatives do. Yet, they do so on a small scale. It is only when "governance" and its characteristics are considered that clear differences between foundations and other nonprofit organizations emerge. Associations and social cooperatives have a democratic form of governance under which members make decisions by majority vote. A foundation, however, has no members and its rules on decision-making procedures, board membership, and so on, are established by the founders and written in to the charter of the foundation itself.

In conclusion, it bears repeating that an important characteristic of foundations, and also of the rest of the nonprofit sector, is its very low level of specialization. Due to its small size and limited development, the Italian nonprofit sector has thus far not been able to create organizations that specialize in particular kinds of operations or develop specific skills and capabilities. Italy lacks organizations whose main aim is to provide financial support to other nonprofit organizations and to provide seed money for deserving causes or projects neglected by both government and the private sector. However, with the so-called "banking foundations," a new type of organization is emerging in the world of Italian grantmaking institutions. They are the outcome of the transformation of many semipublic sector banks, set in motion by Law 218/1990, known as the Amato law.

THE NEW "BANKING FOUNDATIONS"

Origins

Until the end of the 1980s, most of the semipublic banks[7] were incorporated as foundations nor associations. This legal status is very unusual for organizations in the banking industry. To understand the origins of this startling situation, it is necessary to look at the history and role played by government controlled banks in Italy. Each *Istituto di Credito di Diritto Pubblico* has a long and individual institutional history. More general comments could be made about the wider world of the *Casse di Risparmio*. Most of these Italian "savings banks" (they are in fact ordinary checking banks) were set up in the first half of the nineteenth century. Quite often, the start-up capital was provided by rich and enlightened individuals, sometimes (especially in Northern Italy) supported by farsighted government authorities. The main aim of the banks—and their founders—was to stimulate savings of the middle and working classes. Contrary to banking tradition, savings were not considered a requisite for the accumulation of capital or as a means for starting the process of industrialization, but as a "provident" project. The purpose of the savings banks was therefore to help and encourage individuals to save for future economic contingencies.

At first, these banks were therefore more concerned with encouraging deposits than with granting loans. Their lending activity was quite limited, managed with great caution, and aimed at guaranteeing the security of deposits rather than obtaining maximum yields (Clarich, 1984). Sometimes these banks gave credit to particularly deserving (and sound) organizations such as the *Opere Pie,* private charitable institutions generally under direct control of the Church, with estates consisting mainly of legacies and donations acquired over the centuries. Besides interpreting their lending activities as philanthrop-

ic, many savings banks expressed their charitable leanings further: their charters contained clauses that compelled the boards to donate large percentages of
their profits to charity (keeping the remaining profits as reserves).[8]

Recent Changes

In 1990, public banks were still a hybrid of commercial banking and
charitable activity. Several events and developments made the nonprofit status
of public banks seem both anachronistic and restrictive: the competitive conditions resulting from the ratification of European Union directives on banking, the wider recognition of the entrepreneurial nature of banking, and the
conviction that economic development could be better pursued through efficient banking rather than charitable activity undertaken by financial institutions. Having no shareholders, the *Casse di Risparmio,* for instance, found it
difficult to raise the capital necessary to comply with the banking directives of
the European Union and to engage in mergers and acquisitions necessary to
increase their size. Law 218/1990 allowed these banks incorporated as foundations or associations to change their legal status. Thanks to substantial fiscal
incentives, they were allowed to reorganize their banking activities into new
joint stock companies, allowing the creation of financial institutions able to
compete on an equal footing with ordinary private banks. The foundations,
still the majority shareholders of the new banks, could now fully concentrate
on charitable, social, and welfare activities. The share holdings of the new
banks represent the foundations' endowments and the dividends received constitute the income used for philanthropic purposes.

The original version of this law did not allow such foundations to give up
control of the banks, unless control remained within the public sector. This
decision was subsequently reversed in spite of strong opposition from interested parties. In 1993, the government declared it illegal for one person to hold
simultaneous appointments as administrator of a foundation and in the bank it
owned. In 1994, a new law freed foundations from the burden of maintaining a
majority share in the banks and, later that year, new government regulation
forced foundations to sell their majority holdings, although over a lengthy
period of time and with some loopholes. The legislature is therefore moving
toward a permanent separation of banking and charitable activities. The new
banks are supposed to maximize profits in an increasingly competitive market,
while the banking foundations should concentrate on their charitable business, hold their endowments in risk free assets (or in charitable activities), and
behave like true nonprofit organizations and not like financial holding companies.

A new bill is now under discussion by the Italian Parliament. When
passed, the law will give fiscal incentives to those banking foundations that

will lose control of their banks and, moreover, will definitely consider those foundations as private bodies rather than public ones. Moreover, in 1997 and the beginning of 1998, some banking foundations—such as the two largest ones (Compagnia di San Paolo and Fondazione Cassa di Risparmio delle Provincie Lombarde, both with assets in the range of $7 billion)—lost control of their banks (the Gruppo bancario S. Paolo di Torino and the Cariplo bank) by selling the majority of their shares to other private banks or financial investors.

This policy change seems to have been influenced by general economic objectives and did not explicitly aim at creating a strong sector of philanthropic foundations. The sale of the banks owned by foundations has been interpreted as a prerequisite for the privatization of other branches of public sector controlled industries. Nonetheless, this process represents a unique chance for the Italian nonprofit sector, as, for the first time, private foundations are created with considerable assets that are motivated to serve the public interest.

The Banking Foundations: An Overview

By the end of 1997, almost all of the former *Casse di Risparmio* and *Istituti di Credito di Diritto Pubblico* used the opportunity offered by the Amato law to change their legal status. Currently, about ninety banking foundations are struggling to find their way between the banking and charity business, but the link between the two activities is still very strong: more than 95 percent of the net assets of the foundations still consist of their holdings in the joint-stock company banks created as a result of the Amato law.

Banking foundations, as compared to most other Italian foundations, are well-endowed institutions. At the end of 1993, the total net assets of eighty-six of such foundations, analyzed in Ranci and Barbetta (1996), amounted to about 51 trillion lire (about $30 billion), and average assets amounted to 590 billion lire ($350 million). By comparison, only about 3 percent of other nonprofit foundations analyzed by Demarie (1997) could boast assets greater than 50 billion lire ($30 million), while 90 percent of the endowments were smaller than 10 billion lire ($6 million). As shown in Table 10.5, banking foundations in the Northern region of the country represent the bulk of this subsector, with 53 percent of all banking foundations and approximately 66 percent of the net assets. Foundations in Central Italy are relatively few, and smaller, with 34 percent of the foundations but only 21 percent of the assets, and these institutions are comparatively scarce in Southern Italy, with no more than 13 percent of foundations and assets.

The assets are not only concentrated in Northern Italy, but also in just a few foundations: three foundations, or 3.5 percent of foundations analyzed, with individual assets greater than 5,000 billion lire (about $3 billion), ac-

Table 10.5. Geographical Concentration of Foundations
and Assets

Area	Number of foundations	Percent	Assets (billions of lire)	Percent
Northwest	18	21	23,774	46.8
Northeast	28	32.5	9,781	19.2
Center	29	33.7	10,524	20.7
South	11	12.8	6,738	13.3
TOTAL	86	100	50,817	100

SOURCE: Ranci & Barbetta (1996, p. 100).

count for about 45 percent of total net assets, while a large number of small institutions (forty-nine foundations, or about 57 percent of the total number), with individual endowments of less than 200 billion lire (about $123 million), account for only 9 percent of total net assets (Table 10.6). These substantial endowments generate very little income, however: the ratio of interest and dividends to net assets was 1.2 percent in 1993, 1.6 percent in 1994, 1.7 percent in 1995, and 1.8 percent in 1996 [for the slightly different sample analyzed by the Association of Italian Savings Banks (ACRI; 1996, p. 130; 1997, p. 176; 1998, p. 76)]. These strikingly low earnings can be explained by two factors: first, the profitability of the Italian banks is quite low compared to international standards and, in addition, some institutions suffered under the economic recession of the early 1990s; second, the book value of many assets is probably overstated in order to take advantage of the fiscal incentives granted by the Amato law. By implica-

Table 10.6. Concentration of Banking Foundation Assets

Asset range (in billions of lire)	Number of foundations	Percent	Assets (billions of lire)	Percent
More than 5000	3	3.5	23,038	45.3
Between 600 and 5000	12	13.9	15,754	31.0
Between 200 and 600	22	25.6	7,245	14.3
Between 60 and 200	35	40.7	4,287	8.4
Less than 60	14	16.3	493	1.0
TOTAL	86	100	50,817	100

SOURCE: Ranci & Barbetta (1996, p. 100).

tion, the diversification of these foundations' assets is likely to have beneficial effects on their annual revenues, both in terms of stability and level of income.

In 1994, banking foundations transferred about 47 percent of their income into reserve funds in order to increase the capital of the banks they owned without losing control over them; this behavior was the consequence of the law enforcing public sector (or semipublic sector) control of the banks. About 6 percent of income was used for administration, while 7 percent was paid in taxes. As a result, only 40 percent of income was paid out in grants and charitable activities. This figure will increase, however, as foundations are no longer obliged to maintain control of their banks.

Tables 10.7 and 10.8 show the distribution of banking foundation grants (Table 10.7) and the types of activities supported (Table 10.8). The single largest grantmaking domain is "art and culture," followed by "social services," "education," and "health." The foundations show a strong preference for financing the purchase of capital goods, the construction and restoration of buildings, and the conservation or restoration of artworks. The funds granted for buying or restoring architecture and art account for about 50 percent of the total. By contrast, only about 20 percent of the funds support general operating costs.

The figures reflect the great need for funds for restoration (works of art, ancient buildings, and also buildings owned by social services organizations) and the purchase of capital goods, such as advanced technical instruments in the health field. They also reflect the conservative approach of Italian banking foundations to grantmaking. Italy's huge public deficit has forced many organizations (even in the public sector) to seek private funders willing and able to finance expensive projects or the purchase of new equipment. It should not, however, be forgotten that the purchase of new equipment rarely solves the problems addressed by foundations and that the money could sometimes be

Table 10.7. Distribution of Banking Foundation Grants
by Field, 1993–1996

Sector	1993 %	1994 %	1995 %	1996 %
Art, culture, and recreation	30	31	31	35
Education and research	20	19	20	20
Health	16	17	10	10
Social services	26	26	26	26
Environment	1	—	—	1
Development and housing	4	3	8	5
Other	3	4	5	3

Source: ACRI (1996, pp. 153–154; 1997, p. 108; 1998, p. 100).

Table 10.8. Purpose of Banking Foundation Grants, 1993–1996

Purpose	1993 %	1994 %	1995 %	1996 %
Purchase of capital goods	23	24	15	15
Construction and restoration of buildings	22	15	19	16
Conservation and restoration of works of art	15	16	14	16
General operating support	21	22	31	23
Cultural, scientific, and sporting events	11	9	9	9
Research projects	5	5	3	3
Other	3	9	9	18

SOURCE: ACRI (1996, pp. 156).

spent more effectively by helping public or nonprofit bodies solving their organizational problems.

Data published by ACRI (1996) do not allow a precise calculation of average grant expenditures. Nonetheless, it is clear that a large proportion of grants are relatively small. In 1994, grants of less than 50 million lire ($30,000) accounted for 32 percent of all grants made by banking foundations, 43 percent of those made by large foundations, 52 percent for medium foundations, and 65 percent for small foundations. This is striking, considering that more than 50 percent of the grants are given for the purchase of capital goods or construction, restoration, and conservation of buildings. Putting together the data from various different sources seems to confirm conventional wisdom about the charitable behavior of foundations. As many believe, foundations make many small grants to "country parish priests for restoring church bells." There is no definitive evidence to support this image, but the need to rethink the role of banking foundations and the foundation sector at large is quite evident.

A Changing Sector

The new laws and regulations have not yet been able to clarify the future of the Italian banking foundations. Some issues are still open. Are banking foundations part of the public or private sector? The law has not yet decided this crucial question. As public sector institutions, foundations would be subject to considerable legal constraints on their activities, such as hiring personnel and purchasing property, that do not apply to private sector employers. In this case, their operations could be strictly directed and controlled by government authorities.

While some legal experts consider foundations public sector bodies (see Rescigno, 1992, p. 399), board members and representatives of foundations oppose this interpretation and emphasize the private nature of banking foundations. The latter view is mostly based on historical evidence: while most of the *Istituti di Credito di Diritto Pubblico* have received quite a lot of money from the public purse during the course of their history (often as start-up capital), the *Casse di risparmio* almost never required public funds. Requests to recognize the private nature of the banking foundations became more pressing when the Minister of the Treasury issued a directive ordering these foundations to sell most of their bank shares (Merusi, 1995). A quite reasonable suspicion may lie behind these requests: if foundations are considered part of the public sector, then their assets may be expropriated or rigid regulations imposed on their use by the Ministry of the Treasury. Only recognition of their private status would make the assets of these foundations safe.

Should banking foundations thus be forced to sell the stocks of their banks and diversify their assets or should they be allowed to behave as holding companies concentrating their assets in one or just a few companies? Foundations with diversified assets could concentrate on their charitable business, while holding companies would be more interested in managing assets, increasing their size, and acquiring control of new companies, relegating charitable activity to an ancillary role. The outcome of this issue is not yet clear, although the legislature does seem inclined to move banking foundations in the direction of charitable activities. The bill under discussion considers the two issues together, while it is not forcing any foundation to sell the majority of the banks' shares, it will grant private legal status only to those institutions that will lose control.

Should banking foundations become grantmaking or operating foundations, or perhaps play both roles, as the law seems to imply? This is probably the most difficult question that banking foundations will have to answer in the future. The laws and regulations have not yet suggested any clear direction. Events may induce many administrators not to choose any model and to become both grantmaking and operating foundations. Government will probably push in the direction of operating foundations in their desire to get rid of deficit-prone institutions (such as hospitals, nursing homes, or universities) and "sell" them to rich nonprofit organizations, such as a foundation with significant liquid assets from the sale of a bank.

The wide availability of funds resulting from the sale of banks will probably drive the boards of the foundations in the same direction. Without any model of grantmaking organization that they might follow, most administrators will naturally do as most foundations do in Italy: start up—or buy—and manage large operating nonprofit organizations. The widespread notion that grantmaking is not an important and challenging task but, at most, an activity best suited for retired executives, will also encourage foundations to become operating bodies.

On the other hand, demands of local organizations, grassroots groups, and probably of local authorities will drive foundations toward grantmaking activity, as these groups depend heavily on grants from these institutions. The most likely outcome is that the banking foundations will combine the two types of activities. Different skills are required for running grantmaking and operating foundations, and international experience suggests that it is extremely difficult to do both effectively within one organizational entity. Moreover, the needs of the Italian nonprofit sector—with few grantmaking organizations—suggest a high demand for the creation of potent grantmaking institutions.

CONCLUSION

The Italian foundation sector is showing some peculiarities in the international context. Most foundations do not make grants to other organizations but provide goods and services to the public. Their endowments are generally very modest and they have to actively raise funds. Moreover, many of them do not undertake activities on a large scale but concentrate on the local level, performing a limited range of activities. Foundations, at least in this respect, do not differ much from other nonprofit organizations, such as associations or social cooperatives. In contrast to the specialized financial intermediaries that constitute the American or the British foundation sectors, foundation status is still but one of the many possible options for general nonprofit service activities. The limited degree of functional specialization is one of the most striking peculiarities of the Italian foundation field. However, it is not entirely surprising considering the relative underdevelopment of the nonprofit sector at large in Italy.

Several reasons explain the modest role of foundations in Italy and their generally small size. A legal system that until recently has been hostile to any institution that intermediates between citizens and the state is probably the most important reason. Fiscal provisions that do not provide sufficient incentives to donate and make bequests are part of this traditional legal attitude toward foundations. Moreover, one should not forget that, in Italy, it remains easy to avoid taxation on inheritance and bequests, so that fiscal incentives would be quite ineffective unless the enforcement of tax collection would be improved.

The social role of the Catholic Church provides another explanation for the limited role of foundations in Italy, especially grantmaking foundations. In the past and to a lesser degree even today, it was quite common for the wealthy of Catholic background to donate part of their wealth to the Church or church-run institutions. Quite frequently, donations and bequests became part of the wealth of local parishes or dioceses and, although used for charitable purposes, did not give rise to independent organizations.

Nevertheless, foundations are experiencing a new growth period. In fact, more than 70 percent of the foundations studied by Demarie (1997) were founded over the last twenty years, a clear sign that this ancient institutional form is undergoing a revival. The relative absence of grantmaking organizations remains the most substantial and pronounced deficiency of the Italian nonprofit sector. The whole institutional life of the country seems negatively influenced by this circumstance. The problem could be solved by the future evolution of the banking foundations, which are on the verge of transformation into genuine grantmaking organizations. Quite significantly, a country dominated by the French Jacobin tradition of centralization may get a sector of grantmaking institutions as a result of government policies and not from private benevolence.

NOTES

1. For a description of the legal treatment of these organizations, see, for example, Barbetta, 1997a, or, in greater detail, Cartabia and Rigano, 1997.
2. Some legal scholars dispute this principle, however, and believe that a foundation can legally serve the benefit of its founder (for references, see Sanfilippo & Maniaci, 1990, p. 59, 4). This would be the case of family foundations, for example.
3. Many of these laws predate the Civil Code.
4. This option has been available since 1977, after the creation of regional authorities by Presidential Decree 616/1976.
5. For a detailed discussion of the financial treatment of nonprofit organizations, see Cartabia and Rigano, 1997; Sanfilippo and Maniaci, 1990; and Propersi and Rossi, 1995.
6. About 80 percent have endowments of one billion lire or less (approximately $600,000) compared to 43 percent of other grantmaking foundations of that size.
7. Including about eighty *Casse di Risparmio*, or savings banks, and a limited number of credit institutions, or *Istituti di Credito di Diritto Pubblico.*
8. It should be noted that banking itself has long been considered as a public interest activity in Italy. The banking industry played—and still plays—a crucial role in sustaining the process of economic growth; State control of the banks was therefore considered a prerequisite for economic development.

REFERENCES

Association of Italian Savings Banks. (1996). *Primo rapporto sulle fondazioni bancarie.* Rome: Author.

Association of Italian Savings Banks. (1997). *Secondo rapporto sulle fondazioni bancarie.* Rome: Author.

Association of Italian Savings Banks (1998). *Tereo rapporto sulle fondazioni bancarie.* Rome: Author

Barbetta, G. P. (1997a). The nonprofit sector in Italy: A definition. In G. P. Barbetta (Ed.), *The nonprofit sector in Italy* (pp. 20–50). Manchester, UK: Manchester University Press.

Barbetta, G. P. (Ed.). (1997b). *The Nonprofit Sector in Italy.* Manchester, UK: Manchester University Press.

Barbetta, G. P., & Ranci, P. (1995). Le fondazioni bancarie come strumento di crescita civile. *Il Mulino,* n. 6, pp. 1109–1120.

Cartabia, M., & Rigano, F. (1997). The legal and tax status of the nonprofit sector. In G. P. Barbetta (Ed.), *The Nonprofit Sector in Italy* (pp. 51–79). Manchester, UK: Manchester University Press.

Ciriec (1979). *Le fondazioni italiane.* Milan: F. Angeli.

Clarich, M. (1984). *Le casse di risparmio.* Bologna, Italy: Il Mulino.

Demarie, M. (1997). Le fondazioni in Italia: Un profilo empirico. In *Per conoscere le fondazioni,* Edizioni Fondazione Giovanni Agnelli. Turin: Fondazione Giovanni Agnelli.

Guzzi, D. (1996). *Le fondazioni. Perche crearle e come gestirle.* Milan, Italy: FAG.

Merusi, F. (1995). Verso una nuova discipline degli enti conferenti. In Association of Italian Savings Banks (Ed.), *Gli enti conferenti tra il pubblico e il privato: Contribute e proposte.* Rome: Association of Italian Savings Banks.

Onida, V. (1992). Intervento. In G. P. Barbetta (Ed.), *Una discussione su "Non per profitto."* Milan, Italy: Fondazione A. Olivetti and IRS.

Propersi, A., & Rossi, G. (1995). *Associazioni e fondazioni.* Milan, Italy: DeLillo.

Ranci, P., & Barbetta, G. P. (Eds.). (1996). *Le fondazioni bancarie italiane verso l'attività grant-making,* Contributi di ricerca of the Fondazione G. Agnelli. Turin, Italy: Fondazione Giovanni Agnelli.

Ristuccia, S. (1996). *Volontariato e fondazioni.* Rimini, Italy: Maggioli.

Sanfilippo, F., & Maniaci, E. (1990). *Associazioni, fondazioni e comitati.* Rome: Buffetti.

Chapter 11

Foundations in Germany and Their Revival in East Germany after 1989

RUPERT GRAF STRACHWITZ

THE SPECIFIC POSITION OF EAST GERMANY

Like other self-governing bodies, foundations have a major role to fulfill in a civil society. Therefore, the establishment and reestablishment of foundations in Central and Eastern Europe after 1989 were indeed points of particular attention with the new political class and with the advisors from all over the world who assembled in these countries soon after the change of the political system. The development of foundations in Central and Eastern Europe was encouraged and in many cases made possible by the combined forces of the European foundation community and of foundations from the Untied States, Japan, and elsewhere. While the development has not been entirely satisfactory in all of these countries, new foundation legislation is being prepared or has been enacted in every one of them; new foundations, in some countries in larger quantities, have been established; aims traditionally pursued by foundations are indeed being pursued, and the contribution of domestic and foreign foundations to the development of these societies is noticeable and significant (see Quigley & Popson, Chapter 12, this volume).

RUPERT GRAF STRACHWITZ • Director, Maecenata Institute for Third Sector Studies, Berlin, Germany.

Private Funds, Public Purpose: Philanthropic Foundations in an International Perspective, edited by Helmut K. Anheier and Stefan Toepler. New York, Plenum Press, 1999.

Against this background it is an interesting question to examine the case of East Germany, the former German Democratic Republic (GDR), the one Central European communist country with a history substantially different from the others in the region and a very different development after 1989. It must be remembered that the GDR, despite all efforts of the communist regime, never became a nation in the sense that Hungary or Poland are and have been for centuries. After November 9, 1989, there never existed a serious alternative to unification of West and East Germany. Even the discussion as to how long any interim period might last—the last East German Government chosen by the freely elected parliament in April 1990 initially favored a two- to three-year period—was cut short very quickly by the general political development. Within less than a year after the wall opened, the Federal Republic of Germany that hitherto had comprised only the eleven West German federal states had been enlarged by the territory of East Germany in the shape of five new federal states created more or less within the boundaries of traditional political entities. East Berlin was simply amalgamated with West Berlin.

Under these circumstances, it is not surprising that the development of foundations, while adhering to the same basic principle of being welcomed as contributors to society, followed a different pattern than in other Central and Eastern European countries. For one, this matter—as indeed most other matters—was seen by everybody in and outside of Germany as an internal German affair. At no point did there arise a serious debate as to whether the European or World foundation community should make a major contribution, foster networking centers, or the like. European and U.S. foundations did of course give grants to projects in East Germany in individual cases. Although these grants were most welcome, they did not in anyway interfere with the establishment of legal structures, institutions, and the like. Unlike the independent reform states, such as Hungary, Poland or Estonia, to name just a few, neither the post-1989 GDR government nor the governments of the newly established federal states (Brandenburg, Mecklenburg–Vorpommern, Sachsen–Anhalt, Saxony, and Thuringia) ever seriously sought help or advice from outside Germany. In fact, one of the most fundamental rulings of the West German government, representing the opinion of all political parties, was that the new federal states should be modeled as closely as possible on those existing in West Germany.

Special partnerships were established, and 15,000 civil servants were dispatched to help form an administrative framework exactly comparable to West Germany. This system was resented from the beginning by intellectuals in East and West Germany and indeed by a large part of the East German population. The East German people in particular felt they were being treated like colonial subjects. The ill-feeling stemmed from the hopes raised in 1989–1990 that the reunification process would set in motion a general reform of structures. The fundamental question was whether there should be a new Germany or an enlarged West Germany. Politicians and civil servants were adamant that it should be the latter. The efforts of West German foundations that attempted to foster the other alternative remained episodes of no consequence. Thus, in legal and practical terms, the revival of foundations in East Germany must be seen in the more general context of its integration or reintegration into the Federal Republic.

THE GERMAN TRADITION OF FOUNDATIONS

In Germany, the term *Stiftung,* or foundation, has more than one meaning. On the one hand, it is a legal term that defines a legal body necessarily equipped with assets that serve either directly or through their revenue a particular statutory purpose. Ninety-five percent of foundations are registered public benefit organizations (Brummer, 1996), but this qualification is not in itself definitive. The great majority of these foundations are incorporated under civil law, a small minority under public law. On the other hand, the term *Stiftung* is a general term widely used for nonautonomous trusts (*nicht rechtsfähige Stiftungen*) that are similar to foundations proper in terms of their operations; although while not legal entities, they do constitute separate entities under fiscal law. The term is also used by legal entities that—while not being foundations in law—do attempt to act as such. They are usually incorporated as associations (*eingetragener Verein—eV*) or limited companies (GmbH) and have public benefit status. The reason for the difference in their legal framework is usually that they lack the necessary assets to incorporate as foundations and/or wish to avoid government supervision. These foundations in name, provided they operate like foundations, and the nonautonomous trusts are generally regarded as parts of the foundation community (Strachwitz, 1994).

Stiftung also refers to acts of giving that do not necessarily result in institutional foundations as described earlier. Finally, foundations in Germany may be operational or grant-giving. About two-thirds belong to the latter category (Brummer, 1996). Large foundations are quite often both. Whether a foundation operates a hospital or a museum, executes its own projects, awards prizes or gives grants, is laid down in the statutes of teh foundation proper but does not in any way constitute a legal difference.

Foundations have a long and rich tradition in Germany. The oldest of the 8,000 foundations in existence today stem from the tenth century. Over 250 foundations are more than 500 years old (Brummer, 1996). Citizens, aristocrats and princes alike, prided themselves in establishing institutions of aid to the socially underprivileged and later for other purposes, too, that would also serve as a memorial to themselves. Thanks to the extreme diversity of political entities, the tendency of eighteenth-century political thought to monopolize through government any activities for the public good left the German foundation world comparatively untouched, as opposed to France or Austria, where the suppression of foundations took place on a large scale. When, after German unification in 1871, a German civil code was passed by parliament to supplant the individual state codes and traditional legal practices, a special section on foundations was inserted that came into force with the rest of the code in 1900 and is still valid today. In §80–88 of the Civil Code (*Bürgerliches Gesetzbuch—BGB*), incorporated foundations are defined as particular legal entities as are associations. A few very broad legal stipulations follow, while government supervision and indeed all details of a legal framework are left to the federal states to legislate (Seifart, 1987). This reflects the fundamentally federal structure of the German political system. Accordingly, the laws on foundations passed by the individual states differ, not in principle, but indeed in many details. Government supervision may be stricter or less strict; legal terms adhere to diverse traditions; supervisory government agencies may be statewide, regional, or local; and so on.

Up to 1914, when Germany was comparatively affluent, quite a large number of new foundations were established. Especially the large industrial families, like Siemens and Zeiss/Abbe were prone to create new foundations. Most of these are still in existence. Like similar ones of more recent creation, they are quite frequently major shareholders in important business corporations. Between 1914 and 1949, by contrast, the general climate was unfavorable to foundations. Two World Wars, appalling economic conditions, and Nazi dictatorship did not foster the kind of environment that prompts potential founders to become active. The inflation of 1923 brought about the end of a great number of foundations, especially those who were administered, whether autonomous or not, by public bodies. These in particular had adhered to the urgent recommendations of government to invest in government bonds that became worthless by inflation and thus suffered the same fate as millions of private citizens whose trust in government was rewarded the same way. Unlawful acts on the part of the Nazi government and the general political chaos of 1945 had also contributed to the decimation of foundations, some of which had hitherto managed to survive for centuries.

With the reconstitution of German states, broadly speaking between 1945 and 1949, and the establishment of the Federal Republic of (West) Germany in 1949, political and social development created a more favorable climate once again. While the Civil Code still stood as a valid basis, it was now up to the eleven federal states to pass new foundation legislation—Bavaria being the first in 1955, and Bremen the last in 1982 (Burhenne, 1975). Strangely, however, neither the federal civil code nor any of the state laws regarding foundations ever made provision for any sort of publicity, although the improvement of the economic situation and the accumulation of wealth by private individuals in the postwar period let new creations soar. Also, the documentation foundations must file with the inland revenue service is totally protected from any form of publication, as are tax declarations of corporations or individuals.

Accordingly, no empirical data were available, and statistical information was practically nonexistent. In the early 1980s, the federal government attempted to enforce a national register of foundations but was blocked immediately by the state governments on constitutional grounds. It was only in 1989 that the Association of German Foundations (Bundesverband Deutscher Stiftungen), of which all major foundations are members, decided to have information collected for the publication of a first directory of German foundations. From this, a database was established and a number of additional publications ensued. One of the surprising findings was that nearly 50 percent of the existing German foundations had been established after 1949 and that by the late 1980s, nearly 200 new ones were being created each year (Brummer, 1996; Maecenata, 1996; Bundesverband, 1991; see also Anheier & Romo, Chapter 4, this volume).

FOUNDATIONS IN EAST GERMANY BETWEEN 1949 AND 1989

In the German Democratic Republic, also established in 1949, the situation was of course totally different (Franz, 1968). Due to the general lack of historical data (as described earlier), few data are available as to the quantity and size of foundations in that part of Germany as compared to the other part before 1945, but it may certainly be supposed that foundation communities existed in East German cities such as Leipzig, Dresden, and elsewhere that were as active as those in West German cities, such as Frankfurt or Hamburg (Büro Lokale Agenda 21 Dresden, 1997).

The East German communist government was, for obvious ideological reasons, not favorably disposed toward the foundation community. It is therefore not surprising that attempts to suppress foundation activity were made from the very beginning. Landowning foundations were dispossessed along with all other private landowners as early as 1945. Anybody who owned more than 100 hectars of land was totally expropriated without compensation. Quite a few East German foundations thus lost the basis of their income, as farmlands and forests had been the prime assets, especially of older foundations.

In 1953 the Ministry of the Interior in East Berlin issued instructions on foundations and similar groupings of assets. These instructions specified that "all private, public and other foundations which can no longer pursue their aims are to be reviewed as to whether they should be dissolved in accordance with §87 of the Civil Code [of 1900, which at that time was still in force in the GDR]. If a dissolution is possible, the relevant boards are to be induced to take the appropriate decisions. Is there no longer a board in existence or in cases where the board refuses to decide as outlined, the regional government agency (*Rat des Bezirks*) shall decide accordingly." This was the final blow for a great many foundations whose remaining assets were now confiscated by the government. Other foundations were dissolved by individual acts of government agencies, more often than not of very doubtful legality. In some cases, the war and postwar chaos had left foundations without any functioning board to voice any opposition. In a few instances however, board members of foundations with a legal seat in East Germany living in the West managed to transfer the legal seat provided that the assets too were obtainable. Liquid assets that could be claimed with West German banks could in this way be saved for their rightful owners.

The GDR Civil Code that in 1975 replaced the old German Civil Code of 1900 reduced foundations to a mere mention in §9 of the Introductory Act (Einführungsgesetz zum Zivilgesetzbuch, 1975). This act acknowledged the existence of foundations while tacitly admitting that most of them had been suppressed, and invested the regional agencies with the strongest possible powers of interference with the foundations' business. It is apparent that while in West Germany the whole concept of foundations and its practical enactment had thrived substantially since 1949, the development in East Germany was exactly the opposite. No new foundations were established and the existing ones were suppressed, their assets being confiscated to as large a degree as possible.

THE ROLE OF THE CHURCH

The German Catholic and Protestant churches enjoy the right to organize their affairs independently from government. They have the right to pass their own legislation as long it does not conflict with state legislation and they exercise this right quite widely. So, interestingly, we find foundations, some of them very ancient, that are based on church law only, this in turn being based on the autonomy of the churches, which in the case of the Federal Republic is part of the constitutional framework reflecting a long-standing historical development (Menges, 1995; Seifart, 1987).

In the Protestant and Catholic church, the legal entity that acts as proprietor of the parish churches is commonly a foundation of this type. It is estimated that about 50,000 of such church foundations exist in Germany that are not generally regarded as belonging to the foundation community proper. The same applies to the similar number of church tithes. The Christian churches, however, have traditionally also played an important role in attracting nonautonomous trusts and in administering autonomous foundations with charitable purposes relating to the educational and social mission of the church.

This is of considerable importance for the history of the foundation community in East Germany, for the only foundations in the GDR that had any chance at all to survive government action were church-affiliated. Both the Roman Catholic bishops and Protestant church organizations managed to keep the foundations and tithes intact and to take a certain number of other foundations to whom they had strong ties under their protection, thereby resisting government pressure. Considering the adversity of the regime toward the churches, as well as the extreme political pressure, it is indeed surprising that a number of traditional foundations managed to survive forty years of communism in this way.

There is another aspect of church involvement that should not be overlooked: Due to the East German government's policy of rendering contacts between individuals in East and West Germany as difficult as possible, no West German foundation created programs, let alone opened offices, in East Germany. Only toward the very end of the communist regime did a few larger West German research foundations—notably the Volkswagen Foundation—manage to foster a limited degree of scientific cooperation by way of giving grants to very specific projects. Therefore, it was through church channels alone, which remained open right through the communist period, that a limited amount of foundation funding could be directed toward projects in East Germany, particularly in the fields of cultural heritage and social welfare.

FOUNDATIONS AS INSTRUMENTS FOR SOLVING COMPLEX LEGAL SITUATIONS

Before examining how and to what degree the trend was reversed after 1989, it would seem important to draw attention to a particular role of foundations that is quite often overlooked. Traditionally, foundations are seen to be the creation of one or several citizens, be they private or corporate. However, the legal framework of a foundation has also, and very successfully, been used as an instrument to solve complex problems regarding the ownership of assets or other matters. One of the best examples is the Volkswagen Foundation, today the third largest foundation in Germany, with assets amounting to 2.7 billion DM (Volkswagen-Stiftung, 1995). Volkswagen Motor Company was originally a business outlet of a Nazi party organization (*Kraft durch Freude*).

Being situated in the British zone in 1945, it came under the supervision of the British military government. After the state of Lower Saxony and the Federal Republic had come into being, ownership of Volkswagen was the cause of a major dispute between these two constitutional bodies. In 1959, a solution was found by combining a settlement of ownership with government economic and science programs. Volkswagen went public and the shares were sold to private individuals through a complex system designed to involve as many citizens as possible as shareholders. The revenue from this sale was by law turned over to the newly established Volkswagen Foundation, the aim of which is to give grants to research projects, thereby meeting another urgent need of the day (i.e., to support and encourage research). It is obvious that the history of the establishment of the Volkswagen Foundation has nothing in common with that of other foundations that bear the name of large corporations. It is an example of government instituting a nongovernmental institution for very specific reasons.

Another example is the Stiftung Preußischer Kulturbesitz, a foundation established by the Federal Government to assume ownership of, and administer, the art treasures, archives, and State Library of the former state of Prussia abolished by Allied legislation in 1947 without determining a legal successor (Stiftung Preußischer Kulturbesitz, no date). In this case, government decided to draw on the legal form of a foundation under public law. Public Law foundations are formally autonomous legal bodies bearing characteristics of foundations, but that are established by act of parliament or government. Such foundations are in fact instruments of the state. Accordingly, they are legally bound to apply state regulations to staff policies and accounting procedures, and are empowered to act with the authority of a government agency. There are about 400 of these foundations in Germany today.

The case of the Stiftung Preußischer Kulturbesitz is in fact a borderline case. Obviously, the keeping of works of art is not in itself necessarily a government task. Practice shows that around fifty German civil law foundations are perfectly suited to be proprietors and managers of museums; about sixty own and manage libraries and/or archives (Brummer, 1996). The main argument for utilizing the public law foundation was that it should be in the strongest possible position to make claim to former Prussian properties. In addition, since the public showing of the works of art would not yield nearly enough revenue to pay for their upkeep, let alone the building of new museums, libraries, and so on, to replace the old ones that were either in East Berlin or destroyed, subsidizing this foundation became the objective of a very special formal agreement between the federal and all state governments. Since cultural affairs are constitutionally exclusively the task of the states and not of the Federal Republic, again, the foundation was seen to be a good solution to overcome this complication.

EAST GERMANY AFTER 1989

As we will see, these peculiarities of German foundation practice came to play quite an important role in East Germany after 1989. Given the general political framework of the unification process and the very specific fate of traditional foundations in East Germany, a uniform new regulatory system for foundations could not have been established. Loose ends, traditions, and a host of special considerations had to be acknowledged and addressed. The idea of utilizing foundations was rapidly picked up in proposals put forward to reestablish civic institutions in East Germany. For example, as early as February 1990, the author of this chapter was summoned to the East German Ministry of Justice for a discussion concerning issues relating to the following:

- The inclusion of the few East German foundations in the database on German foundations mentioned earlier.
- The establishment of a legal framework for foundations in the GDR by special legislation modeled on West German laws.
- The current status of extinct or dormant East German foundations and the prospects for revitalizing them.
- The establishment of foundations by government or by act of parliament to solve particular problems.
- The encouragement of West German foundations to open programs to East German application or set up operations after the fall of the Berlin Wall.

The word *foundation* seemed to inspire particular confidence with those in East Germany who had preserved their integrity by keeping a distance from the regime. The property of a former, now extinct, local Jewish community was returned to its purpose in the form of a foundation, in this case adopting the West German model of a foundation under public law created by an act of parliament. Also, an ecological advocacy group was set up provisionally as an association, but with the word *Stiftung* as part of its name and with a special provision that it would incorporate as a foundation as soon as this was legally possible. As early as November 1989, Kurt Körber, founder and chairman of one of the largest West German foundations, acquired the lease of a house in Dresden. He established a branch office of the Körber Foundation there, began to hold seminars for special interest groups, and staged a large conference on the basic problems of reunification that took place in April 1990, in the presence of Willy Brandt (former Chancellor of West Germany), Hans Modrow (ex-prime minister of the GDR), and other key players (Körber-Stiftung, 1990).

The Körber foundation also commissioned a former mayor of Hamburg, Klaus von Dohnanyi, to prepare a report on how foundations as legal structures could make a valuable contribution to disentangling ownership problems concerning property. Practically all producers and sellers of goods and services were, in communist times, organized as so-called peoples' enterprises (*Volkseigene Betriebe—VEB*) by government and the socialist party. But by a finesse of terminology, there was supposed to be a legal difference between VEBs and straight state property, resulting in some confusion over the actual ownership under the new political system. Moreover, many of these enterprises had, in the best socialist tradition, come to run branches that had no direct business purpose, such as holiday homes, kindergartens, or even art museums. It was suggested that putting these institutions in the hands of foundations might grant them a stable structure while avoiding the difficult discussion on ownership and relieving the businesses of cost-intensive marginal units (Dohnanyi et al., 1990). The paper prepared by Dohnanyi relied on West German experiences and examples. It drew on the full range of legal options available, generally favoring a nongovernmental approach as opposed to a top-down administrative one.

Unfortunately, by the time of its presentation, the general trend had been reversed. After the first and only free elections in the GDR and the establishment of the new government under Lothar de Maizière, West German politicians and civil servants began to invade the East German ministries and government agencies as advisors. Very soon, few decisions of consequence were made in the GDR government without the consent of the West Germans. This was the time when the anticipated transition period of two to three years was reduced to five months, and it became one of the principles of government policy to hook East Germany on to the West German political and administrative system as smoothly and quickly as possible.

The scope for new ideas for private initiative and experiments, and the range for real and distinctive East German contributions to the new Germany narrowed, and suggestions like the Dohnanyi paper were either turned down or simply disregarded. The VEBs were defined as state ownership and the powerful state agency, Treuhandanstalt, was installed to take full charge and to privatize individual businesses along traditional lines. The Treuhandanstalt never seriously considered foundations as an option in dealing with ownership issues and flatly turned down ideas that might have gone in that direction. It is obviously quite impossible to say today whether the foundation approach would have been more successful in solving East Germany's basic economical problems, but it is certainly reasonable to assume that at least a partial use of these ideas might have alleviated some of the grievances incurred during the process of transformation.

REGULAR FOUNDATION ACTIVITIES INTRODUCED IN EAST GERMANY

There were, of course, other fields where foundations could make an impact. The last GDR government realized that it would be necessary to pass a law on private foundations in the GDR parliament, as it was assumed that it would take years before the then "states-to-be" would enact respective legislation. West German foundation experts were instrumental in formulating a law, advising the East Berlin ministries to push it through parliament. In the end, they were successful in that the East German parliament passed the law in September 1990, and the East German government introduced it into one of the provisions of the unification treaty, so that it would remain the legal basis in the East German states (excluding East Berlin) until they should pass legislation of their own (*Gesetzblatt*, 1990). In principle and wording, it is the best foundation law in Germany, and it is hard to understand why the poorest East German state, Mecklenburg–Vorpommern, decided to pass its own foundation law shortly thereafter, as did Brandenburg in 1994 (Burhenne, 1975).

With the consent of all concerned, the minute East German foundation community had from May 1990 been invited to participate in the database on German foundations and indeed in meetings and activities of the foundation community wherever possible. Probable information sources (e.g., church bodies) were approached. Some were more helpful than others, but considering the odds, the efforts were not entirely unsuccessful and in some cases the simple statement that they were possibly still there enabled foundation managers, quite often self-appointed, to start picking up the pieces and reestablishing themselves. Thus, since 1990, a whole array of old foundations has been brought to life again. In the case of the Franckesche Stiftungen in Halle, it was found that a government act of 1947 had turned the foundation into a nonautonomous trust administered by the state university. The new government of Sachsen–Anhalt simply declared the act of 1947 to be null and void, thus reestablishing one of the most distinguished seventeenth-century civic creations (Raabe, 1995).

Another case, acting under legal advice paid for by the large West German Robert–Bosch–Foundation, challenged the disestablishment of a foundation under the 1953 ministerial guidelines that implied a violation of the Thuringia foundation law of 1924. According to the latter, a disestablishment was to become valid only after official publication. Since this had not happened in 1953, the courts now ruled that the disestablishment had not formally taken place. So, based on this purely formal argument, the St. Georgs–und St. Jakobs–Stift, dating back to the eleventh century, was saved.

The Zeiss foundation is a very special case. Founded toward the end of the last century by the industrialist Ernst Abbe, this foundation not only owned but also actually managed the Zeiss corporation. The seat was moved to West Germany after the war on the economic strength of its largest subsidiary situated in Württemberg. After 1989, the original works in Jena could have reverted back to the foundation, but the financial burden was found to be too great. So, upon the advice of a former prime minister of Baden–Wuerttemberg, Lothar Spaeth, a joint venture was established between the Zeiss foundation and the government of Thuringia.

For many old foundations, the absence of a legal representative presented one of the most difficult obstacles to overcome. Moreover, the state and local authorities were most reluctant to reprivatize institutions or assets that had come under their full control during the communist era. This attitude reflected the overall government position whereby the unification process was to be managed entirely by politicans and civil servants along established West Germans lines, private initiative at the policy level being utterly unwelcome. A rare exception to this rule was the move taken by the East German ministry of culture, toward the very end of its existence, to allot funds for the establishment of three small but totally autonomous foundations: the Kulturstiftung Haus Europa, the Stiftung Neue Kultur, and the Stiftung Industrie–und Alltagskultur. They were established only one week before the GDR formally ceased to exist. To take advantage of the new GDR foundation law, Potsdam, the nearest seat of a future state government, was chosen as legal seat and the application for state recognition was filed with the preparatory office for the establishment of a Brandenburg state government on September 27, 1990. By the time the state of Brandenburg had formally been constituted, a parliament elected, the government appointed, tasks appropriated to various government departments, a foundation department established within the ministry of the interior and, after several unsuccessful attempts, a West German civil servant chosen as its head, nearly eighteen months had passed. Even then, there was no expertise on how to treat the pending applications of these three foundations. Since the establishment as such is a unilateral act and only the legal personality is conferred by government recognition, the three foundations were nonetheless able to operate all through this time as nonautonomous trusts. When recognition was finally granted at the end of 1992, they had long become fully operational (Stiftung Industrie–und Alltagskultur, 1991; Kulturstiftung Haus Europa, 1992).

The ministry of culture also created another much larger foundation out of a former GDR organization, the *Kulturfonds*. It derived its income from a small surcharge on the price of museum and theater tickets—the so-called "*Kulturgroschen*." In the GDR, the means of the Kluturfonds were used both to support art projects and to provide social security for artists. This organization was turned into a foundation under public law because of the social security aspects. Assets of DM 100 million and federal government funding were to ensure the integration of the artists' social security into the West German social security system over a period of four years. Also, there were considerable means to assist local artists so as to enable them to continue working under very different economic conditions (Stiftung Kulturfonds, 1993). Unfortunately, the state government of Saxony has decided to take its share out and thus partially dismantled this "central" institution—incidentally, a step that would not be feasible if the *Kulturfonds* had been incorporated under civil rather than public law.

The euphoria of reunification in 1989 and 1990 naturally prompted West German citizens and institutions to start grantmaking activities for East Germany. A good example is the Robert–Bosch–Stiftung that developed a special grant program for small social welfare organizations in East Germany (Robert–Bosch–Stiftung, 1996). Another particular focus was the restoration of important monuments of cultural heritage, which, after decades of neglect, had been one of the demands of the protest movements in 1989; the issue was close to the heart of people who had historical ties to places such as Dresden or Leipzig, including members of the business community such as the Dresdner Bank. In these cases, new foundations, notwithstanding their East German focus, were usually set up wherever the founder happened to reside in West Germany, avoiding lengthy bureaucratic procedures in East Germany. Some founders, however, thought it right to wait until their foundation could be established in East Germany. In battling the inadequacies of the government agencies, these founders have quite often acted as pioneers and eased the path for successors to come (Campenhausen, 1997). Finally, the efforts of a government-sponsored foundation, the *Kulturstiftung der Länder,* to include East German institutions in its grant program for buying works of art of national importance should not go unmentioned. A famous case was the Quedlinburg treasure, bought back from the heirs of an American soldier who had taken it in 1945 (Kulturstiftung der Länder, 1995).

THE SITUATION TODAY

Today, East Germany's foundations are fully integrated into the West German pattern. Differences are slight. The East German state governments, like their West German counterparts, have themselves begun to establish several foundations, usually for cultural purposes. They have installed many of these under public law for no apparent reason, including the Stiftung Preußische Schlösser und Gärten Berlin und Brandenburg, the Stiftung Schlösser und Gärten (Wistinghausen, 1996). Well-known foundations, like the one that owns and manages the Wartburg—Martin Luther's one-time refuge—which survived as an independent institution during the GDR period, have been revitalized (Wistinghausen, 1996). New creations include the Kulturstiftung Sachsen and the Stiftung Weimarer Klassik, both combinations of operational and grant-giving foundations. The civil servants responsible for the supervision of foundations have been trained by the Association of German Foundations as to their role and especially as regards the limits of their powers.

The churches have usually been cooperative in allowing the foundations they had taken under their wings to reassume their previous autonomy. However, in some cases, managers whose record were not always beyond doubt have kept their hold on power and forestalled necessary changes (Campenhausen, 1995). Some government agencies, and especially local governments, are still toying with the idea of using foundations solely for fund-raising purposes. On the other hand, voluntary bodies established as associations in 1989 and 1990 are now being transformed into foundations in accordance with their original intentions. One fine example of this is the Cranach–Stiftung in Wittenberg, originally created by a civil rights group in the GDR.

Overall, the number of foundations in East Germany has grown considerably between 1990 and 1996 (Brummer, 1996). The general public has accepted foundations as a useful form of not-for-profit activities and as a source of funds for special projects. The proper place for foundations in a modern concept of a society, however, is only slowly being discovered both in West and East Germany (Zimmer, Priller, & Anheier, 1996). Indeed, it may not be an exaggeration to say that a fundamental understanding of the limitations of government and of the importance of nongovernmental organizations is gradually taking hold to the same extent everywhere in the country.

The blessing of private initiative for public affairs is destined to be appreciated more deeply. Empty government coffers and a regular exchange of views with experts from all over the world add impetus, even if concepts developed indigenously sometimes still lack a realistic approach to the vital issue of endowing and funding new foundations. Still, in some instances, the word foundation is taken to be a magic wand to be waved over the financial straights of an educational, cultural, or other charitable institution with expected instant results. But as people adjust to the realities of life in a democracy as its assets—and liabilities—are seen more clearly, the not-for-profit sector in general, and foundations in particular, move into perspective as vital but not all-powerful aspects of a civil society.

REFERENCES

Brummer, E. (Ed.). (1996). *Statistiken zum deutschen Stiftungswesen*. Munich: Maecenata.
Bundesverband Deutscher Stiftungen. (Ed.). (1991). *Verzeichnis der deutschen Stiftungen*. Darmstadt: Hoppenstedt.

Bundesverband Deutscher Stiftungen. (Ed.). (1994). *Bericht über die 50. Jahrestagung.* Bonn: Bundesverband.

Burhenne, W. E. (Ed.). (1975). *Recht der gemeinnützigen Organisationen und Einrichtungen.* Berlin: Erich Schmidt. (updated periodically)

Büro Lokale Agenda 21 Dresden. (Ed.). (1997). *Stiftungen in Dresden.* Dresden: Büro.

Campenhausen, A. Frhr. v. (1995). Alte Stiftungen in den neuen Ländern In J. Goydke et al. (Eds.), *Vertrauen in den Rechtsstand, Beiträge zur deutschen Einheit im Recht, Festschrift für Walter Remmes* (pp. 38–44). Cologne: Heymanns.

Campenhausen, A. Frhr. v. (1997). Zum Geleit. In Bundesverband Deutscher Stiftungen (Ed.)., *Deutsche Stiftungen im Prozeß der Einigung* (p. 5). Bonn: Bundesverband.

Carl–Zeiss–Stiftung. (1985). *Die Carl–Zeiss–Stiftung.* Oberkochen, Germany: Author.

Dohnanyi, K. v., et al. (1990). *Stiftungen und die Privatisierung "volkseigener" Betriebe.* Hamburg: Körber-Stiftung.

Franz, A. (1968). Das große Stiftungssterbern in Mitteldeutschland. In R. Hauer et al. (Eds.), *Deutsches Stiftungswesen—Wissenschaft und Praxis* (pp. 435–445). Tübingen: Siebeck/Mohr.

Gesetzblatt der Deutschen Demokratischen Republik, Teil 1, Nr. 61, 1990.

Körber–Stiftung. (1990). *90. Bergedorfer Gesprächskreis, Wie geht es weiter mit den Deutschen in Europa?* Hamburg: Körber–Stiftung.

Kulturstiftung der Länder. (1995). *Tätigkeitsbericht II.* Berlin: Kulturstiftung.

Kulturstiftung Haus Europa. (Ed.). (1992). *Patronage by the Arts by Foundations and Nongovernment Organizations in Europe.* Berlin: Maas.

Maecenata. (Ed.). (1996). *Stiftungsführer.* Munich: Maecenata.

Menges, E. D. (1995). *Die kirchliche Stiftung in der Bundesrepublik Deutschland.* St. Ottilien, Germany: Eos.

Raabe, P. (1995, September 27). Leuchtturm in der kulturellen Landschaft. *Frankfurter Allgemeine Zeitung.*

Rackow, L. (1997). Deutsche Stiftungen im Prozeß der Einigung; Wirkungen–Leistungen–Handlungsbedarf. In Bundesverband Deutscher Stiftungen (Ed.), *Deutsche Stiftungen im Prozeß der Einigung* (pp. 79–91). Bonn: Bundesverband.

Robert–Bosch–Stiftung. (1996). *Bericht 1994–1995.* Stuttgart: Author.

Seifart, W. (1987). *Handbuch des Stiftungsrechts.* Munich: C. H. Beck'sche Verlagsbuchhandlung.

Stiftung Industrie–und Alltagskultur. (Ed.). (1991). *Einblicke–Ausblicke.* Berlin: Stiftung.

Stiftung Kulturfonds. (1993). *Jahresbericht 1992.* Berlin: Stiftung.

Stiftung Preußischer Kulturbesitz, brochure, Berlin, undated.

Strachwitz, R. G. (1994). *Stiftungen nutzen, führen und errichten—ein Handbuch.* Frankfurt/New York: Campus.

Strachwitz, R. G. (1996). Deutschland in Europa—Der kulturelle Beitrag der ostdeutschen Länder. In B. J. Sobotka & J. Strauss (Eds.), *Burgen, Schlösser, Gutshäuser in Sachsen* (pp. 39–43). Stuttgart: Theiss.

Toepler, S. (1996). *Das gemeinnützige Stiftungswesen in der modernen demokratischen Gesellschaft.* Munich: Maecenata.

Volkswagen–Stiftung. (1995). *Jahresbericht.* Hanover: Volkswagen–Stiftung.

Wistinghausen, M. V. (1996). *Who does what for heritage conversation in Germany.* München, Germany: Maecenata.

Zimmer, A., Priller, E., & Anheier, H. (1996). Der Nonprofit–Sektor in den neuen Bundesländern: Kontinuität, Neuanfang oder Kopie? *Zeitschrift für öffentliche und gemeinwirtschaftliche Unternehemen, 20,* 58–76.

Zivilgesetzbuch der Deutschen Demokratischen Republik. (1989). Berlin: Staatsverlag der Deutschen Demokratischen Republik.

Chapter 12

Rebuilding Civil Society in Eastern and Central Europe
The Role Played by Foundations

Kevin F. F. Quigley and Nancy E. Popson

In the years since the fall of the Berlin Wall in 1989, it has been increasingly clear that building democracy is a complex, uncertain, time-consuming process that is necessarily dependent upon domestic factors. External assistance, however, can play a supporting role in this process. Although there has been considerable attention given to the activities of the international financial institutions and official assistance programs, such as the World Bank and the U.S. Agency for International Development (USAID), there has been relatively little given to the role played by foundations in helping build democracy in Eastern and Central Europe (ECE).[1] In this chapter we hope to begin to remedy that deficit by focusing on one aspect of foundations' recent role, that is, their efforts to help rebuild civil society through their work with the nongovernmental organization (NGO) sector.[2]

Unlike any other events, those in ECE at the end of the 1980s sparked a response from the international foundation community. Perhaps driven by a sense of common heritage and purpose, more than sixty European and North American foundations, most of which had not previously been active interna-

KEVIN F. F. QUIGLEY • Vice President, Policy and Business Programs, Asia Society, New York, New York 10021.   NANCY E. POPSON • Senior Program Associate, Kennan Institute, Woodrow Wilson International Center for Scholars, Washington, D.C. 20523.

Private Funds, Public Purpose: Philanthropic Foundations in an International Perspective, edited by Helmut K. Anheier and Stefan Toepler. New York, Plenum Press, 1999.

tionally, responded to the call for assistance.[3] Between 1989 and 1994, these foundations invested over $600 million in ECE.[4]

Although this amount may not seem especially large either relative to the inflated expectations, to the contributions of the international community, or on a per capita basis, it is significant compared to the $164 million committed by USAID for a roughly comparable period (Agency for International Development, 1996). This overall foundation response represents an unprecedented rallying of resources behind the cause of building democracy and deserves closer inspection. Such an inspection may yield important insights regarding the role played by foundations in strengthening the NGO sector and may enhance their efforts in ECE or other regions of the world.

STRENGTHENING CIVIL SOCIETY THROUGH THE NGO SECTOR

In the first few years after the collapse of communism, both public and foundation assistance to ECE tended to focus on building the structures necessary for a market economy. This was based in large part on the assumption that democracy could not be built without the base of a thriving market economy. However, by 1992 or so, foundations increasingly began to shift their resources from economic reform programs to those geared toward the civil society sector. Foundations generally understood civil society as that sphere of social action situated between the state and the individual that is critical to building democracy.[5]

In particular, foundations emphasized one aspect of civil society—the NGO sector. This is visible in the grants lists of foundations and has been noted by foundation officials and activists.[6] This is not to say that there are no other approaches to strengthening civil society, nor that foundations ignored such alternatives. For example, the Free Trade Union Institute, one of the National Endowment for Democracy's core organizations, has strongly favored programs working with trade unions. In addition, the Soros network of foundations, among others, has emphasized support for independent media. However, foundations' programs aimed at rebuilding civil society placed a particular emphasis on the development of NGOs, including policy research institutions, foundations, charity organizations, community groups, and nonprofits engaged in various societal issues. They also emphasized the creation of an environment conducive to NGO activity. This strategy of working with NGOs was based on foundations' considerable experiences with these organizations, which were quite distinct from those of the international institutions and official assistance programs.

Foundations' emphasis on the NGO sector illustrated a shift in the understanding of democracy and how best to create one. Although foundations espoused no single clear definition of democracy, their focus on NGOs suggested an understanding of democracy as linked to the participation of the citizenry not only in the official procedures of democratic life but also in community activity apart from the state and the economic spheres. This view assures that through NGOs and other institutions of the civil society sector, citizens develop the ways and means—that is, the skills, attitudes, and resources—to function effectively in a democratic society. As one ECE government official remarked, NGOs are the real DNA of democracy, transferring democratic genes to the society.[7]

This shift in foundations' emphasis can be attributed to a practical assessment of their "comparative advantage." Foundations, wielding limited resources in comparison to large government or international financial institution programs, must necessarily search for ways to put their funds to the best possible use. With large and growing publicly funded programs in the economic and state spheres in ECE, foundations recognized that their resources would have more impact in a less crowded arena. Moreover, foundations that had already been active internationally found that their previous experiences in NGO development applied, despite the different geographic area and cultural conditions.

The manner of foundation work also lent itself to NGO development projects. Foundations could more easily work with NGOs directly, bypassing state-to-state arrangements. They could also make smaller and more flexible grants that could be more easily utilized by the NGO sector. Finally, the very nature of foundations as an integral part of Western civil society gave them an advantage in the sector. Simply through the contact ECE NGOs had with foundations, they could gain valuable insights into the world of Western NGOs.

Foundations' general approach was also helpful as part of their strategy of targeting the NGO sector. Foundations perceive their role as society's social venture capital sector, investing in innovative approaches that can be taken to scale by others. Unfortunately, foundations are less successful in this role than they may wish. The general thrust of foundations' work in ECE is an exception to this. Their focus on rebuilding civil society through the NGO sector has been emulated by a number of public funders. For example, USAID launched a $30 million program to support NGOs in the former communist countries. This program, called Democracy Network, has tried to take some of the best practices of foundations and apply them through a publicly funded mechanism. The European Union's Poland and Hungary Assistance for the Restructuring of the Economy (PHARE) Democracy Programme is another publicly funded program geared toward assisting the NGO sector and influenced by foundations' experience. The World Bank has also begun to recognize that relationships forged with NGOs through its poverty and economic programs may be an important strategic goal rather than simply a side effect, and has thus become increasingly aware of foundations and their international activities.[8]

Given this burgeoning interest in working with NGOs, this may now be a good time to step back and assess what foundations have done with NGOs in ECE.[9] This chapter therefore outlines the form, styles, and structure that foundation assistance has taken in the region since 1989. Through examples of different initiatives, it aims to determine what has worked best and why. It then draws conclusions regarding the best practices to assist democracy through the NGO sector. These lessons should be applicable not only to foundation programs in other regions further south and east, but also to publicly funded programs active in the sector.

THE ROLE OF FOUNDATIONS

Between 1989 and 1994, foundations invested more than $50 million in ECE's NGO sector.[10] Although the international community has committed some $76 million to this sector, this represents less than 1 percent of their total programs in the region (Agency for International Development, 1994). The foundation response is therefore quite significant. Only higher education programs received more attention from the foundation community. Of the sixty foundations active in ECE in this time period, more than half conducted programs dealing with the NGO sector in the region. Not surprisingly, given the prominence of the NGO sector in the United States relative to Western Europe, the majority of assistance was given by U.S. foundations. Foundations conducted NGO programs in all of the ECE countries, as well as a number of initiatives that were regional in nature.

After the fall of the Berlin Wall, the call for help in developing civil society in ECE was met with diverse responses from the foundation world. One aspect of this diversity was the style of grantmaking. Generally, there are four types of grants that foundations have used in investing in the broader category of democracy assistance: technical assistance, training, research, and institution building.

In the NGO sector, foundations have initiated technical assistance programs in order to bring experts to the region to assist new NGOs in their fundraising, networking, and public relations campaigns. A number of training programs have also been funded and have taken place both in the region and abroad, usually through short-term study tours. Early on, many foundations relied largely on short seminars to train NGO activists. However, both foundation officials and the NGO sector in ECE realized that such endeavors are often not cost-effective for either side. As a result, grants emphasizing short-term seminars have slowly been replaced by training programs of longer duration with built-in follow-up activities in the region, such as the Civil Society Development Program and Johns Hopkins University's Third Sector Project Training-of-Trainers Program. Foundations also funded some policy-related research and independent research institutions, or think tanks, that are part of the NGO sector.

There is a great deal of rhetoric about the importance of institution-building in the foundation world. Despite this professed strategic goal, institution building in democracy assistance programs has been less of an emphasis than might be expected. It is especially important for the NGO sector to receive institution-building grants that support the operating costs of the organization. Many activists contend that without such support, the fledgling NGO sector will be unable to survive in the long term.[11] To some extent, foundations recognized this. Of those institution-building grants made in the region, a large portion went to the NGO sector. Some foundations, such as Soros, make a point of providing operational support to the NGO sector. Also, certain NGOs, such as Autonomia Alapitvany in Hungary, have been able consistently to garner operational, institution-building support from Western foundations. Those that have received operating support now appear to have better prospects for sustainability.

Besides institution-building grants, foundations have also supported NGOs in ECE indirectly, through operational support for Western intermediaries that conduct programs in support of NGOs. This emphasis on Western intermediaries was understandable in the early years of foundation involvement. Intermediaries had a better understanding of the local atmosphere, had established contacts, and were able more efficiently to deliver funds than foundations that lacked an on-the-ground presence. However, now that many NGOs have matured to the point where they can efficiently develop business plans and handle grants and audits effectively, the continued reliance on Western intermediaries is rapidly losing utility.

In part, reliance on Western partners depended upon the foundation's presence in the region. This is another way in which foundation programs have been diverse. Some funders, such as the Soros network of foundations, the C. S. Mott Foundation (Mott), and the European Cultural Foundation (ECF), have opened offices in the region from which grant programs are designed and implemented. Others have conducted activities from their base offices in North America, Europe, or Japan. Foundations without ECE offices usually relied on intermediaries or funded well-known local in stitutions with internationally successful leaders.

Foundations have also differed in the locus of their programs. By this, we mean not only in which country a foundation operated, but also where grants were made within the country. Even seven years after the fall of the Berlin Wall, much of foundation (and public, for that matter) funds are still invested in the capital cities. With grants to the NGO sector, this means that most organizations without a capital city presence find it extremely difficult to secure funding from international foundations. Some foundations, however, have consistently made a point of reaching outside of the capitals in their grantmaking. Most notable among these is the Soros network of foundations, which has established a network of local foundations in Romania, Slovakia, and Ukraine.

Another important distinction between foundation programs is the extent to which they involve the interested local population or stakeholders in the identification, design, and implementation of the project.[12] This is especially crucial for democracy-building purposes. If a project includes stakeholder participation, the goal of creating a participatory society is served by the process of the project as well as its outcome. In other words, the involvement of local persons with a vested interest in the project is a way to make the means serve the end goals. Ideally, the local population should be involved at every stage of the process, from needs identification through implementation to follow-up activities. To date, however, most foundation programs have emphasized local involvement only during the implementation stages and thus have not realized their full participatory potential.

Foundation activities designed to help rebuild a vital civil society sector in ECE through NGO support have thus approached the issue from many perspectives. We now turn to a few illustrative examples of foundation activity with a view to extracting lessons that can be applied to other regions and other funders.

FOUNDATION PROGRAMS

Foundations have tended to focus their activities in the NGO sector on three types of programs. Great emphasis was placed on the creation or support of information centers for the NGO sectors in each country. Training, sometimes combined with a focus on networking and building cross-sectoral partnerships, has also been a popular tool for grantmakers in the region. Finally, foundations have been more attuned to institution-building needs in the NGO sector than in other democracy assistance programs. They have helped establish a number of organizations and (to a lesser extent) have given grants to cover NGO operational expenses. In supporting individual institutions of the growing NGO sector, foundations have funded both those that directly affect the NGO community through their activities and those that ostensibly focus on another field—such as the environment or human rights—but through their mode of work enhance the sector.

Providing Services for the NGO Sector

NGO information centers are seen by many foundations as essential to the everyday functioning of NGOs. Therefore, it is not surprising that a great deal of foundation attention—especially by American foundations—has been devoted to the creation and maintenance of such centers in ECE. These centers generally provide a variety of services to the NGO community, including training seminars, legal and administrative counseling, database and networking services, and information on domestic and international fund-raising opportunities.

The information center established in Slovakia, the Slovak Academic Inforatmion Agency–Service Center for the Third Sector (SAIA–SCTS), is one example of this type of organization. It has counterparts in Bulgaria, the Czech Republic, Poland, and Hungary.[13] SAIA–SCTS was originally developed as a project of the Ministry of Education, Youth, and Sport of the Slovak Republic to provide information and coordinate educational exchanges. It became an independent NGO on January 1, 1992.[14] SAIA–SCTS's board is exclusively comprised of Slovaks, many with academic backgrounds. In addition to its main office in Bratislava, SAIS–SCTS has branch offices in Nitra, Banska Bystrica, Zilina, Kosice, and Poprad. This is extremely important because it is a break with the centralized, capital-city-dominant pattern of the past.

SAIA–SCTS's mission is to "promote the internationalization, democratization, and modernization of education and research in Slovakia."[15] SAIA–SCTS pursues its mission through a variety of activities. It maintans a database on more than 1,600 nonprofit organizations, trains NGO leaders, provides consultations for NGOs, and publishes and translates material related to the NGO sector. Since 1990, SAIA–SCTS has hosted a series of conferences (known as the Stupava Conferences) on the NGO sector. These conferences are an opportunity for the Slovak NGO sector to gather and exchange information about the state of the sector and to devise strategies for strengthening it. Initially, the conferences relied heavily on foreign trainers and materials. Since 1994, however, SAIA–SCTS has prepared domestic trainers and materials more specifically targeted to the needs of Slovakia's NGO sector.

Although SAIA–SCTS is not directly controlled by the ministry, the government initially provided an important part of its budget. The cancellation, on short notice, of SAIA–SCTS's major contract with the Education Ministry in the fall of 1995 therefore presented a serious institutional challenge. SAIA–SCTS was able to weather the withdrawal of this major contract because it had developed a variety of other programs, some of which produce indpendent revenue streams. In addition, SAIA–SCTS receives support from a variety of foundations including the Ford Foundation (Ford), the Rockefeller Brothers Fund (RBF), Mott, the Foundation for Civil Society (FCS), the Sasakawa Peace Foundation (Sasakawa), and the Bratislava-based Foundation for the Support of Citizen Activity.

Training NGO Activists

Besides support for NGO information centers, foundations have also been active in funding training programs. Perhaps the most ambitious training efforts were parallel efforts undertaken by two American organizations. The first—the Civil Society Development Program (CSDP)—was launched by two American activists who were intially supported by the International Youth Foundation (IYF) to conduct research on young ECE leaders. These researchers, Dan Siegel and Jenny Yancey, developed virtually unrivaled access to young leaders throughout the region, including those outside of capital cities. After authoring a landmark monograph supported by RBF, Siegel and Yancey moved to Budapest to train a small team of NGO sector leaders in Hungary and Poland (Siegel & Yancey, 1992). The concept was to train-the-trainers and leave behind a small cohort that could then continue training after Siegel and Yancey returned to the United States. Siegel and Yancey were initially funded by foundations, including RBF and Mott, and subsequently obtained funding from USAID. Althought this train-the-trainer concept was an important idea, realizing it proved much more difficult than anticipated as the program experienced significant attrition.[16]

The other major NGO sector training effort was the Third Sector Project Training-of-Trainers Program (TOT), launched by Lester Salamon from the Johns Hopkins University (Hopkins). This effort was designed to meet three basic goals: to create teams of skilled trainers and providers of technical assistance for nonprofit organizations in each of the countries in which that program operates; to help create in each country a local institutional base from which the indigenous trainers could operate on a permanent basis; and to improve the information resources for nonprofit management in the region by promoting the development of indigenous resources. To help accomplish these goals, Hopkins opened offices in Budapest, Hungary and Moscow, Russia, housing two full-time regional representative to provide "on the ground" support for the project. By 1997, fifty-six trainers had completed the Hopkins TOT program and partner organizations in seven countries had been established. Although this program has resulted in more than 43,000 person days of training to over 24,000 nonprofit staff and volunteers in the seven countries, the search for local funding for these activities continues to be a struggle for each of the partner organizations.[17]

Another noteworthy NGO training initiative is the Women in Civil Society Programme, funded by the Westminster Foundation for Democracy (Westminster). It is significant in that it is one of few such programs actively seeking to combine training efforts with cross-sectoral networking. The Programme grants funds to the Foundation of the Women of Hungary (MONA) to organize a series of workshops for women NGO activists. Through a series of meetings, MONA seeks to increase communication among women's groups, parliamentarians, local government officials, and representatives from the academic, policymaking, and business worlds in Hungary. Such networking has been lauded by NGO activists as crucial to the sustainability of the sector.[18]

Program and Operational Support for NGOs

These types of networking and partnership-building activities complement the main form of grantmaking that foundations have emphasized in the region—funding the programs of individual NGOs. While institution building per se has taken a smaller role in democracy assistance than hoped, many foundations that are participating in institution-building programs are doing so with the NGO sector. Foundations often support the programs of NGOs, allowing them to continue or expand their activities. This, however, falls short of the operational funds that NGOs need to both conduct programs and maintain day-to-day operations. Fewer foundations have taken that next step and funded the infrastructure of individual organizations.

Soros, however, is an exception. His foundations have been highly visible in their use of institution-building grants to promote the development of NGOs in the region. Soros's very network of national foundations illustrates this fact. Early on, Soros established local foundations in each of the countries in which it was active. One such foundation that has been able to retain that independence, as well as attract funds from other foundations, is the Stefan Batory Foundation (SBF) in Poland.

SBF was formally registered in Warsaw on May 7, 1988.[19] Although SBF identifies itself as part of the Soros network of foundations, according to its annual report, "The Stefan Batory Foundation enjoys complete autonomy in taking decisions affecting its activities" (Stefan Batory Foundation, 1994). This is despite the fact that SBF's Foundation Council is appointed by George Soros. The Council is responsible for oversight of SBF's general affairs, policymaking, and appointment of the board and chair. Aleksander Smolar, a prominent political dissident who emigrated to France in 1969, serves as SBF's chair.

From 1991–1994, SBF's budget was $9.1 million, of which approximately 75 percent was used for programs. SBF is primarily active in the education field, although it also conducts activities in the fields of health care, culture,

the media, and civil society development. It has a strong preference for training the younger generation and cofinancing projects with other interested
funders. Interestingly, the willingness of Soros to give operational support to
SBF has been mirrored with its grantees. Smolar suggests that SBF's most
important work relates to its civil society development program, through
which SBF routinely provides eight to ten operating grants annually to Polish
NGOs.[20] With a $3 million "preendowment" grant from Ford, SBF is well
positioned to become a sustainable independent institution.[21]

Poland has also been the site for two other interesting institution-building
grants. The first is the Forum of Polish Foundations (Forum), which has been
supported by Mott. The Forum is a membership organization bringing together over 150 Polish NGOs. It represents these members to officials of the
national and local governments, to the private sector, and to policymakers in
Warsaw. The Forum also serves as a data clearinghouse for information on
Polish and foreign nonprofit organizations. Moreover, it advocates legal and
fiscal policies that are advantageous to the NGO sector in Poland, and provides
legal, financial, and technical services to the sector as a whole.

Another NGO that has received operating support from the foundation
community is the Fondation de Pologne (FP). Established by the Fondation de
France in 1990, its mission is to promote the development of NGOs in Poland.
FP is governed by a Board of Directors made up of French and Polish citizens
meeting alternatively in Paris and in Warsaw. It supports the activities of
Polish NGOs in the social action, education and cultural action, and local
development fields. Although all of FP's resources originated with the Fondation de France, it is expected to gradually shift over to local sources. By 1994,
it had managed to garner a small amount of its operating budget from French
corporations active in Poland. FP is also still connected closely to Fondation
de France in that all of FP's activities, methodology, fund-raising, and mode of
implementationi rely on the know-how of its French benefactor.

Foundations have also assisted in civil society development through institutional support for NGOs that conduct activities not directly related to the
third sector. One of the most successful of these is the Environmental Partnership for Central Europe (EPCE).[22] EPCE is administered by the German
Marshall Fund of the United States (GMF), and is funded by a consortium of
some fifteen foundations. EPCE was established in 1991 as a regional program
for environmental NGOs in the region. It was envisioned as a long-term
strategy emphasizing broadly based education and training in civic and democratic behavior. By concentrating on the environmental field, EPCE's designers
felt they could extend citizen participation while supporting programs tha
tmight otherwise have been relegated to a lower priority during the economic
transition.

EPCE's administrative structures provide for an efficient grantmaking process and, at the same time, reflect the objectives of the founders as a "fast, flexible, and nonbureaucratic" funding mechanism.[23] It originally established three offices in Czechoslovakia, Hungary, and Poland with staffs of three to four assisted by a support office in Washington, DC. A Slovak office in Banska Bystrica was added after the Velvet Divorce in 1993. Each office is headed by a director familiar with the country and fluent in the local language. An effort has been made to recruit local citizens in all positions, including the directors. These offices act independently, with small grants being decided after a brief consultation with the Washington office. The local offices are assisted by a Board of Advisors, usually consisting of five environmental activists or experts, and, occasionally, lawyers and politicians. The Board of Advisors meet regularly, about every three months, to approve applications.

EPCE has been termed a successful project. An independent evaluation concluded that it was "well designed and well targeted and . . . [was] having an important impact on both environmental reform and democracy building in Eastern and Central Europe" (Wilkinson, 1993). This may be an overstatement, given the lack of clear lines of causation between EPCE's—and other programs'—activities and democracy building. However, EPCE has been able to make its program implementation match its program goals; that is, the open, trusting relationship EPCE has with its local partners has been mirrored in the partners' relationships with their own grantees. Such convergence between ends and means, unfortunately, is relatively rare.

This combination of foundation training, information centers, and institution-building has provided an important stimulus to ECE's NGO sector and to civil society development more generally. Of course, the success of individual programs has varied. Critically assessing the impact and achievements of the foundation response to ECE is therefore crucial to the development of future programs.

LESSONS LEARNED

The NGO sector in ECE is now thriving, although it is facing daunting challenges. Since 1989, the number of NGOs in the region has increased dramatically. In the Czech Republic, for example, between 1989 and 1994, the number of NGOs increased by almost twelve. By 1993, there were more than 35,000 registered NGOs. In 1994, the Slovak and Polish estimates were at 9,800 and 17,000, respectively.[24] While many of these new NGOs are quite small and localized, some have the status of national organizations and many, although not all, implement programs nationally.

Foundations certainly cannot take all the credit or all the blame for the current situation. Nonetheless, foundation initiatives and involvement have had a positive effect on NGO development—perhaps more so than in other fields. While the sector would have expanded without the attention of foundations, the rate and scale of expansion was stimulated by their involvement. Foundation resources have helped young NGOs such as SAIA–SCTS and the Polish Foundation Forum to grow more quickly and expand their activities to an extent that would have taken years longer without these resources.

Foundation training programs—such as CSDP, the Third Sector Project Training-of-Trainers Program, and the Women in Civil Society Programme— have also contributed to civil society development. Study tours and seminars have enabled NGO activists to network with their colleagues domestically and internationally. They have created, to paraphrase one Czech official, individual mini-NGOs that can invigorate the entire sector.[25] Graduates of these training programs are training their ECE colleagues, and some are using the opportunities presented to them by foundations such as Soros and the Charities Know How Fund to train NGO activists in the Newly Independent States and lesser developed countries.

One of the most important aspects of foundation assistance to the NGO sector is simply that foundations were there. While this may seem insignificant, NGO activists in the region stress it repeatedly.[26] Foundations' involvement provided needed resources for a sector that still has difficulty—due to tax laws not encouraging private sector contributions, the embryonic state of the business sector, and a cultural heritage mitigating against charitable giving—obtaining local donations. More importantly, however, foundation involvement offered a psychological means to resist lingering antidemocratic tendencies. Perhaps the best example of this psychological support is how foundations and other external organizations have assisted the NGO sector in Slovakia with its campaign against the controlling tendencies of the Meciar government.

Another contribution foundations have made to the sector stems from the plurality of their response. Each foundation involved in NGO assistance had its own objectives and operating styles. Some, like the foundations that cooperated to create EPCE, took a very proactive approach to grantmaking in the region, developing EPCE on their own initiative once the need was identified. On the other hand, Soros's institutional support for NGOs has been reactive in that its foundations respond to proposals from the sector. Moreover, as the examples of foundation programs shown here indicate, the modality of foundation assistance—training, institution-building, policy research, or technical assistance—has varied by foundation. Foundations have also differed in their locus of programs (i.e., granting to organizations in the capital cities as opposed to local regions or having on-the-ground offices as opposed to running programs from the West). This very diversity carries a crucial lesson for NGO activists in ECE about plurality within the NGO sector.

There is also an evident benefit to foundations' involvement in the sector in contrast to the involvement of public donors. Foundations, by their very nature as an integral part of the NGO sector in the West, assist their ECE counterparts as much by example as by their financial support. The ability of foundations to react quickly to changing circumstances and to take risks also makes them more flexible in their grantmaking than is possible for any institution utilizing taxpayers' money. In addition, foundations have been able to make grants in smaller amounts, facilitating funding of ECE organizations directly. Most importantly, the ability of foundations to make grant agreements without the interference of the state has been crucial to the development of an independent civil society, especially in places such as Bulgaria, Romania, and Slovakia, where the government seems intent on restricting independent voices.

Foundation assistance to NGOs has also had its shortcomings, however. One of these is the continued use of Western intermediaries to distribute foundation resources. For foundations able to grant funds directly to indigenous organizations, this reliance on intermediaries defeats the very purpose of their programs. Not only do intermediaries retain a significant portion of the grant, but also this method deprives indigenous NGOs of the chance to learn about proposal and business plan creation, grants management, and fiscal accountability. Direct funding, on the other hand, channels resources into the NGO sector and also empowers local institutions.

In addition, foundations generally have not paid enough attention to the issue of sustainability in their grants—sustainability both of the individual NGO and of the sector as a whole. This is surprising, given that foundations with experience in democracy assisting in other arenas are aware of the importance of creating sustainable institutions. The absence of this emphasis may stem from an overly optimistic view of how long it would take to consolidate democracy in ECE. It may also result from the difficulty of thinking clearly about designing programs that reflect sustainability concerns in a rapidly changing environment.

Foundations also rarely provided support that reflected a broader understanding of sustainability. The ability of an organization to remain active and vital after the withdrawal of external support depends on more than just financial resources. It depends on effective governance by local individuals with the training to conduct activities and to expand or shift priorities as the environment changes. It also depends on a supportive legal environment for the sector. Absent these, foundations' hopes that NGOs they supported would attract the resources to survive after their withdrawal were unrealistic.

Furthermore, foundation emphasis on the NGO sector, at times to the exclusion of other areas, may have inadvertently hindered the future development of NGOs. As a development officer well versed in past democracy assistance efforts around the world lamented, funders tend to be too purist in their conceptions of the state, commercial, and civil society sectors.[27] Consequently, foundations generally did not pay enough attention to the possibility of strengthening ties among these spheres. NGO activists in the region now are calling for assistance in developing these "cross-sectoral partnerships" that are seen as crucial to their sustainability after the eventual withdrawal of foundation funds. More concerted attention to the possibilities of cross-sectoral partnerships early on in foundations' programs would have been beneficial to the NGO sector.

Another shortcoming of (specifically U.S.) foundations supporting the NGO sector is their Americentric view of civil society. This is seen in the emphasis on creating information centers for a sector that still lacked the legal infrastructure necessary for effective activity. Since information centers are deemed invaluable to U.S. NGOs, it was assumed that they were a necessary element for any civil society. This parochialism has led to what some view as an unrealistically large NGO sector in small countries still in the process of an economic transition. In emulating the United States, which maintains by far the largest NGO sector in the world, ECE activists and their foundation supporters may have fostered a sector that is not sustainable in its current form.

CONCLUSION

Foundation assistance to ECE has been important to the recent development of civil society, especially the strengthening of NGOs. This assistance has made a small, but important, contribution. This contribution should not, however, be equated with the development of a consolidated democracy. Unfortunately, that is still many years away. Nevertheless, foundations' experiences with NGOs and in assisting the NGO sector provide important lessons for both foundations and public donors becoming increasingly involved with this sector.

• *Foundation involvement and diversity are crucial.* Foundations have a comparative advantage over other funders in the field of civil society assistance in general and assistance to NGOs in particular. The nature of foundations as part of Western civil society, as well as their more flexible and nonbureaucratic nature, enables foundations most effectively to assist the NGO sector. Foundations' very involvement gives psychological and financial support to developing NGOs, and the diversity of their programs illustrates the plurality of a healthy civil society.

• *Foundations should concentrate more and earlier on the issue of sustainability* of organizations and of the sector. This involves not only financial support, such as endowments or reserve funds, but also training, local involvement, governance, and attention to the legal infrastructure in which NGOs can effectively work.

• *Foundations should focus more attention on building cross-sectoral partnerships* between the NGO sector, the state, and the business community. These partnerships will foster cooperation and possibly new funding streams once foundation support is withdrawn.

• *Foundations should, at this stage, rely less on Western intermediaries.* There are now a number of mature, fiscally responsible, and internationally well-connected indigenous organizations that can operate just as well, if not better, than Western intermediaries. Not only does direct funding channel resources into the NGO sector, but it also empowers local institutions.

• *Foundations, especially American foundations, should avoid an Americentric view of civil society.* Not all NGO sectors have the domestic resources to be as large and vibrant as those found in the United States. Recognizing this fact should enable foundations to more effectively target their resources in such a way as to develop a sector that will be sustainable with minimal external support.

The lessons learned over the past five years in the field should help foundations more effectively target their resources in those areas in which they choose to remain active. Moreover, these lessons will be beneficial as foundations move farther south and east, and as public funders continue to fine-tune their own initiatives.

NOTES

1. Other scholars have treated the subject of assistance, but most have confined their research to public donors. For example, Tom Carothers and Paula Newberg assessed USAID democracy-related assistance to Romania and the Czech Republic, respectively, and Janine Wedel focused on USAID (Harper & Wedel, 1995; Wedel, 1995; Carothers, 1996; Newberg & Carothers, 1996). Besides the authors, one exception is Michael Dauderstädt (1995), who has examined the role of foundations and other donors in Eastern Europe and the Newly Independent States.

2. There are a variety of terms used to describe the NGO sector, including "civil society sector," "nonprofit sector," "voluntary sector," and "third sector." For the sake of simplicity, this chapter uses "NGO sector" except in cases where another term has been used in the name of a program, such as the Johns Hopkins University's Third Sector Project Training-of-Trainers Program and the "Third Sector S.O.S." campaign.

3. There was also one Japanese foundation involved, the Sasakawa Peace Foundation.

4. This estimate is based on research conducted by the authors using the grants lists, annual reports, and other documentation of foundations. This also draws on information in Ners and Buxell (1995, Annex 3, pp. 109–110).

5. There is a burgeoning literature on civil society. However, it does not provide a clear answer to the question of what is the most effective strategy for strengthening civil society. For further information on the definition and significance of civil society, see, for example, Arato

(1991), Cohen and Arato (1992), Keane (1988), Dahl (1971), Linz (1990), Micou and Lindsnaes (1993), Putnam (1993), and Salamon (1993).

6. For example, this shift was noted by Pavol Demes at the "For Democracy's Sake" workshop, November 2–3, 1995, Bratislava, Slovakia, and by Michael Dauderstädt of the Friedrich Ebert Stiftung, interview, January 30, 1996.

7. Michael Zantovsky, "For Democracy's Sake" workshop, June 5, 1996. Woodrow Wilson Center, Washington, DC. This sentiment was also echoed by Miklos Marschall at the same workshop.

8. Illustrating this, on March 4–5, 1996, James D. Wolfensohn, the World Bank president, hosted a meeting for foundation executives active internationally.

9. The conclusions reached in this chapter are based on research completed through the "For Democracy's Sake" Project at the Woodrow Wilson Center. This research included three workshops—two with Central European NGO activists and one that included American foundation, policy community, and NGO sector representatives. The results of those workshops can be found in Quigley (1996a). The project also encompassed over 200 interviews with foundation and government officials and those involved in democracy assistance programs (Quigley, 1997).

10. This is a conservative estimate based on the research of the authors. Since some foundation data were unavailable and others were in a form that made them impossible to disaggregate by sector, the true amount of democracy assistance generally and of civil society assistance specifically is probably considerably higher.

11. This was a theme discussed in all three workshops conducted as part of the "For Democracy's Sake" project (Quigley, 1996a).

12. There is mounting evidence that the involvement of affected individuals, sometimes known as stakeholders, is essential to the successful implementation of these programs. See, for example, the World Bank (1996).

13. These are the Foundation Center in Bulgaria, the Information Center for Foundations and Other Not-for-Profit Organizations in the Czech Republic, the Nongovernmental Organizations Database (KLON/JAWOR) in Poland, and the Nonprofit Information and Training Center Foundation in Hungary.

14. This information on SAIA is based on numerous conversations with Pavol Demes, David Daniel, and materials produced by SAIA.

15. *Service Center for the Third Sector* brochure.

16. Interview with Dan Siegel and Jenny Yancey, July 17, 1995.

17. Information provided by Carol Dugan, Program Manager, Johns Hopkins Third Sector Project.

18. Networking was mentioned as an essential element of democracy assistance efforts at all three workshops held for the "For Democracy's Sake" project (see Quigley, 1996a).

19. This discussion of SBF draws on Stefan Batory Foundation (1993 and 1994) and an interview with Aleksander Smolar, October 8, 1995, as well as numerous conversation with Jacek Wojnarowski, executive director, Anna Rozicka, media program coordinator, and Krzysztof Michalski, member of the Foundation Council.

20. Interview with Aleksander Smolar, October 8, 1995.

21. Interview with Jacek Wojnarowski, executive director of SBF, July 18, 1996.

22. This section on EPCE is indebted to the research of Michael Strübin, who served as an intern with the "For Democracy's Sake" project.

23. Remarks made by RBF's Bill Moody, "For Democracy's Sake" workshop, June 5, 1996, Woodrow Wilson Center, Washington, DC.

24. The number of 17,000 Polish NGOs represents the low limit estimated by KLON in 1995. The upper limit was given as 45,000 KLON, 1995). For Czech and Slovak figures, see, respec-

tively, Šihánová et al. (1994) and Bútora and Fialová, (1995). For Hungarian figures, see Kuti (1996).

25. Michael Zantovsky, "For Democracy's Sake" workshop, June 5, 1996, Woodrow Wilson Center, Washington, DC.
26. "For Democracy's Sake" workshops, November 2–3, 1995 and April 25–26, 1996, Bratislava (Quigley, 1996a).
27. Catharin Dalpino, "For Democracy's Sake" workshop, June 5, 1996, Woodrow Wilson Center, Washington, DC.

REFERENCES

Agency for International Development. (1994). *Scoreboard of Assistance Commitments to the CEEC*. Washington, DC: Author.

Agency for International Development. (1996). *Seed Act Implementation Report*. Washington, DC: Author.

Arato, A. (1991). Revolution, civil society, and democracy. In Z. Rau (Ed.). *The Reemergence of Civil Society in Eastern Europe and the Soviet Union* (pp. 161–182). Boulder, CO: Westview Press.

Bútora, M., & Fialová, Z. (1995). *Nonprofit Sector and Volunteering in Slovakia*. Bratislava, Slovakia: Slovak Academic Information Agency.

Carothers, T. (1996). *Assessing Democracy Assistance: The Case of Romania*. Washington, DC: Carnegie Endowment for International Peace.

Cohen, J. L., & Arato, A. (1992). *Civil Society and Political Theory*. Cambridge, MA: MIT Press.

Dahl, R. A. (1971). *Polyarchy: Participation and Opposition*. New Haven: Yale University Press.

Dauderstädt, M. (1995). *A Comparison of the Assistance Strategies of the Western Donors*. Bonn: Friedrich Ebert Stiftung.

De Tocqueville, A. (1840). *Democracy in America*. New York: Vintage Books.

Diamond, L. (1995). *Promoting Democracy in the 1990s: Actors and Instruments, Issues and Imperatives*. New York: Carnegie Commission on Preventing Deadly Conflict, Carnegie Corporation.

Di Palma, G. (1990). *To Craft Democracies*. Berkeley: University of California.

Hall, J. A. (1986). Consolidating democracy. In J. A. Hall (Ed.), *States in History* (pp. 271–290). London: Basil Blackwell.

Harper, J., & Wedel, J. R. (1995). *Western Aid to Eastern and Central Europe: What We Are Doing Right, What We Are Doing Wrong, and How We Can Do It Better*. Report from a conference sponsored by the Woodrow Wilson International Center for Scholars, Washington, DC.

Havel, V., et al. (1985). *The Power of the Powerless*, Armonk, NY: M. E. Sharpe.

Huntington, S. P. (1991). *The Third Wave: Democratization in the Late Twentieth Century*. Norman: University of Oklahoma Press.

Keane, J. (1988). *Civil Society and the State: New European Perspectives*. New York: Verso.

KLON. (1995). *Basic Statistics Concerning the Scope of Activities of Nongovernmental Organizations in Poland*. Poland: Author.

Kuti, É. (1996). *The Nonprofit Sector in Hungary*. Manchester, UK: Manchester University Press.

Linz, J. (1990). Transitions to democracy. *Washington Quarterly, 13*, 143–160.

Michnik, A. (1985). *Letters from Prison*. Berkeley: University of California Press.

Micou, A. M., & Lindsnaes, B. (Eds.). (1993). *The Role of Voluntary Organizations in Emerging Democracies*. New York: Institute of International Education, The Danish Centre for Human Rights.

Ners, K. J., & Buxell, I. T. (1995). *Assistance to Transition Survey 1995.* Warsaw: IEWS Policy Education Center on Assistance to Transition.

Newberg, P. R., & Carothers, T. (1996). Aiding—and defining—democracy. *World Policy Journal, 13,* 97–108.

O'Donnell, G., Schmitter, P. C., & Whitehead, L. (Eds.). (1986). *Transitions from Authoritarian Rule: Tentative Conclusions about Uncertain Democracies.* Baltimore: Johns Hopkins University Press.

Perez-Diaz, V. M. (1993). *The Return of Civil Society: The Emergence of Democratic Spain.* Cambridge, MA: Harvard University Press.

Putnam, R. D. (1993). *Making Democracy Work: Civic Traditions in Modern Italy,* Princeton, NJ: Princeton University Press.

Quigley, K. F. F. (1997). *For Democracy's Sake: Foundations and Democracy Assistance in Central Europe.* Washington, DC: Woodrow Wilson Center Press.

Quigley, K. F. F. (1996a). *Conversations on Democracy Assistance.* Washington, DC: Woodrow Wilson Center, East European Studies Division.

Quigley, K. F. F. (1996b). For democracy's sake: How funders fail—and succeed. *World Policy Journal, 13,* 109–118.

Quigley, K. F. F. (1993). Philanthropy's role in East Europe. *Orbis, 37,* 581–598.

Rau, Z. (Ed.). (1991). *The Reemergence of Civil Society in Eastern Europe and the Soviet Union.* Boulder, CO: Westview Press.

Salamon, L. M. (1994). The rise of the nonprofit sector. *Foreign Affairs, 73,* 109–122.

Salamon, L. M. (1993). *The nonprofit sector and democracy: Prerequisite impediment, or irrelevance?* Paper prepared for the Aspen Institute Nonprofit Sector Reserach Fund Symposium on Democracy and the Nonprofit Sector, Wye, MD.

Schumpeter, J. A. (1950). *Capitalism, Socialism, and Democracy.* New York: Harper & Row.

Siegel, D., & Yancey, J. (1992). *The Rebirth of Civil Society.* New York: Rockefeller Brothers Fund.

Šihánová, H., et al. (1994). *Basic Information about the Nonprofit Sector in the Czech Republic.* Prague, Czechoslovakia: Civil Society Development Foundation.

Soros, G. (1991). *Underwriting Democracy.* New York: Free Press.

Stefan Batory Foundation. (1989–1995). *Annual Report.* Warsaw: Author.

Tester, K. (1992). *Civil Society.* New York: Routledge.

Tismaneanu, V. (1992). *Reinventing Politics: Eastern Europe from Stalin to Havel.* New York: Free Press.

Tismaneanu, V. (Ed.). (1990). *In Search of Civil Society.* New York: Routledge.

Weber, M. (1978). *Economy and Society.* Berkeley: University of California Press.

Wedel, J. R. (1995). U.S. aid to Central and Eastern Europe: Results and recommendations. *Problems of Post-Communism, 42,* 45–50.

Weigle, M., & Butterfield, J. (1992). Civil society in reforming communist regimes: The logic of emergence. *Comparative Politics, 25,* 1–24.

Wilkinson, R. C. (1993). *The Environmental Partnership for Central Europe.* Unpublished independent review.

World Bank. (1996). *The World Bank Participation Sourcebook.* Washington, DC: Author.

Part V

Conclusion

Chapter 13

Why Study Foundations?

Helmut K. Anheier and Stefan Toepler

As we mentioned at the outset of this volume, our work in this area began with a concern that from a comparative, cross-national perspective, few types of organizations have received less attention by policy analysts and researchers than philanthropic foundations. While comparative studies of business firms, government agencies, and service-providing nonprofit organizations are increasingly becoming available, little is known in a systematic way about issues of scope and structure, management, or the historical development and the legal environments of foundation communities outside the United States.

Paradoxically, however, at a time when we seem to know little about the roles and behavior of foundations or about the means at their disposal, policymakers are increasingly calling for greater private philanthropic involvement. What is more, not only politicians, but also representatives of corporate and citizen interests, frequently stress the role foundations—along with other forms of private, voluntary engagement such as volunteering—could play in building and servicing civil society.

At the same time, the historic division of labor between the state and foundations is gradually beginning to shift. Traditionally, foundations provided seed money for innovative projects, thus helping innovative projects prove their merit to society, and then usually relied on the state to take over and continue such projects. What has become apparent over the past decade

Helmut K. Anheier • Director, Centre for Voluntary Organisation, London School of Economics and Political Science, London, WC2A 2AE, United Kingdom.
Stefan Toepler • Research Associate and Lecturer, Institute for Policy Studies, Johns Hopkins University, Baltimore, Maryland 21218-2688.

Private Funds, Public Purpose: Philanthropic Foundations in an International Perspective, edited by Helmut K. Anheier and Stefan Toepler. New York, Plenum Press, 1999.

or so, however, is that governments are trying to reverse this order by funding pilot projects on their own in the hope of enticing private institutions—and, namely, private foundations—to step in for continued support. This trend has severe implications both for the self-image of foundations and their operations and policies. Clearly, the reactive-administrative management style that has characterized foundation policies in the past has to give way to new proactive roles for foundations in the future.

What these trends indicate is the need to fill the apparent gap between the hopes and expectations that are put forward toward foundations and the actual knowledge of their operational, economic, and functional capabilities. Interestingly, even in the United States, where data on foundations are relatively plentiful, most policymakers and practitioners fail to realize that foundation grants account for no more than 7 percent of total private giving and an even lesser fraction of total nonprofit revenues (Salamon, 1992a).

As an effort to stimulate a better grounded discussion and further analysis at the international level, this volume therefore offered an overview of philanthropic foundations in different settings and context. While some chapters looked at the historical development of foundations, examined the legal background, or compared the size and activities of foundations cross-nationally, others looked at particular aspects of foundation management and organizations. Finally, several chapters, reporting on specific countries and regions, provided a portrait of the different roles foundations assume across historical and political settings. Yet after having reviewed the various types and definitions of foundation, their size, roles, functions, and regulatory environment across a range of countries and traditions, the question remains: Why is it important to know how many foundations exist where, of what size, and for what purpose?

The material presented in the various chapters of this volume is to support what we regard as a major part of the answer to the question: It is important to know about foundations because they indicate, perhaps more than any other type of nonprofit organizations, long-term directions and shifts in the combined relationships between public and private responsibilities, and between private wealth and the public good. As philanthropic entrepreneurs, foundations can innovate and can nurture new trends and developments; as "niche" institutions, they support constituencies and tastes not included in market and public sector provision. In short, the behavior of foundations may be "seismographic" of these important and often indiscernible features of modern society.

On what grounds does their "seismographic" ability rest? They owe it to *built-in tensions*—perhaps even some form of ambivalence—that characterize foundations in economic, social, and political terms. There are *economic tensions* because foundations have to balance two potentially competing goals: asset preservation and grant promotion (Salamon, 1992b, p. 118); there are built-in *social tensions* because of the very constitution of foundations: Expressing primarily the will of the donor, their organizational structure does typically allow for broad-based participation outside the limited circle of trustees. No shareholder or membership represents the interest of its clients or beneficiaries.

Finally, they are *politically ambivalent* because, as private endowments for public purposes, they operate outside the direct majoritarian public control; foundations represent private agendas in public arenas (see Karl & Katz, 1987; Nielsen, 1972). Thus, due to internal ambivalence, foundations assume a seismographic nature that lets us register changes in values, political preferences, definitions of private and public spheres of responsibility, and new social and cultural deficits, often more clearly than other institutional forms. Thus, analysis of foundations should provide us with interesting insights into the history and constitutions of the economic and political structures of the country in which they operate.

The research presented in this volume supports the view that foundations serve two major functions: The first function is that of complementarity, whereby foundations serve otherwise undersupplied groups under conditions of demand heterogeneity and public budget constraints. For example, a foundation can provide grants for research on issues located outside the set priorities of relevant government funding agencies or corporate interests. Second, foundations can find it easier to take risks and support innovative activities. They may provide the seed money for new initiatives and bypass both the constraints of public budgets and the profitability expectations of the marketplace. It is important to keep in mind that these functions are based on the dual independence foundations enjoy from popular majoritarian control on the one hand, and dominant stakeholders such as shareholders or consumers on the other.

While the innovation and complementarity functions describe demand-side aspects, there are also supply-side considerations to the creation and operation of foundations. The creation of foundations depends on two crucial factors: the availability of financial capital and other forms of assets such as real estate, and the willingness of individuals or organizations to dedicate such funds to a separate entity (i.e., a foundation) and its dedicated purpose. For example, we could suggest that the current foundation boom in the United States represents largely a supply phenomenon, whereby financial assets created during the burst of growth in the stock market of 1980s and the 1990s were transformed into foundation capital by a greater number of people than in the past, indicating a revival of philanthropic and dynastic values in American society. Likewise, the growth in the number of foundations that has been observed in Germany (see Chapter 4, this volume by Anheier & Romo), could be explained by the unparalleled wealth that has been amassed in this country after World War II and the "retirement" of the generation of entrepreneurs and industrialists that has helped create this wealth since the 1950s (Strachwitz, 1994, p. 96). Thus, we can assume that variations in the creation of foundations over time depend not only on the demand for the functions they serve, but also on the extent to which the economy generates—or otherwise makes available—assets that can be transformed into foundations, and the degree of philanthropic entrepreneurship in society.

However, as suggested throughout this book, being large, generally growing, and increasingly important in fields as diverse as education and research, and arts and culture, does not necessarily mean that foundations are well understood, both by policymakers and the general public. In the preface to the recent *Statistiken zum Deutschen Stiftungswesen* (Brummer, 1996, p. 3), Strachwitz writes that foundations frequently confront an ambiguous public image: They are seen as exotic institutions by some, as bulwarks of conservatism by others, or as playgrounds for the rich and selfless expressions for humanitarian concerns. This picture, notwithstanding, is by no means unique to a European country such as Germany: Writing about the United States in *The Big Foundations,* Waldemar Nielsen (1972, p. 3) held that "foundations, like giraffes, could not possibly exist, but they do." As quasiaristocratic institutions, they flourish on the privileges of a formally egalitarian society; they represent the fruits of capitalistic economic activity; and they are organized for the pursuit of public objectives, which are seemingly contrary to the notion of selfish economic interest.

Seen from this viewpoint, foundations are not only rare, but they are also unlikely institutions or "strange creatures in the great jungle of American democracy," to paraphrase Nielsen (1972, p. 3). This volume, as others before (Renz, Mandler, & Tran, 1997; Neuhoff, 1992; Strachwitz, 1994; Toepler, 1996), presents evidence that foundations are becoming increasingly frequent and more common. It seems as if the "golden age" of foundations neither began nor ended when the "big foundations" were established by such industry tycoons as Rockefeller and Ford. More accurate would be a description that links the "golden age," if indeed one must use such expressions, to present times. Within little more than two decades, foundations in many countries have passed from a period of relative decline through a phase of unprecedented growth. Thus, foundations in many countries—and not only in the United States—represent essentially a late twentieth-century phenomenon. Perhaps we will soon have to recognize that the key to understanding the future of foundations lies not in the past, but in the present.

REFERENCES

Brummer, E. (Ed.). (1996). *Statistiken zum Deutschen Stiftungswesen*. Munich: Maecenata.
Karl, B. D., & Katz, S. N. (1987). Foundations and ruling class elites. *Daedalus, 116*(1), 1–40.

Neuhoff, K. (1992). Stiftung and Stiftungsrecht. In R. Bauer (Ed.), *Lexikon des Sozial und Gersundheitswesens* (pp. 1967–1974). Munich and Vienna: Oldenbourg.

Nielsen, W. A. (1972). *The Big Foundations*. New York: Columbia University Press.

Renz, L., Mandler, C., & Tran, T. (1997). *Foundation Giving: Yearbook of Facts and Figures on Private, Corporate and Community Foundations*. New York: Foundation Center.

Salamon, L. M. (1992a). *America's Nonprofit Sector: A Primer*. New York: Foundation Center.

Salamon, L. M. (1992b). Foundations as investment managers: Part I. The process. *Nonprofit Management and Leadership, 3*(2), 117–137.

Strachwitz, R. (1994). Stiftungen—nutzen, führen und errichten: Ein Handbuch. Frankfurt: Campus.

Toepler, S. (1996). *Das gemeinnützige Stiftungswesen in der modernen demokratischen Gesellschaft*. Munich: Maecenata.

Index